Books also by William A. Cook and Sunbury Press

Touring America by Automobile in the 1920s: The Travel Journeys of Hepzy Moore Cook

Lady Moguls: A History of Women Who Have Owned Major League Baseball Teams

Diamond Madness Classic Episodes of Rowdyism, Racism and Violence in Major League Baseball

The Lindbergh Baby Kidnapping

COLLISION COURSE

The Basketball Lives of Bob Cousy and Oscar Robertson
and the fall of the Cincinnati Royals

William A. Cook

Mechanicsburg, Pennsylvania USA

Published by Sunbury Press, Inc.
Mechanicsburg, Pennsylvania

www.sunburypress.com

ISBN: 978-1-62006-210-4 (Trade paperback)

Library of Congress Control Number: 2019940318

FIRST SUNBURY PRESS EDITION: May 2019

Product of the United States of America
0 1 1 2 3 5 8 13 21 34 55

Set in Bookman Old Style
Designed by Crystal Devine
Cover by Terry Kennedy
Edited by Alyssa Vorbeck

Continue the Enlightenment!

For

John Ruschulte

A true Cincinnati Royals fan and friend.

Contents

Introduction

It has been more than forty-five years since the Cincinnati Royals left the Queen City for Kansas City and parts beyond. Today we know the franchise as the Sacramento Kings. There are still a lot of people who are old enough to have supported and remember the Cincinnati Royals, and its players. They still talk about the team and continue to ask the question—what went wrong? What caused the demise of the Royals, a team loaded with All-Stars and former Olympic players that couldn't win a championship and which received only marginal support from ownership, the media, and the fans in Cincinnati?

The answer lies somewhere in the sagas of two Hall of Fame NBA basketball players, Bob Cousy and Oscar Robertson, and how their brilliant careers on the hard-wood collided and destroyed the Cincinnati Royals franchise. It is a basketball story of huge significance.

The lives of Bob Cousy and Oscar Robertson were as much alike as they were different.

Cousy was a white player born and raised in the streets of tough neighborhoods in Manhattan and Queens. He attended college and played basketball at Holy Cross College in Worcester, Massachusetts where he became an All-American.

Oscar Robertson was a black player born and raised in a tough all-black ghetto in Indianapolis. He attended college and played basketball at the University of Cincinnati where he became an All-American.

So it was that destiny brought together the brilliance of Cousy and Robertson to meet at an unharmonious crossing in Cincinnati.

The professional basketball career of Bob Cousy is a paradox in leadership. While Cousy has been credited for saving professional basketball in Boston as a player, he is also credited with destroying professional basketball in Cincinnati as a coach.

Bob Cousy grew up during World War Two, and while going to school he was told that America never lost a war. As Cousy honed his skills on the playgrounds of St. Albans, Queens, New York, he transferred that edict to the basketball court—you had to win every game you played. Going forward Bob Cousy won at every level in which he played. In high school he was an All-City player; he played on outstanding teams at St. Alban's Andrew Jackson High School that almost won the city championship in a very close game his senior year. In college at Holy Cross, he was an All-American and his team won an NCAA championship. Moving on to professional basketball, Cousy was an All-Star and his Boston Celtics teams won six NBA championships, five titles in a row between 1959 and 1963.

Then Bob Cousy retired as a player and began a coaching career. First, he coached at the college level at Boston College with minimal success. Then, in 1969 he was named coach of the Cincinnati Royals in the NBA and failed miserably.

His failure as a coach was just a case of no player being able to rise to the high standards of play that he had set for himself. Cousy quickly learned that the pressure to win as a player as opposed to the pressure to win as a coach was vastly different. The pressure to win as a coach was filled with conflicting demands, to be honest with your players while being honest with the fans, management, and the games' governing body. Success as a coach had a lot to do with relationships and keeping everybody happy and to do that which sometimes caused you to compromise your values.

The story of Oscar Robertson's basketball career from high school to college to the NBA is one of unparalleled brilliance. Oscar Robertson is arguably one of the five best basketball players of all-time at every level.

Still there was something lacking in Robertson's ability to lead and while he played on championship teams in high school and at the end of his professional career with the Milwaukee Bucks, those many years in between with the University of Cincinnati Bearcats and Cincinnati Royals seemed to be more about Oscar than about Oscar's team; there were no championship seasons, and when Bob Cousy became coach of the Royals, that's when the trouble began.

When Bob Cousy became an NBA coach his personality came into play with achieving success with his players. Cousy entered the professional game harboring a deep-seated belief that most players at the pro level were highly pampered products of the college game who, unlike himself as a player, never gave 100% on the court.

Jerry Lucas was one of most successful high school basketball players in history at Middletown High School in Ohio and went on to win an NCAA championship at Ohio State and play on two other runner-up teams. But when Cousy inherited Lucas as a player on the Cincinnati Royals he was deeply disappointed with him.

Cousy felt that Lucas lacked the intensity and desire to win that he had had as a professional player. Although Lucas was an All-Star, Cousy was of the opinion that he used only about 80% of his potential on the court and was often shut off or nullified by players of less talent. After taking over as head coach of the Royals in 1969, Cousy quickly traded Lucas, a fan favorite in Cincinnati, to San Francisco.

Before the season was over Cousy would also attempt to engineer a trade for Oscar Robertson, one of the most storied players in NBA history. Cousy felt that Royals were too much about Oscar rather than being a team. At the end of the season, Robertson would be traded and in return, the Royals would receive a couple of mediocre players and sink further in the standings. Cousy's tenure as coach would ultimately result in the transfer of the Cincinnati Royals franchise to Kansas City.

The fact is that someone or something ruined the promising Cincinnati Royals franchise in the NBA and professional basketball in the Queen City forever. There are plenty of suspects for which to assign blame: the rise of professional football in the city with the Cincinnati Bengals that hogged all the sports dollars in the fall; Major League Baseball was in full-throttle in Cincinnati with The Big Red Machine at the same time the Royals were reeling as Cousy and Robertson wound-up together; the Reds were setting attendance records from April to October drawing over two million fans at home. Also, both the University of Cincinnati and Xavier University basketball programs were fiercely popular and loyally supported by their fans in the city. The annual meeting of the two teams at Cincinnati Gardens usually had an attendance that would equal three of the Royals' home games.

Another prime suspect to be considered was the Royals absentee ownership of Louie Jacobs, the concessionaire king and the Godfather of sports, according to *Sports Illustrated*, who along with his two sons, Max and Jeremy and their Emprise Corporation out of Buffalo, ran the franchise on a short leash for a decade.

But most people considering the demise of the Cincinnati Royals franchise more often than not point their fingers directly at Bob Cousy. When he was hired as the Royals coach in the spring of 1969, he attempted to transform the team overnight and literally began a fire sale for most of the team's most esteemed and skilled players, including Jerry Lucas and Oscar Robertson, not to mention Adrian Smith, the MVP of the 1966 NBA All-Star Game. The salient question is, if Bob Cousy was just taking care of business and attempting to bring a new style of pro basketball to Cincinnati, or if the "Cooz" had a personality conflict with The Big O left over from his playing days and needed to assure himself he was in control of the team.

Both Bob Cousy and Oscar Robertson had developed not only enormous athletic abilities but enormous athletic egos to match their skills. So, it is no surprise that when the two were required to work in an asymmetrical relationship as player and coach it would become a collision of will and rendered the team dysfunctional.

However, in all fairness, it should be remembered, that if it were not for Bob Cousy, George Mikan, Arnie Risen, Joe Fulks, and a few others, there may have not been an NBA for anyone to play in or for the fans to support. They were the round ball pioneers that kept the game alive when it was most vulnerable to total collapse during the period of vast fan suspicion about the honesty of basketball due to the college point-shaving scandals.

The failure of the Cincinnati Royals franchise is a story of the early days of the NBA and two of the league's greatest players. It's a failure that could have been avoided if someone would have seen that the personalities of Oscar Robertson and Bob Cousy were on a collision course.

1

Bob Cousy

& the Holy Cross Crusaders

Bob Cousy was born on August 9, 1928, in New York, six months after his parents Joseph and Juliette (Colette) Cousy had emigrated from the Alsace-Lorraine region of France and entered the United States through Ellis Island.

According to Bob Cousy, he inherited a dual personality from his parents. His father was low keyed and complacent. But his mother, as he described, was as French as Joan of Arc, and was quite emotional and very high strung. Cousy was of the opinion that his father gave him his self-confidence and his mother the overdrive to succeed no matter what the costs.

Joseph Cousy supported the family by driving a cab. Bob Cousy spent his early years being raised in a tenement on the east side of Manhattan in Yorkville.

When he was six years old Cousy donned his uncle's top hat and grabbed his cane then announced to his mother, "Mama I will be a big man someday."[1] But no one could have foreseen just how much celebrity the pint-sized prophet would achieve.

When Cousy was 12 years old the family moved to St. Albans, Queens where his parents had bought a three-story house. The Cousys divided the house into apartments and rented out the first two floors.

Cousy soon discovered O'Connell Park where grounds director Morty Arkin introduced him to basketball. By the age of 13, Cousy started playing basketball on the schoolyard playgrounds or wherever he could find a pick-up game. It was there that Cousy's extremely competitive nature was formed. He played those schoolyard games based on what he later described in his book *The Killer Instinct* as the twin principles that you gave it back "in spades" to anybody who gave it to you and that every loose ball was his.

When he broke his right arm, he showed his budding tenacity by learning to dribble and shoot with his left hand. By the time he recovered, Bob Cousy was becoming a considerable force on the court.

The coach of St. Alban's Andrew Jackson High School noticed him playing in a schoolyard one day and suggested he come out for the team as he could use a left-handed shooter. The coach was stunned when Cousy told him he was actually right-handed.

Cousy tried out for the team and was cut twice from the junior varsity team at Andrew Jackson High School. But Cousy was determined to hang-in-there and learn.

With his extraordinary peripheral vision that allowed him to pass the ball without looking at the other player, Cousy soon became a high school standout and as a senior won the New York City high school scoring title.

Cousy played his last high school game on March 16, 1946, in the New York City Public School Athletic League (P.S.A.L.) championship game at Madison Square Garden before 15,000 fans. At the time, Andrew Jackson High School, led by Cousy, had an 18-game winning streak.

The championship game was against Erasmus Hall High School of Brooklyn. Later, Erasmus would graduate Chicago Bulls and Chicago White Sox owner Jerry Reinsdorf (class of 1953) and Naismith Memorial Basketball Hall of Fame and Philadelphia 76ers basketball great Billy Cunningham (class of 1960).

Erasmus would defeat Jackson for the championship in a close fought game 35–33. *The New York Times* would state in its article on the game, "Andrew Jackson was not so fortunate. Its winning streak was stopped at 18 games by an aggressive Erasmus quintet. Ronnie Nadell was the big gun for the Buff and Blue with 18 points, while Robert Cousy paced the losers with 14."[2]

Cousy was selected for the 1945–1946 *New York Journal-American* All-City Team that included the following first team players: Bob Cousy (Andrew Jackson), Vic Hanson (L.I.C.), George Feigenbaum (New Utrecht), Zeke Sinicola (Benjamin Franklin), and Abe Becker (Lincoln).

While not much is known in regard to what happened to Vic Hanson, the only black player on the 1946 All-City team following high school, Cousy and the other three players would go on to play college basketball and two of three others besides Cousy would play in the NBA.

George Feigenbaum would play college ball at the University of Kentucky and then play in the NBA between 1949 and 1953 with the Baltimore Bullets and Milwaukee Hawks.

Zeke Sinicola became an All-American at Niagara University while leading the Purple Eagles to their first appearance in the NIT in 1950. Following college, Sinicola played with the Ft. Wayne Pistons between 1950 and 1952.

Abe Becker went on to play at NYU and was captain of the 1950–51 squad. While the 1949–50 NYU team finished with a record of 8–11, against their arch-rival in New York, CCNY, the eventual 1950 NCAA champions, they would battle them tooth and nail before losing 64–61 as Becker scored 18 points. Abe Becker would go on to play in the 1951 College East-West All-Star Game.

While Bob Cousy had played less than two years of high school basketball, it seems almost unbelievable by comparison to today's standards that as an All-City Team player he would only be offered two college scholarships. One was at Boston College and the other at Holy Cross College.

A young referee by the name of Lou Eisenstein had first recommended Cousy to coach Alvin "Doggie" Julian who had just taken the Holy Cross job. In the mid-1940s Julian had been the head coach at Muhlenberg College and gave Eisenstein the opportunity to work some of his games. Satisfied with the referee's style, Julian recommended Eisenstein to a few other coaches. Grateful for the opportunity, Eisenstein told Julian that if he ever saw a way to help him, he would.

Doggie Julian came to Holy Cross in the fall of 1945 as an assistant backfield coach for the football team and implemented a two-platoon substitution system. It was then that Lou Eisenstein contacted Julian and told him, "There's a schoolboy on Long Island named Cousy and he's only a sophomore. But he looks like something special."[3]

Julian followed up on Eisenstein's tip and went to see Cousy play, then met his parents. Even though Cousy was not yet a star in New York high school basketball, Julian told Gary Black of the New York Holy Cross Club to keep in touch with the boy, although he was still two years away from graduation.

The Holy Cross basketball program was not doing very well. From 1940 to 1945 the Crusaders had won only 22 games. In 1946, Doggie Julian was offered an extra $500 to become head coach of the basketball team.

Although Holy Cross athletics programs had a solid reputation as a top collegiate performer in football, track, and baseball in the early 1940s, the basketball program was hampered by the fact that the school did not have a gymnasium. The team practiced in an old barn behind a chapel. But the administration made a decision to start building the basketball program and with lots of young athletes starting to return from World War Two (Bob Curran, U.S. Marines; Andy Laska, U.S. Army Air Force; and others) and Julian starting to recruit heavily from New York City high schools, (Joe Mullaney, Chaminade; George Kaftan Xavier; Dermott O'Connell, Cardinal Hayes; Ken Haggerty, Andrew Jackson; and others) they started to acquire some talent.

Holy Cross is located in Worcester, Massachusetts about 40 miles from Boston. At that time the city had a population of approximately 193,694.

In the 1940s, during the winter months, Boston was a hockey town. The city's high schools didn't even have basketball teams until after World War Two. But when Holy Cross, under Doggie Julian, finished with a record of 14–4 in 1945–46 and started to receive national attention, suddenly round-ball was all the rage in Beantown and soon the Crusaders with Bob Cousy would be selling-out Boston Garden.

Holy Cross seemed like a good for fit for Cousy because he had two requirements for selecting a college. First, out of respect for his grandmother's wishes, he wanted to attend a Catholic college. Second, he wanted to go to school outside of New York City.

When Cousy visited Boston College he discovered that it was, for the most part, a commuter school, so he would have to live in rooming houses which did not appeal to him.

Then he visited Holy Cross in Worchester, Massachusetts and found that they had dormitories. So, he gladly accepted the scholarship.

When Bob Cousy enrolled at Holy Cross, the NCAA World War Two regulations were still in effect that permitted freshmen to participate in varsity sports. In 1946–47, Cousy's freshman year, Holy Cross got off to a slow start. In early January 1947, the Crusaders didn't exactly look like a championship team in the making. After being defeated by North Carolina State and

Duquesne, the Crusaders lost their third straight game falling to Wyoming 58–57. At that point in the season, their record stood at 4–3. But all of sudden they caught fire and reeled off twenty-three victories in a row.

As they gained momentum, on February 25 at Boston Garden, Holy Cross walloped Boston College 90–48. The 90 points broke the Holy Cross record for points in a game and also broke the arena record.

On March 20, in the opening round of the eight-team NCAA Tournament, Holy Cross, led by Joe Mullaney with 18 points and George Kaftan with 15, defeated Navy 55–47 to advance to the Final Four. Two days later, they advanced to the finals by defeating CCNY 60–45 at Madison Square Garden in a game witnessed by 18,470 fans.

The Holy Cross victory over the CCNY Beavers was quite surprising considering that after the first 7½ minutes of play the Crusaders had not scored a field goal and after 14 minutes were trailing by a score of 23–12. But then Holy Cross got hot and reeled off 13 straight points and, at the intermission, led by a score of 27–25.

Nine minutes into the second half the score was tied at 38–38. As the Crusaders began pulling away, the work around the basket by George Kaftan led the way. Ultimately, Kaftan scored 30 points to lead the Crusaders over CCNY. At that time the NCAA tournament single-game scoring record was 31 points set by George Giamick of North Carolina vs. Dartmouth in 1941.

George Kaftan, who grew up in Washington Heights and learned to play basketball on the streets of upper Manhattan, where there were no basketball courts, would be named a second-team All-American for 1946–47.

Bob Cousy, coming off the bench, scored 5 points. In his freshman year, Cousy shared playing time with another forward on the team, Joe Mullaney.

Joe Mullaney, a former All-City player in New York, had enrolled in Holy Cross after serving in the Army Air Corps and was captain of the Crusaders' National Championship team. Holy Cross would be the first eastern team to win the NCAA Tournament. Later, Joe Mullaney would become a successful college coach at Providence, taking the program over in 1955 and coaching them to 12 straight winning seasons, including NIT championships in 1961 and 1963. After coaching for a while in the NBA, ABA, and at Brown, Mullaney would return to Providence in 1981 for a second

Bob Cousy – Holy Cross, circa 1949.

stint. For 18 seasons as coach at Providence, Mullaney's record was 319–164. Among the future stars that Mullaney recruited to play for him were Lenny Wilkens, John Thompson, Mike Riordan, Johnny Eagan, and Jimmy Walker.

A few days later, Holy Cross won the 1947 NCAA Tournament defeating Oklahoma 58–47. At the half, the Crusaders had been down 31–28. The Sooners featured two All-Americans, Alva Paine and Gerald "Old Rocking Chair" Tucker who was the center. Tucker was 26 years old, stood 6'4", and was built like a tree trunk. Tucker attempted to intimidate the Crusaders 18-year-old, 6'2" forward George Kaftan by telling him, "So you're the young hotshot." Kaftan quickly replied, "Gerry, this is a young man's game. Time to hang 'em up."[4]

After Tucker pushed Kaftan around in the first half, Doggie Julian put the burly 6'5" Bob Curran on him in the second half. Tucker would score 22 points in the game, but Curran held him to one field goal in the second half and with Kaftan freed-up, the Crusaders rebounded outscoring the Sooners 30–16 to win the championship. George Kaftan once again led Holy Cross with 18 points. Bob Cousy had 2 points both coming from free throws.

Kaftan was the Crusaders leading scorer for the year with 310 points, named the tournament's MVP, and a second-team All-American.

In its national championship season of 1946–47 Holy Cross finished with a record of 27–3. When the Crusaders arrived back in Worcester's Union Station the next day, they were greeted by 10,000 screaming fans.

During his freshman year, Bob Cousy gained a reputation as a slick, ball-stealing, magical-ball-handling, future star of the team. Cousy was not a fast runner, but with his quick reflexes, he just did things fast. In his sophomore year, Cousy would play ahead of Joe Mullaney and teamed up with George Kaftan; the two became the most well-known one-two punch in college basketball. Nonetheless, from time to time, Coach Julian became disenchanted with Cousy's flashy play and his behind the back dribble and benched him. This bothered Cousy, and for a time he considered transferring to St. John's but then reconsidered.

Entering the 1947–48 season, Holy Cross was ranked the third best team in the nation behind Kentucky and Notre Dame.

Holy Cross began the 1947–48 campaign with victories over Valparaiso and Willimantic. On December 13, the Holy Cross Crusaders broke the 100-point barrier for the first time, defeating Eastern Connecticut 104–43. In the first three games of the season, the Crusaders had scored 249 points. Going back into the previous season, Holy Cross had won 26 games in a row.

The Holy Cross winning streak came to an end on December 17 when they were defeated by Columbia 60–53 at Morningside Gym in upper Manhattan. Led by Walter Budko with 19 points and 12 by Bruce Gehrke, the Lions out-hustled the Crusaders on the way to their ninth win in a row as they stole Holy Cross passes and worked hard on the boards grabbing rebounds. Bob Cousy scored 27 points for Holy Cross.

A few days later on December 20, Holy Cross rebounded from the Columbia loss defeating Dartmouth 75–61 before 11,395 fans at Boston Garden. The first half ended with Holy Cross in the lead, 42–26, led by Bob Cousy's 15 points. Cousy would end the game with 22 points made on eight field goals and six foul shots. George Kaftan and Bob McMullan each had 11 points for the Crusaders.

The Sugar Bowl basketball game had begun in 1936 as an added attraction to the Sugar Bowl football game held in New Orleans. In late December the Crusaders went to New Orleans to play in the Sugar Bowl Tournament.

By 1947, the Sugar Bowl basketball game had become a doubleheader and the presence of Holy Cross, the defending National Champion, in the event gave it increasing prestige. In the first game, 967 fans saw Pitt defeat LSU 52–47. Then, Holy Cross defeated North Carolina 56–51 in the event's first overtime game with Bob Cousy scoring 21 points.

As a coach, Doggie Julian was all business. When Bob Cousy had a minor auto accident and missed a Saturday practice, Julian had no mercy on him. At that time, the next game on the schedule was February 28 when the Crusaders met Loyola of Chicago at Boston Arena. Julian kept Cousy on the bench the entire first half. Then, with 8 minutes left in the game and Holy Cross leading 42–38, he finally sent Cousy in. He proceeded to score 12 points in the last 5½ minutes to lead the Crusaders to a 62–46 victory.

By mid-March 1948, Holy Cross had an 18-game winning streak. On March 18, led by Bob Cousy and George Kaftan, the Crusaders defeated Michigan 63–45 at Madison Square Garden in the first round of the NCAA Tournament Eastern Quarterfinals. To advance, the Crusaders would have to conquer Kentucky who had upended Columbia in the quarterfinals.

That was not to be as the following evening the Kentucky Wildcats defeated Holy Cross 60–52. The 18,472 fans at the Garden were thrilled by the scrappy play and individual duels that occurred between the Crusaders and Wildcats players. Kentucky had entered the game as a five-point favorite. But as soon as it was realized that the Wildcats were going to contain Cousy and Kaftan, the outcome of the contest was not in question. Kentucky kept using both its speed on the fast break and size to drive against Holy Cross. The Crusaders could not control either. Bob Cousy had just one field goal and scored only 5 points as two Wildcats, Ken Rotina and Dale Barnstable, did a magnificent job of containing him. Prior to the Kentucky Game, Cousy had scored 472 points in the season. Alex Groza, the Wildcats big 6'7" All-American center, led all scorers with 23 points while wearing down George Kaftan. The loss to Kentucky ended Holy Cross' 19-game winning streak and the Crusaders finished the season with a record of 26–4. Kentucky went on to become the 1948 National Champions.

Despite his lack of brilliance in the Kentucky game, Wildcats coach Adolph Rupp was impressed with Cousy. Later Rupp would remark that Cousy was the best backcourt player he had ever seen and Rupp had seen some truly great ones, including his own Ralph Beard.

Still, it had been another fine season for junior center George Kaftan as he scored 468 points and became the first Holy Cross player to score 1,000 points in his career.

At the conclusion of the 1947–48 season, Doggie Julian left Holy Cross to become the head coach of the Boston Celtics in the Basketball Association of America (BBA). He was replaced as coach of the Crusaders by Lester "Buster" Sheary.

Buster Sheary came into the head coaching job at Holy Cross through the back door. A native of Worchester, he had played college football at Catholic University and was selected as an All-South fullback. He then became a successful high school basketball coach. With the outbreak of World War Two, Sheary assumed scouting duties for the Naval ROTC basketball program. He then served as an assistant coach in the program for two years becoming a head coach in 1947–48.

Bob Cousy later stated that during his career on the hardwood he had played under two master coaches who helped shape his own coaching style. One was Boston Celtics coach Arnold "Red" Auerbach who would help him at the professional level to harness his talents, ultimately developing him into an NBA Rookie of the Year.

The other, at the college level, was Buster Sheary who was his coach at Holy Cross during his junior and senior years. Bob Cousy felt that he had come to college a hungry player, but being around Buster Sheary for a couple of years made him hungrier. Sheary's philosophy was that if you wanted to win badly enough no one could stop you. According to Cousy, at the end of every practice, Sheary always rolled a basketball out of the door of the gymnasium. The gym sat on top of a hill and it was the players' task to chase after it. The player who came back with the ball would be rewarded by being the first one to go to the showers. Cousy stated that he often came back with the ball. "When [Sheary] asked you to run through a wall," said Cousy, "your only question was 'Which wall?'"[5]

However, Cousy freely admits that he may have learned some bad habits from Sheary as well. According to Cousy, Sheary had a habit of smacking steel lockers with his bare fists to emphasize a point and once he even banged his head against a wall.

In the spring of 1973 when Cousy was asked by the AAU (Amateur Athletic Association) to coach a team of college All-Stars against a team of players from the Soviet Union, he accepted and appointed Buster Sheary as an assistant coach. This was the team that had won the Gold Medal in the 1972 Olympic Games in Munich, handing the American team its first-ever loss of the Gold in the games. At that time, Sheary was in his sixties and had been out of coaching for a while. There were critics who believed that Cousy's appointment of his old college coach was nothing more than nostalgia. But the fact was that Cousy truly believed that Sheary would contribute heavily to the competitiveness of the team.

With Buster Sheary's appointment as head coach, going forward the next seven years, Holy Cross teams would win no fewer than nineteen games in a season. In 1954, the Crusaders coached by Sheary would win the NIT, defeating Duquesne 71–62 in the championship game.

1948–49 was Bob Cousy's junior year. That year the Sugar Bowl basketball event became a tournament. The tournament's organizers solidified the legitimacy of the event by bringing both St. Louis, the 1948 NIT champion, and Kentucky, the NCAA tournament champion, to New Orleans. Kentucky coach Adolph Rupp even backed out of the Holiday Tournament at Madison Square Garden to play in the Sugar Bowl Tournament. Holy Cross and Tulane made up the other two entries.

Unfortunately for Holy Cross, they were beaten in the first round by St. Louis 61–52, the eventual winner of the tournament that went on to defeat Kentucky 61–52. Despite 28 points by Bob Cousy in the consolation game, the Crusaders finished fourth, defeated by Tulane 81–70.

In Buster Sheary's first season as head coach, Holy Cross finished ranked 27th in the nation with a record of 19–8. One big pair of gym shoes were left unfilled for Holy Cross when just fourteen games into the season on January 22, the Crusaders lost All-American George Kaftan to graduation. Kaftan would score 162 points in his brief senior year play and wrap-up his career as the leading scorer in Holy Cross history at that time with 1,177 points.

Drafted by the Boston Celtics of the BBA, Kaftan would sign his contract the day after graduation. Actually, his father, a Turkish immigrant, would have to sign the contract as Kaftan was not yet 21 years of age. The contract called for $16,000, a huge sum for a professional player at that time.

With George Kaftan lost to graduation, the major scoring responsibility on the Crusaders now fell on the shoulders of Bob Cousy. In the fourth game of the year, Holy Cross had been unsuccessful in a rematch with Kentucky, this time losing 51–48. Bob Cousy scored 11 points in the game, the lowest total he would score in any game during the season. However, George Kaftan's career record for points scored would be short-lived. By the end of the season, Cousy would take over as the all-time Holy Cross points scored leader with 1,193. Cousy finished the season tallying 480 points, just 6 shy of breaking his school season record of 486 points. In ten games Cousy scored 20 or more points, his highest total of 28 coming in a loss to Tulane, and he was named a second-team All-American.

On February 5, 1949, Holy Cross would defeat Boston College 46–39. Going forward, the victory would have special significance as it would be the start of a 47-home-game winning streak for the Crusaders that would continue until they were defeated on February 27, 1954, by the University of Connecticut 78–77.

1949–50 was Bob Cousy's senior year and the Crusaders started strong, defeating formable opponents such as Bowling Green 71–70, and Kansas 57–53. On January 12, Holy Cross defeated St. Louis 69–55 at Boston Garden to increase their record to 13–0 and become ranked number one in the Associated Press poll. The Crusaders would remain the top-ranked college team for five weeks.

The Crusaders also played several non-NCAA contests on their schedule, and on March 3, the Crusaders would defeat the New York Athletic Club (NYAC) 58–56 to increase their overall record to 27–0 (20–0 NCAA games). At that time the Holy Cross Crusaders were leading the nation in offense with a scoring average of 74.4 points per game. Then they would hit a wall, losing the last four games of the season.

The following day Holy Cross would go up to Morningside Gym and take on a nemesis, the Columbia Lions. The game was widely anticipated in New York and with the Lions' home court limited seating of 3,500, the game would be carried on both television (WOR) and radio (WKCR). So far in the 1949–50 season, the Crusaders had beaten five teams that had topped the Lions (Fordham 75–48, Harvard 102–71, Brown 83–39 and 70–45, Colgate 108–76, and Dartmouth 53–49). In 1947, Columbia had snapped a Holy Cross winning streak of 27 games, and now the Lions did it again, this time defeating the Crusaders by a score of 61–54 to snap their most recent 27-game winning streak.

Next up for Holy Cross was Yale, which defeated the Crusaders 66–62.

With a record of 20–2 (NCAA games) and 27–2 (overall), Holy Cross was invited to the 1950 NCAA Tournament. Bad luck continued for the Crusaders as they were defeated in the opening round at Madison Square Garden by North Carolina State 87–74 despite a strong effort by Bob Cousy with 24 points. The following night Holy Cross lost in a consolation game to Ohio State 72–52 as Cousy finished his collegiate career scoring 14 points.

After losing the final four games of the season, the Crusaders finished the season with a record of 27–4. Bob Cousy had an outstanding senior year averaging 19.4 points per game, was named a first-team All-American and the nation's outstanding college player of the year by the Basketball Writers of America.

During his varsity career spanning four years, Bob Cousy had set the Holy Cross record for most points scored with 1,775. In the Colgate game played on February 7, Cousy had set the Holy Cross scoring record with 36 points, 14 field goals, and 8 free throws. In addition, Cousy had set another Holy Cross record in the Boston College game on February 21 when he sank 14 free throws in 14 attempts. A few years later Cousy's number 17 jersey would be retired.

Several years later Bob Cousy's Holy Cross career scoring record would be broken by Tom Heinsohn with 1,789 points. On March 1, 1956, Heinsohn would rewrite the Holy Cross record book when he scored 51 points and grabbed 42 rebounds as the Crusaders defeated Boston College 111–75.

But time marches on, even in the golden era of Holy Cross basketball, and it wasn't long before Heinsohns' individual game scoring record would fall to Jack Foley. On February 5, 1960, Foley would score 55 points for Holy Cross vs. Colgate. He would follow up that effort by scoring 56 points vs. Connecticut on February 17, 1962, and finish his career with 2,185 points.*

Currently, Bob Cousy's career mark of 1,775 points ranks seventh in the school's history, and he ranks fifth all-time in field goals made with 709.

In June 1950, Bob Cousy graduated from Holy Cross with a Bachelor of Science in Business. Six months later, in December, Cousy would marry his college sweetheart Missie Ritterbach. The couple would have two daughters, Marie and Tricia.

Despite his detractors who pointed out that Holy Cross had not won a major tournament while the Cooz (as he would soon become known) was the school's top star, he was picked in the first round of the NBA draft by the Tri-Cities Blackhawks then traded immediately to the Chicago Stags. When the Stags disbanded prior to the beginning of the 1950 season, Cousy was made available in a special player lottery.

* The current all-time Holy Cross career points leader is Ronnie Perry with 2,524. In addition, Cousy's 14 for 14 at the free throw line has been bested twice. John Wendelken vs. Massachusetts on February 18, 1965, and Ronnie Perry vs. Yale on December 9, 1978; both went 15 for 15 at the charity stripe.

2

A Brief History of the NBA 1946–1951

& the Rise of Bob Cousy and the Boston Celtics

In 2015, eleven NBA teams had a market value of a billion dollars each, due in most part to their lucrative TV contracts. The Los Angeles Clippers were sold in 2014 by embattled owner Donald Sterling for two billion dollars after his racist views were revealed. The sale price of the Clippers surpassed the estimate valuation put on the franchise by *Forbes* by four times.

In the early years, however, professional basketball had been struggling in its attempts to be recognized as a legitimate professional sport, going through a protracted evolution during the late 1930s and early 1940s with the National Basketball League (NBL). But the NBL was a backwater league with teams located in such cities as Hammond, Indiana; Oshkosh, Wisconsin; and Waterloo, Iowa. Playing in such remote communities just didn't afford the league the publicity that it needed to be taken seriously when competing against Major League Baseball and professional football for fan interest.

Then, on June 6, 1946, a group of like-minded sportsmen, most of whom owned hockey teams as well as some of the largest arenas in the country, got together at the Commodore Hotel in New York and formed the Basketball Association of America (BBA), with eleven teams. Each team paid an entry fee of $10,000. Rosters were set at twelve players and a voluntary team salary cap of $55,000 was established. It was agreed that games would be set at forty-eight minutes with four twelve-minute quarters (or periods). The games would be eight minutes longer than all the other professional, barnstorming, and collegiate games being played at that time. Finally, a fixed schedule of sixty games in a season was set; that was sixteen games more than the rival NBL limit.

Maurice Podoloff was a 5'2" white-haired Yale-educated lawyer who had been born in Russia. Given the nickname of "Poodles" by his contemporaries, Podoloff was a former president of the American Hockey League who also operated an arena in New Haven, Connecticut. Podoloff was named President of the BBA, and suddenly there was a rival league with teams located in New York, Boston, Cleveland, Chicago, Detroit, Washington, D.C., Philadelphia, Pittsburgh, St. Louis, Toronto, and Providence. These teams would play in arenas such as Boston Garden and Madison Square Garden, rather than in small towns of various regions of the country.

On November 1, 1946, while Bob Cousy and the Holy Cross Crusaders were starting the march toward the NCAA championship, the first BBA game took place at Toronto's Maple Leaf Garden as the New York Knickerbockers defeated the Toronto Huskies 68–66, and professional basketball as we have come to know it today began.

The early BBA teams traveled by train. Player salaries with the voluntary team salary cap averaged about $6,000. The Philadelphia Warriors won the league championship in that first season led by high-scoring (23.2 points per game), 6'5" Joe Fulks, a former U.S. Marine and Murray State Teachers College player.

While every team in the BBA played its complete schedule in the inaugural season of 1946–47, the league struggled with sparse crowds. With revenues lower than expected it presented a problem in meeting player salaries and every team lost money. Consequently, by the end of the 1946–1947 season, the BBA had lost four teams due to financial difficulties: Pittsburgh, Toronto, Cleveland, and Detroit. Still, Baltimore joined the BBA for 1947–48, and the league continued to gain marginal popularity.

That same year, the BBA had initiated a college draft in which teams drafted the rights to college players with the last place team getting the number one pick. The draft eliminated teams in the same league attempting to outbid each other and strengthened the weaker teams.

Meanwhile, the NBL remained viable and solvent during 1946–47. With a more regional membership in the NBL, there was less travel and the league saved money. NBL attendance was nearly equal to that of the BBA and with lower player salaries several teams managed to turn a modest profit.

But the NBL had an ace in the hole with George Mikan, the most popular professional basketball player in the country. The former DePaul University star had been signed by owner Maurice White to play for the Chicago American Gears in 1946 for a whopping salary package of $60,000 over five years.

George Mikan, standing 6'10", was a titan under the basket, and while other teams attempted to harass him, he remained steadfast. When he decided to take the ball to the basket, no one could stop him.

There was temporary high anxiety in the NBL during 1946–47 when George Mikan walked away from the Chicago team and the NBL for a month. Maurice White had attempted to back out of certain incentive clauses in Mikan's contract. When Mikan returned, everyone gave a sigh of relief, and he then picked up where he had left off, spear-heading the American Gears playoff charge.

Due to George Mikan's extreme popularity, Maurice White came to the conclusion that he could really cash-in by using him to launch a new league that he would have complete control over. So, at the beginning of the 1947–48 season, White withdrew the American Gears from the NBL and organized the Professional Basketball League of America (PBA). The league began with sixteen teams. White hoped to expand it to twenty-four teams, and he would own all the teams and the arenas. But within only a few weeks it was apparent that the PBA was going to fail and did. Maurice White lost approximately $500,000 dollars in the fiasco, went bankrupt, and lost his business.

With Maurice White and the Chicago American Gears defunct, the Chicago players were distributed over the eleven remaining NBL franchises. George Mikan's contract was awarded to the Minneapolis Lakers. Mikan joined two other very talented players on the Lakers: forward Jim Pollard and guard Herm Schaefer.

Jim Pollard, a 6'5" forward, became one of the first players in professional basketball capable of playing the game above the rim. Nicknamed the Kangaroo Kid Pollard, he had a tremendous jumping ability, and although he seldom dunked the ball in games, he would leave his teammates thunderstruck by dunking from the foul line in practice.

All three, Mikan, Pollard, and Schaefer, became a dominating force as the Lakers went on to defeat the Rochester Royals in four

George Mikan – 1948 Basketball Card. (Courtesy of Bowman via WikiMedia Commons.)

games for the 1948 NBL title. For the season, George Mikan averaged 21.3 points per game.

Even with George Mikan's popularity and small sold-out arenas, the NBL was on the verge of folding. Likewise, entering the 1948–49 season, the BBA was still losing money. But it was willing to take a chance on expanding by rescuing four of the NBL teams: the Minneapolis Lakers, the Ft. Wayne Zollner Pistons, the Rochester Royals, and the Indianapolis Kautskys (later named the Jets). Two other NBL franchises, the Oshkosh All-Stars and Toledo Jeeps, had also sought to jump to the BBA but were turned down.

While the BBA was now a bloated circuit with the inclusion of the four NBL teams, the upside was that those teams brought with them several star players capable of enhancing gate receipts.

With quality players joining the league, the BBA's popularity would immediately grow to a point where the league was considered marketable. In 1948, the Bowman Company issued a 36-card set of basketball cards featuring BBA players. The cards were in color and measured 2⅟₁₆ x 2½ inches. The set included a George Mikan rookie card that is today highly coveted by sports card collectors.

Mikan had an immediate impact on the league, and for the 1948–49 season, he averaged 28.3 points per game, which amounted to one-third of the Minneapolis Lakers point production.

In the 1949 BBA playoffs, the Minneapolis Lakers advanced to the finals to face the financially strapped Washington Capitals coached by former high school coach Arnold "Red" Auerbach. The Lakers won the first three games of the best of seven series. Then, in game four, George Mikan broke his wrist and the Capitals won. While Mikan played with a cast on his wrist in game five and scored 22 points, the Capitals won again, but the Lakers won game six played in St. Paul to wrap-up the championship. Mikan averaged 27.5 points per game in the series.

The NBL, left with only a few star players such as Dolph Schayes of the Syracuse Nationals and Don Otton of the Tri-City Blackhawks, played through the 1948–49 season, then sought to merge its remaining teams into the BBA. Almost without objection, every remaining NBL franchise was merged into the BBA.

In the fall of 1949, the BBA would begin play as the National Basketball Association (NBA). The league would have seventeen teams that year in three divisions. Going forward, notwithstanding that the Minneapolis Lakers had won the BBA championship in 1949, the first six years of the 1950s would see a former NBL team win the NBA championship.

Racial integration in professional basketball had a long journey to traverse. While there had been several black players who had played professional basketball going back to the mid-1930s, with 6'4" center Hank Williams of the Buffalo Bisons in the Midwest Basketball Conference, the first black pro in basketball was probably Buck Lew who played in 1904 for the Newbury team in the New England League.

All-black professional teams would occasionally meet all-white professional teams. One of the more memorable meetings took place in 1939 at Chicago Stadium as the all-black New York Rens defeated the all-white Oshkosh All-Stars 36–25 in the finals of the World Tournament with 20,000 fans in attendance.

The Rens, named for the Renaissance Ballroom in Harlem, were owned by Harlem businessman Robert Douglas who had organized the team in 1922. He paid his players $150 a month and $3-a-day meal money. Between 1932 and 1936, the Rens rolled-up a won-lost record of 473–49. At one point in 1933, the Rens won 88 straight games. Many of those games would end in fights as all-white teams could not accept losing to an all-black team. In 1948, Douglas broke the team up.

The Rens had advanced to the finals in the 1939 World Tournament by defeating the Harlem Globetrotters in the semifinals. The event was the world's first integrated tournament championship. John Isaacs, who stood 6'3", was a member of the Rens. Later, Isaacs stated that as a reward for winning the tournament, the Rens were given jackets that had the words "Colored World Champions" stitched on the back. Offended by the implication, Isaacs went into the office of Rens owner Robert Douglas and said, "Do you have a razor blade I can borrow?"[1] Douglas gave Isaacs a single-edge razor blade; he put the jacket on the back of one his teammates and cut the word "Colored" out of the back of it. "So it just said World Champions," said Isaacs, "because that's what we were."[2]

John Isaacs remained extremely irritated until the day he died on January 26, 2009, by the implication of various New Yorkers, fans, and sportswriters that the 1970 Knicks were the first professional team to win a basketball championship for the city.

John Isaacs, like most of his black contemporaries, never played in the ABL, NBL, or NBA, but rather played in an era of basketball that was billed as the Black Fives. The teams were sponsored by churches, businesses, colleges, YMCAs, and social clubs and were comprised of black amateurs and professionals playing in well-organized barnstorming circuits. The New York Rens and the Harlem Globetrotters were the most famous of these teams. The Rens often played against all-white teams, most notable being another New York team, the Original Celtics, that featured Nat Holman and Joe Lapchick, and the Indianapolis

Kautskys that featured future legendary U.C.L.A. coach John Wooden as a player.

The Original Celtics refused to join the ABL in 1925 because the league would not admit the Rens as a member. However, the following season in 1926, the Celtics reconsidered and joined the ABL. The league had been organized by George Preston Marshall, who later would own the Washington Redskins, and due to his racial intolerance would become the last NFL team to integrate its roster in 1960.

The early history of the Harlem Globetrotters was similar to that of the Rens. Abe Saperstein, the son of a Jewish tailor on Chicago's south side, became a black sports promoter. He was instrumental in promoting Negro league baseball and also assembled a team of highly talented black basketball players he called the Savoy Five. He had them barnstorm all the way across the country to the west coast in the 1930s. Later, the team's name was changed to Globetrotters. The competition that the Globetrotters usually faced was not very good and to keep the interest of the fans seeing the games, Saperstein began having them employ clowning routines in the team's format. But the Globetrotters were far more than a basketball vaudeville act, they played superior basketball. Although they were defeated by the New York Rens in the 1939 World Championship Tournament, in 1940 they returned to the tournament and beat the Rens in the quarter-finals.

By 1943, with Reece "Goose" Tatum doing a clown routine at center with his incredible 84" arm span, sometimes looping in twenty-five-foot hook shots, and Marques Haynes playing spectacular legitimate basketball dribbling through multiple defenders, the Globetrotters were a force to be reckoned with when they played the game for real.

In 1948 and 1949, the Harlem Globetrotters, with Tatum and Haynes playing the game for real, would defeat that season's eventual BBA champion the Minneapolis Lakers and George Mikan twice in exhibition games. The first game in 1948, was played before 17,823 fans at Chicago Stadium with the Globetrotters victorious 61–59. The second game in 1949, also played at Chicago Stadium, drew even a larger crowd of 21,866 and saw the Globetrotters prevail again 49–45.

The Globetrotters would continue to play some very serious and competitive exhibition basketball into the early 1950s, but due to losing an increasing number of black stars to the NBA the club began to focus its brand more on a clowning game that was enormously entertaining and became financially successful on an international stage and that survives until this day. Over the years the Globetrotters have played before kings, queens, popes, behind the Iron Curtain, and in Africa and Australia. In Berlin, the Globetrotters played outdoors before the biggest basketball crowd in history with 75,000.

It wasn't until the 1950–51 season that the first black players came into the NBA. In 1950, Chuck Cooper of Duquesne University became the first black player to be drafted in the NBA when he was chosen by the Boston Celtics as the 13th player picked in the draft.

Bob Cousy has always proudly pointed out that he played with the first black player to reach the NBA. Celtics owner Walter Brown, making Cooper his second pick in the 1950 NBA college draft, stated, "I don't give a damn if he's striped or plaid or polka dot, Boston takes Charles Cooper of Duquesne."[3]

Chuck Cooper had attended Duquesne on the G.I. Bill and his legacy is celebrated in civil rights history due to an incident that occurred while he was a player on the Duquesne Dukes squad. On December 23, 1946, in Pittsburgh, Tennessee coach John Mauer refused to put his team on the court with a black player. Dukes coach Charles "Chuck" Davies was adamant about adhering to the long-time administrative policy of the school to not discriminate on the basis of race in its athletic programs. Duquesne had been allowing black players to compete in its athletic programs since the 1920s. One of the first blacks to play sports at the school was Cumberland Posey, who later owned the Homestead Grays in the Negro Leagues. When Tennessee remained steadfast in its decision to not take the court, Duquesne was awarded a 2–0 forfeit of the game.

While Nat "Sweetwater" Clifton became the first black player to sign an NBA contract when he signed with New York Knicks in 1950, it was Earl Lloyd who became the first black player to play in an NBA regular-season game because the schedule had his Washington Capitals team opening one day before the others.

Nat "Sweetwater" Clifton had played college ball at Xavier of Louisiana during 1942 and 1943. He then joined the U.S. Army and served for three years during World War Two. Following the war, Clifton played for the New York Rens and Harlem Globetrotters before joining the Knicks.

Several players chosen in the 1950 NBA college draft would go on to have careers in the NBA that would take them all the way into the Naismith Memorial Basketball Hall of Fame and immediately upon entering the league, help the NBA to keep its footing as a national professional sport while it was still unstable in fan support.

Aside from the issue of black players entering the NBA, the 1950 draft would be a pivotal event in forging the league's legitimacy by bringing some of its early stars into the game.

In the 1950 draft, the Philadelphia Warriors exercised their territorial draft rights to pick Paul Arizin of Villanova. Arizin, who suffered from asthma, played hard despite his disability and had an immediate impact on the league. In only his second season in 1951–52, Arizin, a line drive shooter, would become the leading scorer with an average of 25.4 points per game. Ultimately, he played ten years in the NBA, missing two years while serving in the armed services during the Korean War and was an All-Star every year he played in the league.

George Yardley of Stanford University was taken by the Ft. Wayne Zollner Pistons and would become the first player in the NBA to score 2,000 career points.

Bill Sharman of USC was taken by the Washington Capitals in the second round as the number 16 pick. Within a year Sharman would be a member of the Boston Celtics; he would be instrumental in helping the Boston Celtics to become one of professional sports' first dynasties and go on to be named as one of the fifty greatest players in NBA history in 1996.

But the player taken in the 1950 NBA draft that would have the biggest impact on NBA history, was Bob Cousy of Holy Cross. Cousy was hopeful that the Boston Celtics, who had the number one pick in the draft, would select him. He had even made plans to settle down in Worcester, Massachusetts.

Although Cousy was well-known in Boston, Walter Brown was not eager to draft him. Brown had drafted several other well-known players from New England colleges in the past few years and been burned. Former Holy Cross players Joe Mullaney, Dermott O'Connell and even All-American George Kaftan had failed miserably wearing a Celtics jersey. In addition, Wyndol Gray and Saul Mariaschin of Harvard and Tony Lavelli of Yale had been busts in Boston.

While Holy Cross had won the NCAA tournament in 1947 when Cousy was a freshman, there was a group of hardcore, very vocal Cousy detractors who were quick to point out that the Holy Cross Crusaders had never won a tournament while Cousy was the leading player on the team. Furthermore, it was alleged that he had never played a good game at Madison Square Garden, the prime basketball task environment that supposedly separated the average players from the good ones or great ones. While all that was not exactly true, the Crusaders had won the Sugar Bowl Tournament in Cousy's sophomore year, the damage was done.

Of course, there was also the belief among some of the supposedly informed analysts that all the fancy stuff that Cousy exhibited with the behind the back passes and through-the-legs passes would not work in the NBA. Celtics coach Red Auerbach had seen Cousy play with the college all-stars against the Harlem Globetrotters and he advanced the opinion that Bob Cousy was a one-dimension player, all offense and no defense.

Arnold "Red" Auerbach, born September 29, 1917, in the Williamsburg section of Brooklyn, was the son of Jewish immigrant parents from Minsk, Russia. He was a standout basketball player at George Washington University. Auerbach began his coaching career at the high school level at St. Albans Prep School in Washington, D.C. After serving in the U.S. Navy in World War Two, Auerbach became coach of the Washington Capitals in the BAA, winning division titles in 1947 and 1949. Red Auerbach would become an NBA legend coaching the Boston Celtics, and his rise to fame began with Walter Brown drafting Bob Cousy.

While Bob Cousy may have been the most popular player in New England, Walter Brown had been urged by Red Auerbach to get him a big man that could neutralize George Mikan.

The 1950 NBA draft was held at the Biltmore Hotel in New York and when it came time for Walter Brown to make his number one pick for the Celtics, he took a big man, 6'11" Chuck Shares of Bowling Green State University.

The Boston press was outraged that Cousy had been passed up by the Celtics and blamed it on Red Auerbach. According to Bill Russell writing in *Red and Me—My Coach, My Lifelong Friend,* one reporter confronted Auerbach by saying, "You asshole! Don't you realize you've insulted everyone in New England by not drafting Cousy! He's the best player in the country! Anyone with brains knows that. Besides that, you're a Jew, and we don't like Jews either!"

Chuck Cooper. (Courtesy of The Sports Museum.)

The Celtics second draft pick was even more surprising as well as ground-breaking. Boston selected 6'5" Charlie Cooper of Duquesne, a black player. The NBA was still an all-white league and there had been no discussion among the owners about integrating the league. The draft of a black player by the Celtics was especially concerning to Abe Saperstein who owned the Harlem Globetrotters. Saperstein had a monopoly on black professional players and his team was the biggest draw at the gate in the game. Those games were played in arenas owned by NBA teams and meant considerable revenue. Saperstein was keenly aware of what the integration of Major League Baseball in 1947 with Jackie Robinson and Larry Doby was doing to the sagging attendance at Negro League games.

Befuddled by Walter Brown's selection of a black player, the NBA team owners called a recess and discussed the matter. They quickly came to the conclusion that there were no grounds to prevent the Celtics from drafting a black player and resumed the draft.

In the ninth round, the Washington Capitals took a black player, Earl Lloyd of Washington State University.

Later that summer, the New York Knicks convinced Nat "Sweetwater" Clifton to abandon the Harlem Globetrotters and sign an NBA contract. Abe Saperstein was furious and threatened Walter Brown with a boycott of Boston Garden. But Brown ignored him.

The racial integration of the NBA seems archaic today as the league is made up by an overwhelming majority of black players. By the 1970s, the demographics of the NBA showed that 70% of the players were black. In 2013, 76.3% of the players in the NBA were black and 43% of the coaches were black.

Bob Cousy was the number three choice in the draft and taken by the Tri-Cities Blackhawks. The Blackhawks consisted of three small towns (Moline, Davenport, and Rock Port) where Illinois and Iowa come together. They were one of the former NBL franchises that were merged into the NBA and are the forerunners of the Milwaukee Hawks, St. Louis Hawks, and Atlanta Hawks.

Blackhawks owner Ben Kerner had also seen Bob Cousy play for the College All-Star team against the Harlem Globetrotters, but unlike Red Auerbach, he was convinced that he had a lot of talent. Although very disappointed with not being drafted by the Celtics, Cousy signed a contract with the Blackhawks for $9,000. But before the season began, Cousy was dealt to the Chicago Stags for guard Frank Brian who had been the third leading scorer in the former NBL with the Anderson Packers team which had folded following the 1949–50 season.

Today, most writers offer a rather simplistic and almost magical account of how Bob Cousy became a Boston Celtic. They advance the notion that, during a meeting of gentleman club owners, Cousy's name with two other players were dropped into a hat and his was pulled out by Celtics owner Walter Brown. Voila!

The rest was history—right? Not exactly. The reality is that the process of Bob Cousy joining the Celtics is a little more complex.

Tri-Cities owner Ben Kerner also wanted Frank Brian for a reason other than his scoring ability. Kerner had owned the concessions program at Anderson, and Brian sold the advertising for him; Kerner was glad to bring Brian to Tri-Cities where they could continue their dual sports-business relationship.

But soon after the Brian-for-Cousy trade, the Chicago Stags folded before the 1950–51 season began. All of the Chicago players were put into a draft pool. But Ben Kerner was told that he could either keep Frank Brian or give up his number one draft choice, who happened to be Bob Cousy. He chose to keep Brian.

While all the NBA team owners were informed that Cousy would replace Brian in the player draft pool, Cousy himself, who was staying with his parents on Long Island, was never informed.

The draft pool meeting was held in October at the Park-Sheraton Hotel in New York. Boston Celtics majority owner Walter Brown and coach Red Auerbach attended the meeting and knew that Bob Cousy was available, but neither was interested in him as the first pick. It wasn't that Brown or Auerbach had no regard at all for Cousy as a player; it was just that they had a preference for another player. The blue-chip player in the draft that most teams wanted was Stags guard Max Zaslofsky, a four-time All-Star. Brown thought that he would have first choice and Auerbach gave him instructions to take Zaslofsky.

The process for this draft turned out to be a little different than any that had previously taken place. Valuations had been placed on the players to help pay off the Chicago club's debts. So, the regular draft order was dropped. Players were named almost at random and assigned to teams by general agreement. Everything went smoothly until the three top-priced players were left—the three Stags guards; Max Zaslofsky ($15,000), Andy Phillip ($10,000), and Bob Cousy ($8,500).

When Zaslofsky's name came up Brown confidently asserted his claim. But he was immediately challenged by Ned Irish of the New York Knicks and Eddie Gottlieb of the Philadelphia Warriors.

Ned Irish attempted to establish *ex-post facto* territorial rights to Zaslofsky stating that he belonged to the Knicks because he had been born in New York, educated in New York and would be a huge favorite with the Jewish population in the city. But Irish's territorial rights claim was weakened by the fact that Zaslofsky had been playing in Chicago for four years.

Eddie Gottlieb's claim on Zaslofsky was a bit far-fetched. Gottlieb claimed that his good friend and minority partner Abe Saperstein, who owned the Harlem Globetrotters, had a phantom deal to take over the Chicago franchise. In anticipation of that move, Gottlieb claimed that Saperstein had traded Zaslofsky to the Warriors for Joe Fulks.

Brown, Irish, and Gottlieb argued into the night over their right to Max Zaslofsky. With all the other parties becoming extremely bored, at 10:30 P.M., NBA Commissioner Maurice Podoloff slammed his fist on the table and said enough is enough. "I'm sick and tired of all this," said Podoloff. "There's three of you and three players, all backcourtmen, so I'm going to put the names into a hat, and whoever you draw, that's who you got."[4]

Irish said OK, so did Brown, although he personally felt that he had just been jobbed out of getting Zaslofsky, believing he had the legitimate draft choice claim. Gottlieb was dissatisfied and screaming. He said that before proceeding he had to call the owner of the Philadelphia arena. When he returned, he agreed, and the drawing was on.

Maurice Podoloff wrote out the three names of the players and put them into the legendary hat that was supplied by Syracuse Nationals owner Dan Biasone.

As a consolation to Walter Brown, he was given the first pick from the hat, but he felt it was unlucky because previously he had the first pick in two other drafts and got a player that didn't do too much for the Celtics. So, Brown asked Ned Irish to draw the first name. Irish put his hand in the hat came out with Zaslofsky.

Well, Andy Phillips was still in the hat. He along with Bob Davies was considered to be the best playmakers in the NBA, so Brown thought he might still come out all right. "When I drew Cousy I could have fallen through the floor," said Brown. "No there was no secret feeling that maybe it would all turn out for the best in the long run."[5] Brown was sure he had gotten the dirty end of the stick all the way around.

With one name left in the hat, Ed Gottlieb didn't bother to draw. But the Warriors would do well with Andy Phillips as he would be highly instrumental in leading them to an Eastern Division championship in 1950–51.

That night, shortly after midnight, Walter Brown called Bob Cousy and told him to report to the Celtics office in Boston. Cousy was jubilant, but he still knew that he was going to have to convince Red Auerbach that he belonged on the Celtics.

The Boston training camp was tedious that year as Red Auerbach set about transforming the Celtics into a winning team. He traded players and cut two former Holy Cross players, George Kaftan and Joe Mullaney, that were both popular with the Boston Garden crowds, but Bob Cousy made the team.

The arrival of Bob Cousy, along with Bill Sharman, also new to the NBA, and center-forward Ed Macauley, picked-up from the defunct St. Louis team, would revitalize the Boston Celtics, a team that had been playing mediocre basketball for several years. It seems ironic that Bob Cousy as a player would be credited by many with saving professional basketball in Boston and later as a coach be accused by many of ruining professional basketball in Cincinnati.

The Celtics had not only been struggling in the league standings but also financially. Following the 1949–50 season, the board of directors of Garden Arena Corporation that owned both Boston Garden and the Celtics intended to get out of professional basketball. It was then that Walter Brown, who had been employed as the general manager of Boston Garden, saw an opportunity. Brown was a true sportsman from a family with a deep history in sports. His father George V. Brown had organized the Boston Marathon and for more than thirty years, Walter had fired the starting gun.

At first, Walter Brown didn't think that professional basketball had much of a chance of succeeding. But after witnessing Holy Cross sell out Boston Garden regularly for college games, he changed his point of view. Now with the Celtics about to become defunct in 1950, Brown took out a mortgage on his home and solicited other investors, raising about $200,000. One such investor was Lou Pieri of Providence, Rhode Island.

Lou Pieri owned the Rhode Island Auditorium and had also owned the Providence Steamrollers in the NBA before the team folded in 1949. Amazingly, Pieri agreed to invest $50,000 in the Celtics. However, there was one condition, that Walter Brown hire Arnold "Red" Auerbach as coach.

According to Pieri, if it had not been for the support of Providence banker Clarence "Bud" Gifford who came up with additional loans, the Celtics franchise would have folded. "For three years when Walter and I were short of money and in danger of having to drop out, he came up with the loans that kept us in business," said Pieri. "If we had been forced to quit, Cousy would have wound up in another city."[6]

Bob Cousy would become one of the greatest playmakers and passers in NBA history. His dizzying behind the back and through the legs passes and ball handling would earn him the nickname "The Houdini of the Hardwood." Albeit sometimes he was too much of a wizard for his teammates, and some of his passes would hit them in the head. In the early part of Cousy's career, Red Auerbach thought he was too tricky for his own teammates. "He wasn't that good for two, three years," said Auerbach. "We were losing the ball; he'd make great plays but he'd lose the ball a lot."[7]

On the other hand, Cousy believed that after a player played with him for a couple of weeks, there was no excuse for him being fooled. He told Celtics rookies to be ready for a pass anytime. Most players, even if they had been playmakers themselves on other teams or in college like Sam Jones and K.C. Jones, got used to Cooz, and when they started to score a lot of points from his passes, they liked him even better.

Of course, there were some in the NBA who were not impressed with Cousy's showboating. For one, Les Harrison, owner-coach of the Rochester Royals who called Cousy's ball handling bush league stuff. Harrison stated, "I've got Bob Davies who can do all those things, but I don't let him. This is professional basketball and you don't make a fool of other pros."[8]

When Bob Cousy joined the Boston Celtics, he had a concern about his style of play as well. So, he asked Red Auerbach if he was OK with his style of passing the ball. Auerbach replied, "Cooz, I don't care how you pass the ball. You can pass it through your ass if you want to. Just be sure somebody catches it."[9]

Eventually, everyone, Red Auerbach included, came to realize that Cousy's fancy ball flinging on the court put fannies in the arena seats. That was what the fans were coming to see. The Boston fans were familiar with Cousy from his days with Holy Cross and loved his style.

On December 9, 1950, Bob Cousy and Marie "Missy" Ritterbusch were married. But due to a schedule change, the newlyweds spent their first night together in Boston Garden as the Celtics were defeated by Syracuse.

In 1950–51, the NBA would drop some of the teams located in smaller cities and become more manageable with eleven teams playing in two divisions with Minneapolis, Rochester, and Fort Wayne reverting to the five-team Western Division. The Eastern Division would begin the season with six teams, but Washington, which had been on the brink of bankruptcy and lost Coach Red Auerbach at the end of the 1949–50 season when he left to become coach of the Boston Celtics, folded after going 10–25.

The first NBA All-Star game was played that season on March 2, 1951, at Boston Garden. There were 10,094 fans in attendance for the game that saw the East defeat the West 111–94. The East squad was led by Boston's Ed Macauley, the game's MVP, with 20 points. The Syracuse Nationals Dolph Schayes had 14 rebounds and Bob Cousy had 8 assists. For the West, Alex Groza of Indianapolis had 17 points and 13 rebounds, while George Mikan of Minneapolis added 12 points and 11 rebounds. Jim Pollard of Minneapolis and Bob Davies of Rochester each had 5 assists.

The Philadelphia Warriors, with Andy Phillips feeding the ball to Paul Arizin and Joe Fulks, won the Eastern Division by 2½ games in the 1950–51 season. However, Philadelphia was quickly dispatched 2 games to 0 by the Syracuse Nationals in the Eastern Division Semi-Finals.

Also in the Eastern Division, the Boston Celtics with Bob Cousy finished in second place and made the playoffs. From that point on, the Celtics would not be out of the playoffs until 1970. But the New York Knicks with Max Zaslofsky quickly dispatched the Boston Celtics in the semi-finals then barely got by the Syracuse Nationals in the East finals to reach the championship series.

In the Western Division, Minneapolis finished ahead of the Rochester Royals by three games. Still, it had been a solid season for the Royals led by Arnie Risen, Bob Davies, and Bobby Wanzer. During the regular season, the Royals had played a couple of memorable overtime games. On January 6, the Royals were edged by Indianapolis in a game that went six overtime periods, still the longest game on record in the NBA history. Then a little over two weeks later the Royals battled the New York Knickerbockers through four overtime periods before winning the game.

In the West Division Semi-Finals, the Royals defeated Ft. Wayne 2 games to 0 and then beat the Minneapolis Lakers 3 games to 1 to reach the finals.

In 1951, for the first time, the NBA Finals would require a seventh game to determine the outcome of the championship. The Rochester Royals proceeded to square-off against the New York Knicks for the NBA championship as well as bragging rights in the Empire State. The Royals would jump out to a 3–0 lead in the series. But the Knicks would fight back with determination and force a seventh game with the Royals played at Rochester's Edgerton Park Sports Arena. With the score tied at 75–75 with 40 seconds left in the game, Bob Davies hit two clutch free throws to give the Royals the lead 77–75. The rules at that time mandated a jump ball after two successful free throws during the final three minutes of a game. The Royals controlled the tip and Jack Coleman's lay-up made the score 79–75, sealing the victory and NBA championship for Rochester.

While the Rochester Royals would continue to play winning basketball over the next few seasons, their 1951 NBA Championship would be their last title in the twentieth century and beyond. Going forward, the Royals would be moved from Rochester and bought and sold in a transcontinental odyssey that would take them to new homes in Cincinnati, Kansas City/ Omaha, and eventually in Sacramento, where the team remains in the new millennium.

Ten years in the future, the basketball lives of a kid by the name of Oscar Robertson, who was about to start to playing high school basketball in Indianapolis, and Bob Cousy, a player who had just finished his rookie year in the NBA, would collide in an attempt to revitalize the Royals franchise.

3

Scandal Revealed in College Basketball:

The NBA Escapes the Fallout

Throughout the 1930s and 1940s, college basketball had been a ball hog when it came to coverage of its games in the newspapers, leaving minimal space to the pros. Then, just as professional basketball was getting a solid footing in the sporting world, a dark cloud was about to descend upon the collegiate game. In February 1951, a scandal was revealed that showed widespread game fixing in college basketball. The event made major headlines that threatened to undermine the entire legitimacy of the collegiate game and seriously damage the growing popularity of the professional game.

The City College of New York (CCNY) had won both the NCAA and NIT tournaments in 1950, a truly outstanding achievement. While most of the same squad returned for the 1950–51 season, the first two months, CCNY had only achieved a record of 11 wins and 7 losses. Something didn't seem right.

The answer to the lackluster play of City College came on February 18, 1951, when three of the CCNY players that had played on the 1950 championship teams were arrested for bribery. All three of those arrested admitted receiving up to $1,500 each to fix three games played at Madison Square Garden during the current college season of 1950–51.

The method used by the players to fix the games was point-shaving where the players participating in the conspiracy are supposed to lose or keep the margin of victory below the point spread. Simply stated, even the most casual fan will understand that something is wrong with the game's outcome when a good team suddenly underperforms and an average team overperforms. It creates suspicion of a fix.

Three CCNY players, Co-captains Ed Roman and Ed Warner along with Al Roth, were taken into custody when they returned to New York with Coach Nat Holman after a Saturday night 95–71 victory over Temple in Philadelphia. When confronted with the evidence all three confessed to the wrongdoing.

Others implicated in the scandal would soon be arrested, including Salvatore Tarto Sollazzo, a 45-year-old jewelry manufacturer and ex-con known as a sure-thing gambler. Also arrested was Eddie Gard, a Long Island University senior and former LIU player named as an intermediary with the CCNY players.

Also taken into custody that day was Harvey "Connie" Schaff, a New York University player who had attempted to line up players at NYU to fix a game against Cornell at Madison Square Garden on New Year's Day in 1951, but failed. NYU, the pregame favorite, lost to Cornell 69–56.

In the NYU fix, Connie Schaff was approached by former outstanding LIU player Jackie Goldsmith working on behalf of Daniel "Dutch" Lamont, known as the biggest bookmaker in Altoona, Pennsylvania, and racetrack follower Joseph Serota. Goldsmith, Lamont, and Serota had offered Schaff $2,000 to hold down his team's score against Cornell. Within a month, Connie Schaff was convicted and sentenced to six months in prison. The others would go through a series of appeals facing other charges. Goldsmith was also charged with attempting to bribe four LIU players to throw a game against Duquesne at Madison Square Garden on January 1, 1949.

In the days that followed, the scandal would widen as others would be arrested for bribery and attempted bribery of college players. One of those implicated was Henry E. Poppe, former co-captain of the Manhattan College team that was involved with fixing three Manhattan games during 1949–1950.

But it was the CCNY fixers that were the leading story in the scandal. The plot to fix the CCNY games is believed to have originated during the summer of 1950 when several of the college's players were entertained by Salvatore Sollazzo at a hotel in the Catskills where college players from all over the country earned money in the summer by working at various jobs and playing unofficial basketball games in the tongue-in-cheek "Borscht Circuit" league for the entertainment of the hotel guests.

Prior to the 1950–51 college basketball season, an invitation was extended by Sollazzo to Gard to visit his home where it was suggested to Gard that he attempt to entice current New York City college players to fix games. Eddie Gard had known Al Roth since high school, he sounded him out and he was agreeable. At the beginning of December 1950, Ed Roman was approached by Roth and he agreed to visit Sollazzo's home with Roth. Following a game at Madison Square Garden, Roman and Roth met with Sollazzo and he told them they could make a lot of money if they agreed to fix some games. The players were easy prey for the gambler. To entice the naïve players, Sollazzo asked them, what's the difference if you win by ten points or seven points. Still, Roman and Roth were concerned that they might be detected if they didn't feed the ball to Warner who they considered critical to follow through on the plot. Warner might suspect something and go to coach Holman. So, they approached Warner, and to their surprise, he wanted in on the action.

The three tainted games in question had been the CCNY games with Missouri on December 9, Arizona State on December 28, and Boston College on January 11. In all three games, the fix was for the CCNY players to keep their margin of victory down to no more than six points. They did better than that as they lost all three games.

In the Arizona fix, CCNY lost 41–38 and Roth, Roman, and Warner each received $1,000. In the Boston College game, lost by CCNY 63–59, Sollazzo had promised Roth and Roman $1,000 each. Warner was hurt and didn't play, but Sollazzo said that he would still give him $500. However, after giving Roth $1,400, Sollazzo failed to honor his promise to Warner and Roman and at the time of their arrest, they were still attempting to collect. Nonetheless, all three CCNY players did receive incentives from Sollazzo, such as a payment of $500 each following the Washington State game that wasn't fixed and won by CCNY 59–43. The game was played at Madison Garden and one of the CCNY conspirators bet all the money he received from Sollazzo on his own team.

While Al Roth, Ed Roman, and Ed Warner would all receive suspended sentences for their parts in fixing games, Commissioner Maurice Podoloff and the NBA took swift action to protect its brand banning all three from ever playing in the league.

Salvatore Sollazzo wouldn't be as lucky as the players he used. He was sentenced to twelve years in prison and handed a lien of $1,128,493 for evasion of taxes.

By March 1951, three more CCNY players would be arrested and charged with fixing games by a gambler other than Sollazzo. Those players, Irwin Dambrot, Norman Mager, and Herbert Cohen, were charged in a conspiracy to fix games against SMU, UCLA, and Niagara University and enticed Ed Roman and Al Roth to join them. But upon their arrest, the three stated that they had been involved with fixing games as far back as 1948.

The initial bribe of $4,500 made to five players for fixing the SMU game on December 8, 1949, was to be split as follows; Dambrot, Mager, Ed Roman, and Al Roth $1,000 each. Cohen, a substitute who played only a little, was to receive $500. However, the money was never received by the players because the final outcome of the game against SMU in which CCNY won 67–53 resulted in a financial loss for the gambler. It was just a case of SMU playing so badly that the CCNY players would have to lie on the floor to lose.

However, the UCLA game played on December 27, 1949, and won by CCNY 60–53 met the fixer's specifications and the players received the $4,500 payoff.

In the Niagara game, played February 16, 1950, at Madison Square Garden, Roman and Roth backed out saying they'd had enough. So Dambrot, Mager, and Cohen did the dirty work. CCNY had been a big favorite but was upset by Niagara 68–61 in overtime.

One of the most unfortunate individuals to be implicated in the scandal was 6'8" Sherman White, a forward on the LIU team. White, an All-American, had just been named *Sporting News* Player of the Year when he was arrested for point shaving in February 1951. In the game against John Marshall College on February 28, 1950, White had scored 63 points. At the time of his arrest, White was the leading college scorer in the nation with a 27.7 point-per-game average and LIU had a record of 20–4. White was certain to be the New York Knicks number one draft choice in the 1951 NBA draft.

According to Sherman White, he had been recruited into the point shaving plot through peer pressure. In a 2001 interview with Dave Anderson of *The New York Times,* White stated, "Peer pressure. It wasn't the money, it was just peer pressure. I didn't handle it well."[1] White was implying that he joined the LIU team right out of high school not long after World War Two and most of his teammates were older having served in armed services. One of those older teammates just happened to be Eddie Gard, the connection between the CCNY players and Salvatore Sollazzo.

"I was naïve," said White. "I think Leroy Smith and I were the only ones who were right out of high school. Socially and mentally, the other guys were ahead of us. At times you could tell the fans knew. They knew you like a book. And when I finally got caught, it was a relief."[2]

For his part in the point-shaving scandal, Sherman White served eight months in the New York City prison on Rikers Island and was banned from ever playing in the NBA and possibly becoming one of the league's first black superstars.

In the months that followed, the college basketball scandal continued and within a year it would be revealed that game fixing in college basketball had taken place not just in New York City but was widespread. An investigation of the sport during the period of 1947 to 1950 resulted in the disclosure that eighty-six games in twenty-three cities and seventeen states had been fixed or tampered with.

The NBA would also ban another potential star, Gene Melchiorre of Bradley, who was the number one pick in the 1951 NBA draft by the Baltimore Bullets. On July 24, 1951, soon after the draft had taken place, Melchiorre, along with two of his former Bradley teammates, pleaded guilty to point shaving in one game played in 1951 vs. St. Joseph's University in Philadelphia and Oregon State University in Chicago.

Irwin Dambrot, the 6'4" center on the 1950 CCNY team, had been chosen the Most Valuable Player in the NCAA Tournament. In the 1950 NBA draft, Dambrot was the number seven pick by the New York Knicks. With the scandal breaking several months later it would have been a short career for Dambrot, so it's good that he passed up the chance to play professional basketball and instead enrolled in Columbia Dental School.

The most shocking revelation uncovered in the scandal investigation was that Frank Beard, Alex Groza, and Dale Barnstable, stars on Adolph Rupp's University of Kentucky Wildcats, had been involved in point shaving. Kentucky had won consecutive NCAA titles in 1948 and 1949 as well an NIT title.

The charges against Beard, Groza, and Barnstable stemmed from them accepting bribes to shave points in games played in 1949 against Loyola University of Chicago in an NIT game played at Madison Square Garden and a month prior against The University of Tennessee in Lexington. The Wildcats team had been on its way toward winning its second consecutive NCAA title. The three Kentucky players received $3,500 for their parts in the fixed games.

Coaches of the college teams caught up in the scandal were hardly exempt from scrutiny and administrative action. Nat Holman, the coach of CCNY, a victim of circumstances, was suspended by the New York City Board of Higher Education for "conduct unbecoming to a teacher."[3] Holman contended that he had no knowledge of his players' actions and when offered early retirement he declined. Instead, Holman fought and won. In 1953, he was reinstated, but by that time, CCNY had de-emphasized its basketball program and banned its team from playing any games in non-college-controlled arenas. Nonetheless, since he was a member of the Original Celtics, Nat Holman's legacy was assured, and in 1964, he was inducted into the Naismith Memorial Basketball Hall of Fame.

Kentucky coach Adolph Rupp came under fire after it was revealed in a sixty-three-page report issued by Judge Saul S. Streit, one of the primary jurists investigating the scandal, that Rupp had meetings with Ed Curd, a well-known bookmaker in Kentucky. According to the report, Rupp admitted that he knew Curd and "had visited him at his home on at least two occasions and had telephoned him once to learn what the point spread was on a game to be played by Kentucky against the University of Alabama."[4]

The report further stated that following a game played at Madison Square Garden in the 1947–48 season, Rupp had an after-supper snack with Curd at the Copacabana. The judge was particularly interested in who had picked up the check. Rupp said he didn't know who paid for it.

Judge Streit stated that his inquiry showed that both Rupp and the University of Kentucky should share in the plight of the three defendants, Groza, Beard, and Barnstable. It was the opinion of Judge Streit that intercollegiate basketball and football at Kentucky "had become highly systemized, professionalized and commercialized enterprises. I found covert subsidization of players, ruthless exploitation of athletes, cribbing at examinations, illegal recruiting, a reckless disregard of their physical welfare, maturation of unqualified students, demoralization of the athletes by the coach, alumni, and townspeople and the most flagrant abuse of 'athletic scholarship.'"[5]

The Southeastern Conference shut down the Kentucky Wildcats basketball program for the 1952–53 season for recruiting practices and providing secret payments to some of its star players. But in the end, it was all ignored by Kentucky, swept under the rug, and Adolph Rupp was soon back in business. By 1958, the Wildcats had won the school's fourth NCAA championship.

At the time, the NBA had been informed bookies were skeptical of professional basketball, they saw it as a bad investment. While the players were very good, any one of them that had a bad game would come under heavy scrutiny by the media. Still, the bookies were sure that it wasn't impossible for games to be fixed; the players were not only good but clever. But after the NBA had been in business for a couple of seasons, the bookies came to the conclusion that professional basketball was an honest game and began accepting bets on professional games. In a very short time, fans would begin betting heavily on professional basketball. Bets would even be taken in the arenas.

Then, the depth of the college basketball scandal cast doubt over the entire spectrum of the game and as a result, there was collateral damage to the NBA.

In the 1949 NBA player draft, Alex Groza, the brother of Pro Football Hall of Fame member Lou Groza of the Cleveland Browns, and Frank Beard were taken by the Indianapolis Olympians.

Alex Groza was sure to be a major gate attraction in the NBA and in his first game as a pro, played at Madison Square Garden on November 10, 1949, he scored 41 points as Indianapolis defeated the New York Knicks 83–79 before a packed house of 18,135.

In the 1950–51 NBA season, the Indianapolis Olympians finished in fourth place in the Western Division with a record of 31–37, but good enough to make the playoffs. In the Western Division Semi-Finals, the Olympians faced the powerful Minneapolis Lakers and led by Alex Groza, nearly knocked off the division champs in a best of three games series.

In game one, Minneapolis defeated Indianapolis 95–81. In the game, Alex Groza had 19 points while George Mikan had but 12. Then, in game two, the Olympians ran all over the Lakers, 108–88, as Groza scored 40 points while holding Mikan to just 2.

Game three was a shoot-out with the Lakers prevailing by a score of 85–80. George Mikan had 30 points and Alex Groza 38. It would be Groza's final game in the NBA.

That summer, Alex Groza, along with former Kentucky teammates Ralph Beard and Dale Barnstable, would admit that they had accepted bribes amounting to $3,500 in the Loyola and Tennessee games played in 1949. Immediately, NBA commissioner Maurice Podoloff would ban all three players from playing in the league for life.

Bill Spivey, a seven-foot All-American center on the Kentucky Wildcats in 1949 and 1950, was charged with perjury when he refused to testify against his teammates Groza and Beard. Although the case against Spivey was dismissed, Maurice Podoloff decided to put the kibosh on another potentially great player for the NBA and banned Spivey before he had to chance to play in the league.

With the door to the NBA slammed in his face, Bill Spivey joined the Boston Whirlwinds, one of the Harlem Globetrotters' patsy teams that accompanied them on tour. Spivey would continue to play theatrical basketball for several years eventually being moved to the Trotters' opponents "A-Team," the Washington Generals.

Then, the Indianapolis Olympians folded after losing their star players Alex Groza and Ralph Beard, along with Wallace "Wah Wah" Jones, all caught up in the college basketball scandal.

New York had been the epicenter of the college basketball scandals and the fallout had a devastating effect on the game in the city. Following the public exposure of the scandals, New York City colleges began to curtail their recruiting and the best high school players in the city left for colleges across the country. Highly touted Sihugo Green, of Boys High School in Brooklyn, enrolled at Duquesne University in Pittsburgh and became an All-American and NBA first-round draft choice.

With the taint of the scandal and lower quality of players competing, the number attending the remaining college games at Madison Square Garden began dwindling to 3,000 to 4,000. LIU would not schedule another game in the facility for nearly twenty years, and CCNY de-emphasized its program and would not allow its team to play in any arenas that weren't college controlled. Many fans began to watch pro basketball for the first time.

Despite the loss of some potential major star players and the collapse of the Indianapolis franchise, the college basketball scandals would actually benefit the NBA, at least in New York. In 1950–51, the New York Knicks had only18 home games scheduled at Madison Square Garden; now, with fewer college games at the Garden, they would expand that schedule. The Garden had preferred booking college games as they attracted a much larger gate—sometimes as many as 18,000 fans for a game. So, the New York Knicks saw a window of opportunity to grab the fans and closed it.

Entering the 1951–52 season, the NBA would become a solid ten-team league and have a very competitive season. It would be that season that one of the first major changes would be made to improve play in the league. The lane was widened from six to twelve feet to prevent the big men from clogging the middle. The most notable big man clogging the middle was, of course, George Mikan.

In the Western Division, the Rochester Royals were champions and had the best record in the regular season in the NBA. The Royals proceeded to defeat Ft. Wayne in the Western Semi-Finals 2 games to 0, before being defeated in the division finals to their perpetual nemesis, the Minneapolis Lakers, 3 games to 1.

In the Eastern Division Semi-Finals, Syracuse finished on top and defeated Philadelphia 2 to games 1 while New York defeated Boston 2 games to 1. Then, in the East Finals, the Knicks surprised the Nationals 3 games to none.

The New York Knicks, who had finished third in the Eastern Division with a record of 37–39, suddenly found themselves playing in the NBA Finals against the Minneapolis Lakers in a city still tainted by the college basketball scandals. But the series would rejuvenate the fans in New York as the Knicks took the powerful Lakers to seven games before losing.

The finals were not without controversy, both warranted and irrelevant. To begin with, games one, two, and five of the finals had to be played at St. Paul Auditorium as the Lakers home arena, Minneapolis Arena had been booked. It was a circumstance that would be repeated time and time again in the NBA into the 1960s with teams being pre-empted by circuses and ice shows.

It could be argued that playing in St. Paul might have cost the Lakers the home-court advantage. If any NBA team ever had a bigger home-court advantage it was the Lakers. Minneapolis Arena (Auditorium), the 10,000-seat facility where the Lakers played their home games, was narrower by a few feet than the other arenas where NBA games were played at that time. The saying among a lot of the players was that 6'10" George Mikan, 6'7" Vern Mikkelsen, and 6'4" Jim Pollard would stretch their arms across the narrow court and nobody could get through.

In the first quarter of game one, played at Minneapolis, Knicks guard Al McGuire drove inside for a basket and was fouled. But neither referee, Stan Stutz nor Sid Borgia, had seen the ball go in the basket and McGuire was given two free throws. There was, of course, no video at that time for refs to check. While Knicks coach Joe Lapchick pleaded emphatically with commissioner Maurice Podoloff seated at courtside the call was allowed to stay.

The game wound up in overtime and the Lakers won 82–77. Of course, had the extra two points been on the scoreboard at the end of regulation time from McGuire's shot the Knicks would have won. The Knicks All-Star forward Harry Gallatin later remarked, "If they had counted that shot, it would have made a big difference in the series."[6]

The Knicks won game two sending the series to New York, tied at one game each. Games three and four, scheduled to be played in New York, took place at the 69th Regiment Armory located on Lexington Avenue between East 25th and 26th Streets. Madison Square Garden had been booked by the Barnum & Bailey Circus for those dates. The Armory is a 5,000-seat facility that actually served as the Knicks primary home venue between 1946 and 1960.

The Lakers won game three 82–77 by forcing a slower game that disrupted the Knicks fast-break offense as George Mikan scored 26 points and had 17 rebounds. Two days later, in game four at the Armory, the Knicks rebounded to win 90–89 while limiting George Mikan to just 11 points to even up the series 2 games each.

Over the years, much speculation and ballyhoo have been made that the Knicks lost the home-court advantage by being trumped by a circus at Madison Square Garden. But the facts are that both games were close. Furthermore, the 1952 playoffs would not be the last year that an important NBA playoff game would have to vacate its home arena to permit a circus to take place. Another memorable displacement of an NBA playoff game by elephants and clowns would take place in 1963 at Cincinnati during the Eastern Division Playoffs between the Royals with Oscar Robertson and Boston Celtics with Bob Cousy. In that series, the Cincinnati Royals lost a hard-fought series 4 games to 3 to Cousy and the Celtics.

Game five of the 1952 championship series was played again in St. Paul as the Lakers downed the Knicks 102–89. For

Minneapolis, both George Mikan and Vern Milkkelson scored 32 points each.

The series returned to New York for game six and only 3,000 fans showed up at the Armory to witness Max Zaslofsky score 23 points and sink the Lakers 76–68.

The Minneapolis Lakers won the 1952 NBA Championship in game seven on April 25, defeating the New York Knicks 82–65 at the Minneapolis Auditorium in front of 8,600 delirious fans. Game seven was the only game in the finals that was played on either team's home court. The win gave the Minneapolis Lakers their fourth title in five years as they became the NBA's first dynasty.

In the 1952–53 Bob Cousy began to demonstrate dominance in his play. For the first time, he would lead the NBA in assists, then proceed to lead the league in that category every year going forward through 1960 while also always finishing near the top in scoring and free-throw percentage. At the conclusion of the season, when the writers and broadcasters picked their NBA All-Star Team, Bob Cousy led the balloting and just missed being a unanimous choice by one vote.

Joining Cousy on the All-Star Team were Celtics teammate Ed Macauley, George Mikan of Minneapolis, Dolph Schayes of Syracuse, and Neil Johnston of Philadelphia.

The addition of Bob Cousy on the Celtics had transformed the team into competitors. In 1952–53, the Boston Celtics finished third in the Eastern Division with a record of 46–25 behind division champion New York Knicks 47–23 and second place Syracuse Nationals 47–24. Therefore, Boston was scheduled to play Syracuse in the best of three games in the Eastern Division Semi-Finals. At that point in their history, the Celtics had never won a playoff series. Bob Cousy's emerging brilliance would be personified by his performance in game two of the 1953 Eastern Division Semi-Finals.

The Celtics won game one by a score of 87–81 led by Bob Cousy with 20 points and Bill Sharman with 15, while Dolph Schayes had 10 points for the Nationals.

Game two of the series, witnessed by 11,658 delirious fans at Boston Garden, turned out to be a four-overtime affair and is arguably Bob Cousy's greatest game in the NBA, although he had only 2 assists and was playing on a bad leg.

With less than a minute to play in regulation time, Cousy uncharacteristically missed an open man under the basket. Luckily,

Bob Cousy in action. (Courtesy of The Sports Museum.)

the Celtics got the ball back; Cousy was fouled and sank two free throws to tie the game at 77–77 and send it into overtime. At that point in the game, Cousy had 25 points.

In the first overtime, Bob Cousy had six of the Celtics nine points including another game-tying free throw. With the score tied 86–86, the game entered the second overtime. At the four-minute mark, Syracuse lost Dolph Schayes, the team's top scorer, when he was tossed out of the game for fighting with the Celtics' Bob Brannum. The Nationals and Celtics scored just 4 points each in the period, but once again it was a basket by Cousy that kept the Celtics in the game.

The Celtics and Nationals proceeded into the third overtime with the score knotted at 90–90. The Nationals had only five men who had not fouled out. Then, Paul Seymour, the Nationals 6'1" guard, sprained his ankle. Now Syracuse coach, Al Cervi, was confronted with the dilemma of choosing between sending an ineligible man back in and giving the Celtics a technical or leaving Seymour in the game. The decision was to leave Seymour in the game stationed under the basket. So, in effect, the Celtics were playing against four men on the court but found themselves in trouble and trailing by two points with 18 seconds left to go.

Then, Bob Cousy tied it again with two foul shots. Syracuse then hit a basket with five seconds to regain the lead at 99–97. Once again, it was the Cooz to the rescue as he raced up court and sank a 25-foot one-handed push shot as the gun sounded to tie the score 99–99.

The game entered the fourth overtime and in the first 2½ minutes of play, Syracuse used its four mobile players to take a five-point lead, 104–99. Then Cousy got hot and scored nine of the Celtics' 12 points, and in the end, Boston won the game 111–105 as Cousy finished with 50 points.*

A total of 107 fouls had been called in the epic contest, 55 against Syracuse and 52 against Boston and in the end, despite Cousy's heroic effort, it would be fouls that caught up with the Nationals, as seven men reached the limit of six, resulting in a technical every time they committed a foul.

Unfortunately, the success of the Boston Celtics would be short-lived, as they would fall to the New York Knicks 3 games to 1 in the Eastern Division Finals.

Despite the dominance of George Mikan and the Minneapolis Lakers, the Syracuse Nationals had been the most popular team in the early 1950s, but having a solid team in New York, the nation's largest media center, did much to increase interest in professional basketball.

The New York Knicks and Minneapolis Lakers would once again meet in the 1953 NBA Finals. But after winning game one, the Knicks would lose four straight to the Lakers. For the third year in a row, the Knicks had reached the finals only to lose having been defeated by the Royals in 1951 and the Lakers in 1952 and 1953.

* Playing the game on that bad leg, Bob Cousy had scored 50 points, 10 out of 18 from the field and 30 out of 32 foul shots. Cousy's 50 points set a new record for a playoff game surpassing the old record of 47 set by George Mikan in the 1952 playoffs.

It was anticipated that 1953–54 would be a banner year for the NBA. George Mikan announced that he intended to retire at the end of the season and everyone was anticipating a repeat in the finals of Lakers vs. Knicks. Unfortunately, just as the NBA was legitimizing its game and building a larger following, problems began to occur.

First, fourteen games into the season the Baltimore Bullets went bankrupt. Then, scandal would enter into the picture. Although the NBA had dodged a bullet in the college point-shaving scandals, it was almost inevitable. The skullduggery had been so widespread that somehow an undetected part of it would leak into the league through a crack in the wall.

That occurred on September 16, 1953, when Jack Molinas, a former Columbia University star, signed an NBA contract with Frank Zollner's Ft. Wayne Zollner Pistons for $8,500 and a $1,500 signing bonus. But Molinas wouldn't last half a season in the league. Jack Molinas played his last NBA game on January 7, 1954, as Ft. Wayne lost to Syracuse 79–67. The following day, NBA Commissioner Maurice Podoloff suspended Molinas indefinitely. In addition, he was declared ineligible to play in the NBA All-Star Game for which he had been chosen. At the time, Molinas was playing well, averaging 12 points and 8.2 rebounds per game, playing an average of 32 minutes per game.

George Yardley was Molinas' Ft. Wayne teammate in 1953, both were rookies. Yardley was to state that, while Molinas was on the telephone a lot, he never saw him dealing with bookies nor did his roommate.

After being arrested by the Ft. Wayne police, Jack Molinas signed a statement that he had bet on his team, the Ft. Wayne Pistons, to win games. In Indiana, it was not unlawful for an athlete to bet on himself. But due to legislation enacted in New York in the wake of the 1951 collegiate scandals, Molinas was declared culpable because he had made calls to Stanley Ratensky in New York to bet on NBA games which were in violation of anti-bribery codes. The Bronx Assistant District Attorney announced that he intended to take Jack Molinas to a grand jury in an effort to determine whether a widespread gambling ring was operating in the NBA.

NBA president Maurice Podoloff, in his official statement on the matter, said that Jack Molinas had bet on a total of ten games and won six of the bets netting a total of $400 profit.

Following the shocking revelation of Jack Molinas' connections to gamblers, Ft. Wayne owner Fred Zollner obsessed over the character of his players. He was convinced that a couple of other players, Mel Hutchins and Monk Meinke, were also on the take because they were friends of Molinas. So, he hired a detective and followed them both at home and on the road while checking their telephone records. When they came up clean, Zollner told Pistons coach Charley Eckman to trade both players.

The exile of Jack Molinas from the NBA hardly stopped gambling in professional basketball, there was widespread gambling by fans on almost every game played. Syracuse Nationals center Johnny Kerr stated that fans at Boston Gardens would shout, "Hey, we doubled our bets on you shmucks, so you better beat the spread."[7] Some fans with wagers placed were so brazen that they were of the opinion they could influence the outcome of the game by yelling at and intimidating the refs and by littering the court with debris. Some zealous bookies even set up shop under the stands at half-time.

The NBA players were warned to avoid hanging out with gamblers or face being banned from the league, but when it came to the fans, especially in New York City, it was a different matter. At Madison Square Garden it was estimated that about half the fans at any given game were more concerned about the point spread than the actual outcome of the game.

Alex Hannum, a 6'7" power forward, who played for seven NBA teams between 1949 and 1957, was of the opinion that player's salaries were being paid indirectly by gamblers due to the fact that a lot of the fans buying tickets were there to bet on the games. "In my first game at Madison Square Garden," stated Hannum, "we were up by eight points over the Knicks and the fans yelled like hell. Then the score was tied and the place was quiet. We later learned the point spread was eight."[8]

A few years later, Jack Molinas would surface again at the center of another college basketball scandal. Legal authorities would allege that Molinas was involved with paying over $70,000 to fix forty-three college games throughout the country between 1957 and 1961. It would be revealed that in the chicanery, forty-seven players were believed to have been approached and thirty-three admitted to taking bribes from twenty-two schools that amounted to between $75 and $4,500.

Jack Molinas would be convicted and sentenced to 10–15 years in prison for attempting to fix the outcome of a game between North Carolina State and Wake Forrest in 1959. Several others would receive prison sentences and six former players received suspended sentences.

On August 5, 1975, in Los Angeles, Jack Molinas was shot in the back of the head by a sniper and killed while standing on the patio of his luxurious Hollywood Hills home. He was 43 years old and his murder remains unsolved.

Despite the shenanigans of Jack Molinas, the NBA had an exciting season in 1953–54. Fans in Boston were accustomed to seeing the Bruins engage in hockey fights at Boston Garden. But on November 11, a capacity crowd of 13,909 fans at the Garden witnessed a huge round-ball donnybrook between the Celtics and Philadelphia Warriors. The fight started between Bob Cousy and Neil Johnston of the Warriors when the two collided chasing a loose ball in the first half. Cousy still went after loose balls with the same fervor that he had chasing balls rolled out the door by coach Buster Sheary at the end of practices at Holy Cross. Cousy was no pansy, he had grown-up on some tough streets and playgrounds in lower Manhattan and Queens and gallantly held his own with Johnston. The scuffle quickly escalated into a full-fledged, free-swinging brawl between all the members of both teams. It took two minutes and twenty policemen to stop the fight. While it was hard to tell who won the fight, Boston ultimately won the game 78–72.

As was anticipated, the Minneapolis Lakers made sure that George Mikan hung up his gym shoes in a grand finale at the end of the season. The Lakers reached the NBA Finals by defeating the Rochester Royals in the Western Division Finals.

The Rochester Royals were still a good team and had one of the best records in the league, finishing the 1953–54 campaign in second place in the Western Division with a record of 44–28. But the Royals were an aging team with the oldest roster in the league, averaging 29.1 years old. Bobby Wanzer was 33, Bob Davies was 34, and both Arnie Risen and Jack Coleman were 30.

The Lakers won their fifth NBA championship in seven years defeating the Syracuse Nationals in the finals 4 games to 3.

The New York Knicks had won the Eastern Division and were expected to meet the Lakers again in the finals, but were swept by Syracuse Nationals in the Eastern Semi-Finals.

The NBA was then seven years old and George Mikan left the league as the career leader in points scored and points per game. Mikan then became general manager of Lakers and opened a law practice in Minneapolis.

Although they failed to reach the finals, it had been quite a year for the Boston Celtics and Bob Cousy. The Cooz finished as the second highest scorer in the league with an average of 19.2 points per game and had been named the All-Star Game MVP.

The Celtics finished as the league leader in points per game (87.7), assists (1,773), and total rebounds (3,867), while finishing in a second-place tie in the East with Syracuse. But once again, the Celtics were swept by those nagging Nationals in the Eastern Division playoffs.

4

The Shot Clock Ushers in the Modern NBA

& Bill Russell Joins the Celtics

Throughout the early years of the NBA, the games were, for the most part, a battle for position, lots of shoving, pushing, and blocking. It allowed a big slow man like George Mikan to control play and slow the game down. As a result, it had become a common strategy for teams with a substantial lead to freeze the ball in the closing minutes of the game. This, of course, would lead to constant fouling in order to get the ball back, low scoring, and depriving the fans of exciting endings to the games. One of the most ridiculous incidents of this type of play occurred on November 22, 1950, when the Minneapolis Lakers defeated the Ft. Wayne Zollner Pistons 19–18. Pistons coach Murray Mendenhall had decided that rather than attempt to contain George Mikan, his team would hold the ball, not run it, and wait until the end of the game to score the winning basket. Many fans, infuriated with this strategy, demanded their money back.

The stall game did have its supporters, including Red Auerbach, who felt it benefited the Boston Celtics. On many occasions toward the end of the game, to slow the pace, Auerbach would pull Bob Cousy out and replace him with Sonny Hertzberg whose job it would be to just hold on to the ball. The Rochester Royals also benefited from the stall game as they played a slow defensive posting game. But by 1953, it was apparent that such a molasses strategy as stalling the ball was killing the professional game. Play needed to be sped up and made more exciting.

So, in 1954, the NBA adopted the idea of Syracuse owner Danny Biasone to implement a 24-second shot clock to speed up the game by eliminating stalling. The shot clock was adopted and the intervention was an instant success with fans as it increased scoring and the pace of the game. Immediately, in the 1954–55 season, scoring in the NBA increased from 79.5 points per game to 93.1. But most importantly, the shot clock ensured that the excitement in the game never lessened. In essence, the modern NBA game had been born.

With the fast pace of the game created by the shot clock, the league's games were becoming more mainstream in the sporting world. One single game, in particular, would put the NBA over the top with fan interest. It would be a game played at Boston Garden on February 27, 1959, in which the Boston Celtics defeated the Minneapolis Lakers by a score of 173–139. In the game, Bob Cousy scored 31 points and had 29 assists for the Celtics, and Tom Heinsohn had 43 points. The Lakers leading scorer was Elgin Baylor with 28. In the fourth quarter, the two teams scored a remarkable 96 points (Boston 52, Minneapolis 44).

In the 1954–55 season, a player just coming into the league would immediately take advantage of the shot clock—Bob Pettit. Drafted out of LSU by the Milwaukee Hawks, Pettit would be named Rookie of the Year while finishing fourth in scoring, averaging 20.4 points per game.

The Boston Celtics finished in third place in the Eastern Division in 1954–55 with a record of 36–36 behind the New York Knicks and the division winner, the Syracuse Nationals.

Despite the third-place finish of the Celtics, Bob Cousy had played like a champion. The Cooz finished first in the NBA in assists with 557 and assists per game 7.8. He was second in the league in six categories, including scoring with 21.2 points per game and third in two categories, points (1,504) and free throws (460).

While the Celtics got by the Knicks 2 games to 1 in the Eastern Division Semi-Finals, they just couldn't get over that final hurdle to the championship finals as they fell again to the Nationals 1 game to 3 in the Eastern Finals.

In the West Semi-Finals Minneapolis got by Rochester 2 games to 1, then, without the retired George Mikan, lost to Ft. Wayne 3 games to 1 in the West Finals.

Syracuse went on to win the championship as they defeated Ft. Wayne 4 games to 3 in the finals.

Following a last-place finish in the Western Division for a fourth straight year, the Milwaukee Hawks moved to St. Louis for the 1955–56 season. With new fans, the Hawks were a reinvigorated franchise and finished second in the Western Division. Bob Pettit was named the NBA's first MVP and led the charge, finishing first in eleven statistical categories including scoring with 25.7 points per game, 1,846 total points, and 1,164 total rebounds.

The Hawks entered unfamiliar territory in the playoffs and made it to the second round before being defeated by Ft. Wayne. The Pistons would then advance to the championship finals to be defeated by the Philadelphia Warriors.

Meanwhile, Bob Cousy's star continued to rise in the NBA. In 1956, Cousy would become the first NBA player to appear on the cover of *Sports Illustrated.*

The Boston Celtics finished in second place in 1955–56, but once again they were knocked out of the playoffs by the Syracuse Nationals. While the Celtics had the best offense in 1955–56, scoring a league-leading 106.0 points per game, they finished last in defense, giving up 105.3 points per game to the opposition. Coach Red Auerbach came to the conclusion that in order to win a championship he had to plug a big hole in his team. Since 1950–51, the Boston Celtics led by their core three, Bob Cousy, Bill Sharman, and Ed Macauley, and had been competitive in the Eastern Division, finishing second three times (1951, 1952, 1956) and third three times (1953, 1954, 1955), but they couldn't make it to the championship finals, either being knocked off by the Syracuse Nationals or the New York Knicks. The reason for the Celtics coming up short each year was that those teams had a fatal flaw. While they were a high scoring and exciting teams, they just couldn't get the ball enough to finish the job.

Red Auerbach wanted a big center that could rebound, block shots, and start his fast break; the man he wanted was Bill Russell, a 6'10", 220-pound All-American about to graduate from the University of San Francisco, a small Jesuit school team coached by Phil Woolpert. Bill Russell had led the USF Dons to 60 consecutive victories and back-to-back NCAA Championships in 1955 and 1956.

Red Auerbach had first heard about Bill Russell from Bill Reinhart, his old college coach at George Washington University. In December of 1955, Reinhart had seen Russell play that year in a holiday tournament in Oklahoma City. Everyone associated with Russell, officially or otherwise, that knew of his play at the University of San Francisco, assured Auerbach that while Russell could not shoot well, he was the most brilliant defensive player they had ever seen and was very good at running the fast break. Furthermore, Russell's ability to block shots and rebound made him an intimidating force for opposing players just by his presence on the court. Red Auerbach began to track Bill Russell's senior year at USF, and in April, as the 1956 NBA draft drew near, he set his agenda and began to move on a plan to get him.

Since the earliest days of the NBA through 1965, the very first order of business in the draft each year was for any team with standing to exercise its territorial draft rights on a player. The rules were that a team could opt to relinquish its first-round choice to claim a player who had played within a 50-mile radius of its home arena. There were instances of this rule being bent, and the most classic is the case of Wilt Chamberlain who played his college ball at Kansas but was taken as a territorial draft pick by the Philadelphia Warriors because he had played high school basketball in Philadelphia.

So, the Boston Celtics quickly exercised their territorial right to Tom Heinsohn of Holy Cross. Heinsohn had been a member of the Holy Cross NIT championship team of 1954. A power forward, standing at 6'7", he had broken Bob Cousy's career points record at Holy Cross scoring 1,789 points while averaging 27.4 points per game in the 1955–56 season.

It was expected that Bill Russell would be the number one pick in the 1956 draft. That pick belonged to the Rochester Royals. However, Russell informed Royals owner Les Harrison that he wanted $25,000 ($232,431 in 2018 money) to sign, which included a signing bonus.

At the time, the Royals were a cash-strapped franchise and besides, they already had 6'7", 250-pound Maurice Stokes, the 1956 NBA Rookie of the Year. In his rookie season, Stokes had averaged 16 points and 16 rebounds per game. He was so agile that he could rebound the ball and then, instead of passing it out, could bring the ball down court himself. A lot of pro-basketball experts and analysts at the time believed Maurice Stokes to be the best rebounder in the game and destined to be the NBA's first black superstar.

At the same time, Abe Saperstein was offering Bill Russell a considerable sum to sign with the Harlem Globetrotters. The estimated offer was as high as $50,000 ($464,862 in 2018 money). But there was a problem—Bill Russell did not personally care for Abe Saperstein and had very little interest in playing theatrical basketball for him.

Also, there was tension still existing between Russell and Coach Phil Woolpert held over from his playing days at the University of San Francisco. It wasn't anything personal between the two; Russell just never liked the way he was coached by Woolpert who wanted him to play a flatfooted stationary game under the basket like George Mikan had as opposed to Russell's preference of playing above the rim and leading a fast break.

In addition, Russell had been offended when he, along with Coach Woolpert and USF Assistant Coach Ross Giudice, met with Saperstein in Chicago and negotiations for his services became a one-on-one dialogue between Woolpert and Saperstein. It was as if Russell wasn't even in the room.

Nonetheless, with Saperstein entering the process, the ante for signing Russell had been raised, and Les Harrison, who had a team experiencing financial problems and playing in a small market in Rochester, just could not meet the price. Also, Harrison had seen Russell play in the College All-Star Game and was less than impressed.

So, Boston Celtics owner Walter Brown made Harrison an offer too good to ignore. Brown told Harrison that if he passed on selecting Bill Russell in the first round of the draft, he, being president of the Ice Capades, would guarantee a two-week run of the show in his building in Rochester. The deal may have smacked of collusion, but with an assurance of a sell-out crowd every evening in a building that sat mostly empty, Harrison grabbed it.

So, Les Harrison came to the conclusion that the Royals needed a player who could score points and compliment the rebounding of Maurice Stokes. He passed on Russell and took Sihugo "Si" Green of Duquesne instead as the first draft choice. That left the door wide open for the St. Louis Hawks, who had the number two draft pick, to select Bill Russell.

At that time, the Boston Celtics were having financial problems as well. In fact, Walter Brown had withheld the player's playoff money. He would not make good for another year before he paid them back with interest. While Bob Cousy, the team's star, remained silent, Red Auerbach was so unsure of his future that he began working an off-season job as a sales representative for a plastics manufacturer.

Regardless of the fact that the Celtics were in a financial crisis, the thought of the St. Louis Hawks having Bill Russell in the frontcourt along with Bob Pettit, who had burst into the league and began to dominate everything, made Red Auerbach sweat bullets! So after Auerbach consulted with Walter Brown, the Celtics made an offer to St. Louis.

The Hawks had the number two pick in the draft and in exchange for it, the Celtics offered to trade All-Star center Ed Macauley, the Celtics leading scorer. It seemed like a win-win situation; Ed Macauley had been a star at St. Louis University, was bound to draw a lot of fans, and could still play a lot of basketball in the frontcourt. Also, Macauley lived in St. Louis and had an ill son. He wanted to be closer to his child while continuing to play professional basketball.

Hawks owner Ben Kerner didn't have any serious intention of drafting Bill Russell for one reason in particular—he was black. St. Louis was a very racially insensitive city and he believed it was in his best interest at that time to keep his team all-white. Nonetheless, Kerner knew they had Walter Brown and Red Auerbach over a barrel and wasn't satisfied with Macauley alone for their second draft pick. So, Auerbach agreed to include Cliff Hagan in the deal. As a sophomore, Cliff Hagan had helped the University of Kentucky to win a national championship in 1951. He had been picked as the number three player in the 1953 draft by the Celtics. But Hagan decided to play one more year at Kentucky as a graduate student and helped the Wildcats to a 25–0 record. Then, he entered the military service for two years.

With the inclusion of Cliff Hagan in the deal, Ben Kerner agreed to give up the Hawks number two pick in the draft. Going forward, the Hawks would become a dominating force in the Western Division for several years. Cliff Hagan would become a five-time All-Star and in 1978, be selected to the Naismith Memorial Basketball Hall of Fame.

Now, Boston had the number two draft choice and could select Bill Russell. However, Russell wanted to play in the 1956 Olympics Games being held in Australia before entering professional basketball. The draft was in April and the Olympics were in November so Russell could not sign a contract at that time and jeopardize his amateur status. The Celtics agreed to give Russell $22,500 which was an astonishing sum for a rookie, but $6,000 would be deducted because he would miss the first two months of the 1956–57 season. However, Walter Brown thought it was unfair and split the $6,000 deduction with Russell. Nonetheless, Russell's contract before the deduction made him the second highest paid player in the NBA behind Bob Cousy who was making $25,000.

By 1965, Bill Russell's contract with the Boston Celtics would call for $100,001 a year ($802,817 in 2018 money). The extra dollar was included to make his contract higher than that of Wilt Chamberlain. In the end, it would be a bargain as having Bill Russell as their center the Boston Celtics would proceed to win 11 NBA championships in 13 years.

Following the 1955 college season, in which Russell's University of San Francisco Dons had won the NCAA title, he was invited by President Dwight D. Eisenhower to the White House for a conference on physical fitness along with several other former and active athletes that included Bob Cousy, Major League Baseball Greats Hank Greenberg and Willie Mays, former heavyweight champion Gene Tunney, and others. President Eisenhower, a former collegiate football player at Army, addressed him as Mr. Russell and prodded him with questions about whether or not he intended to turn pro before his college eligibility was exhausted thereby making him ineligible to play in the 1956 Olympics in Australia. Russell was in awe of the White House and the respect displayed toward him by the president.

However, at the time Bill Russell joined the Celtics, he was in cultural shock having recently been exposed to some extreme racism.

Russell, along with his father, stepmother, and fiancée had all driven from California to Washington. They decided to make the return trip by driving to the old family home in Louisiana. The motor trip through the "Jim Crow" deep-south deeply affected Russell emotionally with the indignities that he experienced during the journey.

Actually, it wasn't Russell's first experience with the segregated south. During his college career, the University of San Francisco booked a game with Loyola University New Orleans, another Jesuit college. There were two other black players on the Dons and the only time they and Russell saw the rest of the team was at the arena. While all the white players stayed in a hotel, the black players were quartered in dorm rooms at Xavier University of Louisiana.

The blatant segregation in public accommodations Russell experienced in the deep-south, such as separate drinking fountains, restaurants, and bathrooms for blacks and whites, severely depressed him. Russell, in regard to his experience in the deep-south, stated that he was treated as "just another black boy, just so much dirt, with no rights, with no element of human courtesy or decency shown to me or mine."[1]

While determined to be respected as a man just as much as a player, the experience of his deep-south sojourn would haunt Bill Russell and follow him into the NBA during his rookie season. When the Celtics played against the Hawks in St. Louis, which in the mid-1950s was still a city deeply influenced by southern customs, Russell would have to endure vile racial epithets of the cruelest kind, and he was refused service in the hotel coffee shop. While Russell played well in St. Louis, there were times when the taunts hurt him so bad that he felt like quitting the professional game.

The racial abuse that Russell endured wasn't just in St. Louis, he was subjected to racial insults on his own home court by the fans in Boston Garden where often the words "Nigger" and "Coon" came roaring down upon him on the court from the stands. Bob Cousy told Russell, "If you let the names people call you bother you, you don't belong in this business."[2]

Bob Cousy was personally offended by racial segregation and had a progressive attitude about equal rights that he had gone on record with. In 1950, Red Auerbach booked a Celtics game in the segregated city of Charlotte, North Carolina. When Chuck Cooper found out that he was going to be confined to a segregated hotel, he took a midnight train out of town. Bob Cousy went with him.

Cousy was keenly aware of the fact that at the Worcester Country Club, where he played golf, Bill Russell would not be welcome—so he never invited him. Race relations in the United States were changing by the late 1950s but ever so slowly. While Cousy had empathy for Bill Russell's circumstances he was also keenly aware that he had a limited platform in the Boston area to bring about social change.

Boston, supposedly the epicenter of progressive thought in the nation's northeast corridor, had a flaw in its philosophical reputation. Bostonians were more in favor of racial integration in theory rather than practice. Boston talked a good game in racial tolerance but came up short on the practice side. If you were black in Boston in the 1950s you lived in segregated areas of the city such as Roxbury and, for the most part, were rejected from employment in the mainstream economy. Even the Boston Red Sox were the last Major League team to field a black player in 1959. When Bill Russell and his wife bought a modest suburban home in Boston, vandals would knock over his trash cans when he was on road trips.

Bill Russell took Cousy's counseling to heart and began to focus on his game—blocking shots, getting rebounds, asserting himself for position under the boards, and starting the fast break. Although Russell wasn't scoring many points, Red Auerbach had told him to not worry about scoring points, play his game, get a lot of rebounds, and he would consider the rebounds as points. "When we talk contract down the line," said Auerbach, "I will never discuss statistics. All I'll discuss is if we won and how you played."[3] In fact, Russell never knew what his statistics were, and furthermore, as a team player, he didn't care. The modus operandi of Red Auerbach was simply about results that led to winning.

According to Russell, at least a third of the shots he blocked were off the men that Bob Cousy was guarding. But he never criticized Cousy behind his back or to his face. "The way I looked at it," said Russell, "was that [Cousy's] flaws on defense triggered our offense. I'd block a shot and outlet it and get it going the other way, turning it into a strength."[4]

Red Auerbach's straightforward, unconventional approach to coaching stunned Russell. He quickly came to the conclusion that he had never encountered a coach with such wisdom and consideration. It would be the beginning of a friendship between the two that would be everlasting.

While Bill Russell demonstrated that he had some incredible, if not magical moves, like any other rookie coming into the league, he was soon being tested by the other teams. They needed to see if he could be intimidated or if he would fight back after being roughed up under the basket. Did he really have the guts for the pro game?

The answer came sooner rather than later in a game against the New York Knicks at Madison Square Garden. The Knicks center was brawny 6'11" Ray Felix who made it his personal business to put Russell to the test, elbowing him, jabbing him, and pushing him for position under the basket. Red Auerbach called a timeout and reprimanded Russell for being bullied by Felix and telling him that he didn't have to take any of that.

When play resumed and Felix continued elbowing Russell, he elbowed him back. After a couple of minutes of experiencing "what goes around comes around" from Russell, Felix decided to escalate the intimidation by making a fist and acting as if he was about to lay a haymaker on Russell. But it was Russell who proved to be quicker on the draw, landing a solid punch to Felix's jaw, dropping him on the floor where he laid knocked-out cold.

The 1956 NBA draft for the Boston Celtics had personified the axiom "Luck of the Irish" with Bill Russell and Tom Heinsohn joining the team. Their presence filled in the missing pieces needed to create the NBA's second and most famous dynasty. The Celtics began 1956–57 with Tom Heinsohn at center. When Bill Russell finally joined the team in December, they were well on their way to winning their first division championship.

Bill Russell played his first game for the Celtics on December 22, 1956, at Boston Garden against the St. Louis Hawks. It was a Saturday afternoon game attended by 11,000 fans. NBC even sent a TV crew to Boston for national coverage. Red Auerbach put Russell in the game with five minutes gone in the first period to guard Bob Pettit. Russell was amazed and exhausted by the pace of the pro game but he hung in there and hauled down 19 rebounds and scored 6 points in sixteen minutes of playing time as the Celtics defeated the Hawks 95–93. While Russell blocked three of Bob Pettit's jump shots, he still scored 28 points for St. Louis. Bob Cousy scored 16 for Boston.

From that point on, Bill Russell just got better with every game, and his style fit Red Auerbach's game style perfectly. When he would come down with a rebound, he would fire the ball down court to Bob Cousy already streaking toward the basket. If the man guarding Cousy was covering the basket he passed off with lightning speed to Bill Sharman or Tom Heinsohn.

Boston won the Eastern Division with a 56–37 regular season record and then advanced to the NBA Finals by defeating Syracuse 3 games to 0 in the Eastern Finals.

As was expected by all the experts when Red Auerbach traded Ed Macauley and Cliff Hagan to St. Louis, thereby joining player-coach Alex Hannum, Bob Petit, Slater Martin, and Jack McMahon, the Hawks would win the Western Division Championship. But it wasn't an easy road to the championship for the Hawks. They finished in a three-way tie for the Western Division championship with Minneapolis and Ft. Wayne, all having records of 34–38. The Hawks reached the finals by defeating both the Lakers and Pistons in one game match-ups.

The 1957 NBA championship series would be a see-saw affair with each team winning a game, then losing a game until it was all tied-up three games each.

In the first game of the finals at Boston Garden, the Hawks defeated the Celtics 125–123 in double overtime. Bob Cousy scored 26 points for the Celtics but with three seconds to go in the second overtime period, he missed a shot.

The second game also played in Boston was won by the Celtics 119–99.

Game three was in St. Louis at Kiel Auditorium and the bad blood between Hawks owner Ben Kerner and Red Auerbach reached a climax. The ongoing hostility between the two had begun when Red Auerbach quit as coach of Kerner's Tri-City Black Hawks mid-season in 1950.

Prior to the game, Red Auerbach complained about the beat-up basketballs that the Kerner had given the Celtics to practice with. Then, as Bill Sharman shot free throws, they all fell short. Bob Cousy tried a few shots and got the same result. So Sharman complained to Red Auerbach that the basket on the Celtics end of the court was not regulation height. Auerbach, in turn, complained to referees Sid Borgia and Arnie Heft. The referees measured the basket height and determined that it was regulation compliant.

All the while, Ben Kerner had been watching the chaos from the sideline. He came to the conclusion that the whole affair was a cheap trick created by Auerbach to throw the refs off track. All at once, Kerner came running out on the court toward Auerbach incensed that he would accuse the Hawks of cheating. Auerbach's response was to turn around and punch Kerner in the face, bloodying his lip and knocking a tooth out. Later, Bill Russell alleged that Ben Kerner's tooth landed at center court. Immediately, both Auerbach and Kerner were restrained.

The fracas had hardly been noticed by fans starting to fill the stands. Commissioner Maurice Podoloff was already in the arena and decided he couldn't throw Red Auerbach out of the game because the game hadn't started. Instead, Podoloff fined Auerbach $300.

Recalling the Kerner incident, Red Auerbach stated, "Before the game, a couple of our players told me that the basket was too low, so I had the referees check it. The basket was actually at an angle. All of a sudden Kerner comes running out the stands screaming, saying I'm up to my old tricks. He started calling me every name in the book. I hit him with a left hook—boom."[5]

While the Celtics had created a lot of pre-game excitement, the Hawks won the game 100–98 to take a 2–1 lead in the series.

The Celtics came back to take game four, played at St. Louis, 123–118, to even the series 2–2.

In the next two games, both teams won on their home courts, the Celtics taking game five in Boston 124–109 and the Hawks taking game six in St. Louis 96–94. So, the stage was set for a deciding seventh game played on April 13, 1957, a Saturday afternoon in Boston, before a packed house at Boston Garden and a national TV audience.

The seventh game turned out to be one of the most exciting NBA finals ever. The lead in the game changed 38 times and there were 28 ties requiring a double overtime to decide the winner. The game had been sent into the first overtime by two free throws made by Bob Pettit in the closing seconds of regulation time. Then, during the first overtime, a basket by the Hawks' Jack Coleman forced a second overtime.

The game was finally decided in the second overtime when the Celtics Jim Loscutoff made two shots to give Boston a 125–123 lead. Alex Hannum called a timeout and set up a play to get the ball to Pettit. Hannum threw a long pass that intentionally hit the backboard sending Pettit high for the rebound who then attempted a shot that bounced off the rim at the buzzer.

Jubilant fans poured onto the court and Red Auerbach lit up a victory cigar. It was the beginning of the Boston Celtics NBA dynasty and the first of nine championship banners in the next eleven years that would be raised to the rafters and hang high over the aging parquet floor,

Tom Heinsohn, a rookie, led the Celtics in the championship game with 37 points and 23 rebounds. Bob Pettit led the Hawks with 39 points while Cliff Hagan dropped in 24.

Boston Celtics, 1957 NBA Champions. (Courtesy of The Sports Museum.)

There were no individual surprises in the series, everyone did their job as expected; Bob Pettit was the leading scorer with 298 points, Bill Russell the leading rebounder with 244 boards, and Bob Cousy was the assist leader with 93.

Tom Heinsohn was named the NBA Rookie of the Year for 1956–57, an award that personally irritated Bill Russell, believing that the selection of Heinsohn had a whiff of racism connected to it. For Bill Russell to object to a teammate winning an award seems out of character for him, a player who always put the team ahead of individual performance, but the facts were that Russell had joined the team mid-year and Heinsohn's scoring and rebounding had just as much to do with the Celtics championship as did the arrival of Russell. However, it seems certain that the Celtics would not have won the championship without having both players on the team. On the other hand, there remain many who believe that the award should have gone to Russell and it's very doubtful that Tom Heinsohn would have objected if it had.

Bill Russell would eventually receive more awards than he could count. One of the most prestigious was being named the Associated Press Player of the Decade, covering 1960–70. A golden decade for the NBA that saw such players as Wilt Chamberlain,

Elgin Baylor, Jerry West, and Oscar Robertson compete on the hardwood.

With the Celtics' first NBA championship on the books, Coach Arnold "Red" Auerbach had a lot more than just bragging rights, he was about to establish himself as the John McGraw of professional basketball. In fact, the Celtics coach had much in common with the legendary manager of the New York Giants. Both had a fiery personality and didn't give pep-talks but would berate you, for instance, for a bonehead play or a lack of hustle. He didn't teach fundamentals to his players either. Like McGraw, he believed that if you were a professional player you should know how to play the game. Players either loved Auerbach and McGraw or they hated them. Bob Cousy and Bill Russell were two players that would always have great affection for Red Auerbach.

5

The Rochester Royals Move to Cincinnati

& Maurice Stokes Suffers Career-Ending Injury

By the 1954–55 season, the NBA was struggling financially and was forced to downsize to an eight-team league. In order to survive, toward the end of the 1950s, the NBA started to seek greener pastures and began to abandon its last small market cities that had been the genesis of the league. Small market teams started to move to cities that featured Major League Baseball.

Following the 1957 season, Fred Zollner moved the Ft. Wayne Pistons to Detroit. The move immediately increased the Pistons fanbase from a metropolitan area population in Ft. Wayne of 216,853 to one in Detroit with 3,421,766.

Then, the Rochester Royals were moved to Cincinnati at the end of the 1956–57 season, increasing their fanbase from a metropolitan area population of 487,632 to one of 1,051,605.

The relocations of the Ft. Wayne and Rochester franchises left Syracuse as the last small market team in the NBA.

The Rochester Royals had never been a profitable entity but owner Les Harrison had a passion for professional basketball and continued to operate the fledgling franchise in one of the NBA's smallest markets. Even after the Royals had won the 1951 NBA Championship on the opening night of the 1951–52 season, attendance was only 2,316 at Edgartown Park Arena.

In 1951–52, Royals games were televised for the first time, but only about one in four families owned a television set. By the time the Royals left Rochester for Cincinnati in 1957, the percentage of families owning TV sets in Rochester had jumped to about 80%.

Les Harrison always blamed the poor attendance on the rise of television. "We played Tuesdays and Saturdays opposite Milton Berle and Imogene Coca," said Harrison. "Attendance went down after our title year [1951]. It was just a matter of time before we had to give up."[1]

In 1954–55, the Rochester Royals had finished third in the NBA Western Division with a season record of 29–43. While the Royals' record was good enough to get them into the playoffs, they were quickly eliminated by the Minneapolis Lakers 2 games to 1.

The 1954–55 season had been a disaster at the gate with the Royals averaging just 1,633 fans per game which resulted in a net loss for the franchise of $34,600.

But it seemed like there was hope on the horizon. The 1955 NBA draft was good to the Rochester Royals. The Royals drafted 6'7", 240-pound center Maurice Stokes from St. Francis College (PA). At St. Francis, Stokes had become a small-college All-American. In his junior year, he averaged 23.3 points and 22.2 rebounds per game. St. Francis had a 22–9 record and played in the National Invitation Tournament. Then, in 1955, his senior year, he led St. Francis to a fourth-place finish in the NIT. In the semifinals, Stokes scored 43 points in a 79–73 overtime loss to Dayton and was named the NIT's MVP.

The Royals also drafted 6'6" forward Jack Twyman, an All-American from the University of Cincinnati. Twyman led the Bearcats in scoring his sophomore year through his senior year and finished his college career as the school's all-time scoring (1,598 points) and rebound (1,242) leader. In his senior year, Twyman scored 49 points against Western Kentucky and led Cincinnati to the semi-finals of the NIT where the Bearcats lost to eventual tournament champion Duquesne.

With Stokes and Twyman on the roster, the Royals moved their home games into the 8,000-seat War Memorial Arena for the 1955–56 season, built by the city at a cost of $7 million. On November 5, a total of 5,723 fans showed up for the opening game of the season as Maurice Stokes put on quite a show scoring 32 points in his NBA debut in a 100–98 loss to the New York Knicks.

But in the end, the Royals finished in fourth place (last) in the NBA Western Division with a record of 31–41. Stokes was selected the NBA Rookie of the Year, finishing with an average of 16.8 points and 16.3 rebounds per game. While attendance nearly doubled over the previous season, averaging 2,325 fans per game, once again the Royals showed a loss of $25,000.

In 1956, the Rochester Royals had the first draft pick but due primarily to the team's financial problems, Les Harrison passed on selecting defense-oriented Bill Russell, who had just led the University of San Francisco to consecutive NCAA championships, in favor of high scoring Sihugo Green, who had led Duquesne to the 1955 NIT title.

Harrison had considered drafting Bill Russell but he didn't look particularly good in a game that he had scouted. When confronted with the fact he had passed on drafting Russell, Harrison always maintained, "We found out later he knew we were watching him and did poorly so he wouldn't end up in Rochester."[2]

The facts were that there was more to the Royals failure to get Russell than a poor scouting report. The super racially sensitive Bill Russell has always maintained that he didn't want to play for Les Harrison after he had approached him with Dolly King tagging along. King was a black player who had formerly played for the Royals. Russell resented having another black man used as a pawn in an attempt to recruit him. Also, Russell supposedly had told Harrison that he would have to match the $25,000 plus that the Harlem Globetrotters were offering him. The figure caused Harrison to immediately abandon all hope of drafting Russell.

In the 1956–57 season, although Maurice Stokes set a new single-season record with 1,256 rebounds for the second straight season, the Royals finished last in the Western Division with a record of 31–41. Attendance was slightly up with an average of 2,313 customers per game despite the fact that, for a time, the Royals were displaced in the War Memorial Arena by the ABC (American Bowling Congress) Tournament and had to play their games back at the Edgartown Park Arena that Harrison referred to as a glorified warehouse. So once again, the Royals lost money—$17,500.

To add insult to injury, Les Harrison had to endure the fact that the Rochester Americans, a new professional hockey team in the city, outdrew the Royals in attendance at War Memorial by a ratio of two-to-one.

With failing attendance in Rochester, Les Harrison had moved thirteen of the Royals home games to other cities for the 1956–57 season. Three of the Royals home games were played in Boston and three others in New York. Other cities included Albany, New

York; Camden, New Jersey; Louisville, Kentucky; and Ft. Wayne, Indiana. Also, three cities in Pennsylvania hosted Royals games: Hershey, Johnstown, and Philadelphia. But the city that stood out above the others was Cincinnati, Ohio.

Two of the Royals players, Jack Twyman (University of Cincinnati) and Dave Piontek (Xavier University), had played college ball in Cincinnati. The two approached Les Harrison and convinced him to schedule a Royals game in Cincinnati. On February 1, 1957, the Royals played the Ft. Wayne Pistons at Cincinnati Gardens before a sell-out crowd of 10,000. The Royals won the game 96–80 with Jack Twyman scoring 23 points and Dave Piontek, 7. Les Harrison was extremely impressed with the huge turnout for the game and began to consider Cincinnati as a possible new home for his Rochester Royals.

Since 1951–52, the net losses of the Rochester Royals franchise had totaled $131,263. Les Harrison and his brother Jack, co-owners, decided they had to do something with the franchise. Harrison wanted to sell the Royals and was asking $240,000, the amount he believed that he needed to get even. He was committed to his hometown of Rochester so his first choice was to sell to a local group and stated he would take less to keep the Royals in the city.

While the Royals had won three championships and five division titles in twelve years in Rochester, on March 14, 1957, Les Harrison issued a press release announcing that the Royals were definitely seeking a new home.

Harrison had been in negotiations with several potential buyers and announced to the press, "I will check thoroughly into at least five possible buyers in Milwaukee, Cleveland, Chicago, Cincinnati, and Kansas City."[3] He added that he had been offered a job with a $25,000 yearly salary ($ 224,986 in 2018 money) by the Marty Marion-Milt Fishmann combine of Kansas City which was also interested in an NBA franchise.

On April 4, 1957, Les Harrison announced that after being in negotiations with Tom Grace, the executive vice president of Cincinnati Gardens, he had formally signed contracts moving the Royals franchise from Rochester to Cincinnati for the 1957–58 season.

In moving from Rochester, Les Harrison stated that the Royals needed an average home attendance of 3,500 to break even. One of the attractive aspects of moving the Royals to Cincinnati was that

Cincinnati Gardens.

the team's home games would be played in Cincinnati Gardens. The arena, which cost $3 million to build, opened in early 1949 and consisted of 24,000 square feet with a seating capacity for basketball of 11,000. At the time the facility was opened, it was the seventh largest indoor arena in the United States.

The inaugural event at Cincinnati Gardens had taken place on February 22, 1949, when 11,144 fans witnessed an exhibition hockey match between the Montreal Canadians and their minor league affiliate, the Dallas Texans.

Six days later, one of the first major sporting events held in Cincinnati Gardens took place on the night of February 28, 1949, when local heavyweight boxer Ezzard Charles defeated Joey Maxim of Cleveland in a 15-round bout. The win for Charles set up a heavyweight championship bout in which he outpointed Jersey Joe Walcott on June 22, 1949, at Comiskey Park in Chicago. Charles retained the heavyweight crown until July 18, 1951, when he lost the title in a rematch with Walcott, held at Forbes Field in Pittsburgh.

Prior to the Royals coming to town, Cincinnati Gardens had been used sparingly for minor league hockey, professional wrestling matches, several basketball games played each year by the University of Cincinnati and Xavier University, the annual visit by the Harlem Globetrotters, and such popular attractions as the Ice Capades shows and the Shrine Circus, so the lights in Cincinnati Gardens were frequently turned off. But that would change in the fall of 1957 when Royals came to town.

The Cincinnati Royals played their first game at Cincinnati Gardens on October 26, 1957, defeating the Syracuse Nationals 110–100. Jack Twyman led the Royals with 32 points, big Clyde Lovellette, known as the "Terre Haute Terror" had 28, and Maurice Stokes had 10. Dolph Schayes led the Nationals with 32 points.

During their first month in Cincinnati, the Royals achieved a slightly better than .500 record. But any hope of a division championship went down the tubes when they lost nine straight games between December 10 and 27. The Cincinnati Royals finished 1957–58 with a four-game winning streak that put them in third place with a record of 33–39, good enough to make the playoffs.

On March 12, in the final game of the season, the Royals pulled a 96–88 victory out of the fire over the Lakers in Minneapolis that was needed to make the playoffs. The victory came in the closing minutes by a pair of three-point plays by Jack Twyman and Maurice Stokes.

However, a monumental tragedy had occurred in the game when Maurice Stokes was injured. In the game, Stokes, who had 24 points, had gone up for a rebound, fallen on the hardwood court, and hit his head, knocking him unconscious. At the time, NBA teams had no trainers or doctors as part of the everyday team and knowledge of sports head trauma injuries was in its infancy, so Stokes was revived and remained with the team with only a cursory examination. There was hardly a mention of Stokes injury in the newspapers, which said that he was being treated for a boil on his neck.

A coin toss took place to determine home-court advantage for the Western Division Semi-Finals playoff between Detroit and Cincinnati with Pistons coach Red Roche calling it correctly.

The first of the three-game series, nationally televised by NBC, was played in Detroit at the University of Detroit Memorial Gymnasium before 2,482 spectators. The Pistons defeated the Royals 100–83.

Despite his injury, Maurice Stokes flew with the team to Detroit and played in the opening playoff game against the Pistons.

Something seemed wrong with the Royals as they had a frigid first half, letting the Pistons roll to a 56–36 halftime lead. Jack

Twyman, who had led the NBA in field goal percentage during the season, didn't score a point in the first half and, according to coach Bobby Wanzer, Maurice Stokes looked sluggish and scored only 12 points in the game. Even Clyde Lovellette was off his game. In twelve previous games vs. the Pistons, Lovellette had averaged 22.1 points per game; he scored just 15 in this one.

On the flight home from Detroit, Maurice Stokes became ill and upon the plane's landing at Greater Cincinnati Airport in Boone County, Kentucky, was rushed to St. Elizabeth Hospital in Covington, Kentucky.

Stokes had first become ill on the bus going from Detroit to the airport and while the team waited for their plane to take off. On the plane, Stokes seemed to recover slightly and began to read a book he had brought with him. Then, at about 10:05 P.M., as the plane neared Cincinnati, Stokes passed out. Immediately, a stewardess on the TWA plane, Jeanne Phillips, administered oxygen attempting to keep Stokes alive until the plane landed.

On Sunday afternoon, March 16, at Cincinnati Gardens before a crowd of 2,508, while Maurice Stokes lay unconscious in a hospital bed in Covington, the Pistons eliminated the Royals, winning the second game 124–104 to a complete a sweep in the best-of-three game series.

Meanwhile, Maurice Stokes lapsed into a coma and laid unconscious for several weeks. Following tests, Stokes would be diagnosed with having suffered encephalopathy, a traumatic brain injury that affected his motor control functions. At that time, diagnostic technology such as CAT Scans and MRIs were a couple of decades in the future, so the primary diagnostic tests included ECGs and X-rays. Samples of Stokes' blood were sent to the U.S. Public Health Service in Louisville.

Today's analysis of Stokes' head injury suggests that it caused swelling in his brain, then complications occurred on the plane with a change in cabin pressure that resulted in the injury mimicking symptoms of encephalitis.

At the time of Stokes' injury, Dr. Benjamin Hawkins, who served as the Royals team physician, stated in a press release, "[Stokes] is holding his own in a light coma. He opens his eyes slightly occasionally but has shown no real signs of regaining consciousness."[4]

Royals owner Les Harrison was deeply concerned over Stokes' circumstances and he, along with Stokes mother, twin sister, and brother, who had arrived from Pittsburgh, maintained a vigil by his bedside. Soon they were joined by Stokes' teammates, Dick Ricketts and Jack Twyman. Even opposing players started to arrive, such as Ed Fleming of the Minneapolis Lakers. Everyone was concerned about "Big Mo," it was very difficult to conceive such a strong man could be in such a state of helplessness.

A few days later, Les and Jack Harrison had to leave town, but they did not abandon Stokes; they sent a check to the hospital to cover the cost of 24-hour nursing care and left word that any other bills necessary for his care should be forwarded to them in Rochester.

With the motor control center in his brain damaged, Stokes became a quadriplegic, was confined to a wheelchair, and would never fully recover from his injury. The medical bills for his care became astronomical. Jack Twyman and Maurice Stokes were both from Pittsburgh and had faced each other on the hardwood as teenagers in high school. Going forward, Jack Twyman would act as Stokes' legal guardian and raise funds for his care through such events as benefit games and golf tournaments that amounted to more than a couple hundred thousand dollars. Also, Twyman taught Stokes to communicate by blinking his eyes for each letter.

Today, a lot of sports writers, too young to have witnessed the Maurice Stokes story, feel a compulsion to point out that Jack Twyman, a white player, had helped out Maurice Stokes, a black teammate. But the fact was that there was no black-white connection to their friendship. The friendship between Twyman and Stokes was one with a strong human bond and race was never a factor. Not one of the sportswriters and broadcasters of the time ever suggested that there was a racial connection to the Twyman-Stokes friendship. It wasn't part of the story.

On April 6, 1970, after a courageous twelve-year battle for recovery from his injury, Maurice Stokes died at the age of 36 with Jack Twyman by his side.

For years, following Stokes' death, Jack Twyman advocated on his behalf for induction in the Naismith Basketball Hall of Fame. Finally, in 2004, Maurice Stokes was inducted posthumously.

While Maurice Stokes remained in a semi-coma in a Kentucky hospital, back in Rochester, Les and Jack Harrison were undecided as to what to do with the Royals. The Royals' move from Rochester to Cincinnati had not turned out to be the land of "milk and honey" that the Harrisons had hoped it would be for their financially ailing franchise. The Royals attendance for 1957–58 in Cincinnati had been a dismal average of 3,641 fans per game.

A group from Washington D.C. was offering the Harrisons $225,000 for the team, which it intended to move to the nation's capital.

Then, the Harrisons received another offer from local businessman Norm Shapiro, to buy the Royals for $250,000 and return the team to Rochester. Shapiro even sweetened the pot by offering Les Harrison a job in the Royals organization as a scout and consultant. So Les Harrison was being given an opportunity to remain in professional basketball and not have any financial profit and loss concerns. The Shapiro offer was made public in Rochester and as expected, fans in the city rallied behind it, circulating petitions. Of course, this was a bit of a surprise to some observers; these were the same fans that had failed to provide adequate support in ticket sales for the Royals while they played in Rochester for over a decade.

Anyway, a move of the Royals from Cincinnati to Washington or back to Rochester would require an affirmative vote of three-quarters of the NBA Board of Governors made up of the team owners to approve the transfer. It was doubtful that the Board of Governors would approve a shift of the franchise back to Rochester as it had already made it clear to all concerned that they wanted the league's teams to play in major league cities. Also, contract talks with NBC for televised games were in progress and the network had also stated that they wanted a league that played only in major markets.

In Cincinnati, no one was rushing forward to save the Royals. One of the reasons for the lack of support for the Royals in the Queen City was that most basketball fans were focused on the University of Cincinnati Bearcats that featured one of the most talented and exciting players to ever play the college game—Oscar Robertson—who had just completed his sophomore year.

It was because of Oscar Robertson, known as "The Big O," that the NBA Board of Governors would have been reluctant to move the Royals back to Rochester or to Washington. The Cincinnati Royals were in a position to exercise territorial draft rights on Robertson when he completed his senior year in 1960. With Robertson playing for the Royals, the Board of Governors was certain that fan interest in the Royals would increase significantly, not just in Cincinnati but in every city in the league. So, it was worth waiting and letting the franchise lose money for a couple of years.

At first, no sports-minded entrepreneur in Cincinnati came forward with an offer to buy the Royals from the Harrisons, but as soon as the Washington offer became public, reality set in, and various Cincinnati businessmen and basketball fans of means realized that the city could lose the team. Rapidly, an eclectic group of investors was formed, ranging from millionaire insurance magnate Thomas E. Wood to Bill Powell, co-proprietor of Shipley's, a popular neighborhood bar and grill near the University of Cincinnati campus, that collectively ponied-up an offer of $200,000 for the team.

The Board of Governors approved the Cincinnati offer and the Royals became a public corporation with Thomas E. Wood becoming the majority partner.

Despite having the number two pick in the 1958 NBA draft, the Royals did not fare well. Their first pick was 6'8" center-forward Archie Dees from Indiana University. Dees would be traded after one year with the Royals and last just four years in the NBA, playing on four teams and one additional year in the newly formed ABL.

Other draft picks by the Royals were players taken from colleges within their potential territorial fan base of 100 miles of which no one would have an immediate impact: Arlen "Bucky" Bockhorn (University of Dayton), Larry Staverman (Villa Madonna College/ now Thomas Moore College), Adrian "Odie" Smith (University of Kentucky), and Wayne Stevens (University of Cincinnati).

With Maurice Stokes hospitalized and struggling to recuperate, the 1958–59 Royals would be led by Jack Twyman. After the Royals lost 15 out of their first 18 games, Bobby Wanzer was replaced as coach by Tom Marshall. Without Maurice Stokes, the Cincinnati Royals became the doormat of the NBA, finishing with a league-worst record of 19–53. During the 1958–59 season, the 11,000-seat-plus Cincinnati Gardens had been an empty house. Attendance was so bad the season before, it had caused Les Harrison to sell; the team now had dropped in attendance by 33% in 1958–59 to an average of 2,445 per game. So sparse were the crowds that a fan could hear a conversation of another fan sitting in the stands across the court.

Of course, finishing last did have a benefit, it gave the Royals the first non-territorial draft pick in the 1959 NBA draft. The

Royals took advantage of that fact and selected 6'8" All-American forward Bob Boozer from Kansas State University. In 1958, Boozer had led the Wildcats to the Final Four in the NCAA Tournament. However, the Royals would have to wait a year for Boozer to join the team as he wanted to sit out the 1959–60 season to remain eligible to play in the 1960 Olympic Games.

Meanwhile, the Royals continued to pick other players in the draft of local interest such as 6'5" forward Joe Viviano (Xavier University) and Mike Mendenhall (University of Cincinnati). Both of these players would have no impact on the Royals in the standings and both would have short careers in the NBA.

In 1959–60, the Cincinnati Royals would finish with a record of 19–56, despite the fact that Jack Twyman finished second in the league in scoring with a 31.2 points-per-game average. Once again, attendance for the Royals was abysmal, falling to a pre-NBA low of just 1,878 fans per game.

But help was on the horizon and following the 1959–60 college season, the Cincinnati Royals would be able to exercise territorial draft rights on Oscar Robertson.

The big prize in the 1959 draft was Wilt Chamberlain, another player like Oscar Robertson, that the NBA was hoping would be a franchise saver and a marketing giant for the NBA.

The 7'1" Chamberlain had been recruited out of Overlook High School in Philadelphia by University of Kansas coach Forrest C. "Phog" Allen. Ed Gottlieb who owned the cash-strapped Philadelphia Warriors had been waiting five years to exercise territorial draft rights on Chamberlain with high hopes that he would save the franchise.

Chamberlain had led Kansas to the NCAA Finals in 1957 where the Jay Hawks lost to North Carolina 54–53 in triple overtime. In his senior year in 1958, Chamberlain averaged 47.2 points per game.

Chamberlain was controversial because he was using the dunk to change the game. Boston Celtics owner Walter Brown had said that Wilt Chamberlain should be banned from the NBA "because he proselytized himself at Kansas. No NBA team can afford to pay him what he gets at Kansas."[5]

There was at least a half-truth to Walter Brown's assertion. No NBA team could afford Chamberlain—the salary cap was $25,000. So, Chamberlain passed on joining the Philadelphia Warriors to accept a contract to play for Abe Saperstein's Harlem

Globetrotters calling for $46,000 plus an attendance clause that had the potential to add another $20,000.

In 1959, the Globetrotters became the first team to play in Moscow where Soviet General Secretary Nikita Khrushchev greeted the team.

But Chamberlain really wanted to test himself against the best players in the game, so he left the Globetrotters after one season and signed with Philadelphia. At that time, only a few players made the $25,000 league limit, Bob Cousy, Bill Russell, etc. Ed Gottlieb got the salary cap raised to $27,000 and then included an attendance clause in Chamberlain's contract. Wilt Chamberlain immediately lived up to his billing and was named NBA Rookie of the Year in 1960.

6

Oscar Robertson
& the University of Cincinnati Bearcats

Before joining the Cincinnati Royals in 1960–61 and beginning an NBA career that would lead him to the Naismith Memorial Basketball Hall of Fame, Oscar Robertson had a storied college basketball career at the University of Cincinnati (UC) where, during his three varsity years, the Bearcats had a record of 79–9 and played in two NCAA Tournament Final Fours.

Oscar Palmer Robertson was born November 24, 1933, in Charlotte, Tennessee. His parents, Bailey and Mazell Robertson, had three sons Henry, Bailey, Jr., and Oscar. When Oscar was four, the family moved to Indianapolis, Indiana to seek better employment opportunities. Bailey worked at various jobs as a security guard, butcher, and sanitation worker. Mazell, an aspiring gospel singer, worked part-time.

In Indianapolis, the Robertson family lived in Lockefield Gardens, a government-subsidized housing project, and Oscar grew up dirt-poor. It was there in the projects that Oscar Robertson began playing basketball on the inner-city dirt courts against his older brothers and neighborhood kids. He would practice his game endlessly shooting tennis balls and rags bound with rubber bands into a peach basket behind his family's home.

Oscar also liked playing baseball and was a shortstop until he got too tall. Eventually, he gave up baseball because it interfered with basketball in the summertime.

Oscar's brother Bailey, Jr. turned out to be a pretty good basketball player, too. He went on to set scoring records at Indiana Central College that was coached by Ray Crowe, brother of Milwaukee Braves and Cincinnati Reds first baseman George Crowe.

Oscar Robertson attended the all-black Crispus Attucks High School in Indianapolis where his natural ability and unique skills would be honed by coach Crowe.

Indiana is a state with a blighted racial past. In the 1920s, Indiana had more Ku Klux Klan members per capita than any state in the union. At the Klan's pinnacle in 1923, it had more members (178,000) in Indiana than the Methodist Church.

Crispus Attucks High School, named for a runaway slave believed to be the first American killed by British soldiers in the Boston Massacre, had been founded in 1927 by Indiana KKK Grand Dragon D.C. Stephenson along with a group of Klan supporting politicians that wanted a segregated high school for black students in the city.

The day that Crispus Attucks High School opened its doors the Ku Klux Klan led a parade past the school that lasted for an hour.

The *Indiana Magazine of History* describes D.C. Stephenson as "a charming personality and powerful orator; he was also arrogant, cunning, evil, and hedonistic. Early in 1925, he assaulted, raped, and held captive his young secretary Madge Oberholtzer, who took poison and died one month later. Stephenson was indicted, and when Governor Jackson (who had now distanced himself from the Klan) refused to pardon him, Stephenson leaked information to Jackson's trial for bribery (the governor was acquitted on a technicality)."[1]

When Crispus Attucks High School was founded the Indiana High School Athletic Association ruled that it was not a public school because it had no white students in its enrollment. In fact, it was not until 1933 that member schools in the Association were permitted to play in sporting events vs. Crispus Attucks. Finally, in 1942 Attucks was granted membership and permitted to play in the state basketball championship tournament.

By the 1950s, Indianapolis was still a heavily de-facto segregated city and Oscar Robertson has never overcome his early experiences with racism in the city. From the time Robertson's Crispus Attucks High School basketball team won back-to-back championships in 1955 and 1956, becoming the first all-black high school team in Indiana to win the state title, throughout his brilliant All-American collegiate career at the University of Cincinnati, and into the NBA, he thought of himself as a victim.

These deep-seated feelings were fueled by various episodes of overt racism Robertson had experienced. When Crispus Attucks won back-to-back state basketball titles it was an unsettling event for many people in Indianapolis. They considered the victories by an all-black team a threat to the tradition of the state's game. According to Zak Keefer of the Indianapolis Star, "They saw their horizontal game shifting vertical, a group of bigger, faster, stronger athletes uprooting convention and burying their white teams along the way."[2]

Following Attucks' first championship in 1955 the victory parade for Oscar Robertson's team was rerouted in Indianapolis toward the predominately black residential area (or ghetto) because the city fathers didn't trust the blacks to behave themselves along the traditional route. This event left an indelible mark on Robertson's psyche.

In winning back-to-back state championships in 1954–55 and 1955–56 the Crispus Attucks teams had a record of 60–1. While Oscar Robertson was the most famous player on those teams, the squad also included Hallie Bryant and Willie Gardner, both of whom would go on to play for the Harlem Globetrotters.

Besides his basketball prowess, Oscar Robertson was a better than average high school student and heavily recruited. More than seventy-five schools expressed an interest in him and forty schools contacted him directly, including UCLA, Duquesne, Kansas, NYU, Duke, Marquette, Nebraska, Illinois, Purdue, Notre Dame, Arizona State, Cincinnati, and Indiana.

Oscar was no different than most kids in Indiana, black or white—most kids who played basketball in the state had a dream of playing for Indiana University. However, during a recruiting visit to Bloomington, Oscar was disappointed and promptly left the Indiana campus after being confronted by coach Branch McCracken who stated, "I hope you're not the kind of kid who wants money to go school."[3]

The insinuation that he was out for money deeply insulted Robertson. He was to say later that if McCracken had just said something as mundane as "Oscar, we really want you to come to Indiana and play basketball for us," he would have grabbed a pen and signed on the dotted line to become a Hoosier.

Oscar Robertson wasn't the only talented black basketball player to have misgivings about Branch McCracken. Wilt Chamberlain had been offered a scholarship by Indiana and made a campus visit but left convinced that McCracken had racist tendencies, so he signed with Kansas.

Robertson ultimately decided to enroll at the University of Cincinnati for several reasons: it was close to home, only a hundred miles from Indianapolis; he intended to study business, and liked the fact that UC had a business administration program that included a co-op program; the Bearcats played a lot of eastern teams and he always wanted to play in such venues as Madison Square Garden; and the clincher was that his parents, Bailey and Mazell Robertson, liked Bearcats head coach George Smith.

After enrolling in the University of Cincinnati and entering the business administration program, Oscar began his co-op job in the accounting department at the Cincinnati Gas & Electric Company. But he quickly felt that the racism of Indianapolis had followed him to Cincinnati. The racial environment of the UC campus and community at large didn't improve much and considerably reinforced his negative feelings about America's racial conscious.

Most writers chronicling Robertson's early days at UC state that his professors harassed him. The fact is that most college freshman, regardless of their race, are routinely, although mildly, harassed by their professors and instructors to socialize them into an environment of higher learning. But Oscar maintained in his own biography, *The Big O—My Life, My Times, My Game,* that he was ridiculed by his professors who attempted to make him feel stupid. One could make a case that it was Oscar once again conceptualizing himself as a victim.

Oscar arrived in Cincinnati to play basketball amidst considerable ballyhoo in the press and tickets for Bearcats home games quickly became scarce. Robertson's freshman team, that included Ron Dykes, Ralph Davis, Spud Hornsby, and Larry Willey, averaged 99.6 points per game and finished with 13–12 record.

Following Robertson's freshman year, all the Bearcats home games were sold out for the next three years. Beginning in his sophomore year and through his senior year, Oscar filled the 8,000-seat Armory Fieldhouse to capacity. Unprecedented large crowds also showed up for his freshman squad games that preceded the varsity contests. Every Bearcat fan, whether young or old, was filled with optimism and the mantra became wait till next year.

Haldane Dosher Higgins was a Bear Kitten with the University of Cincinnati Band when Oscar Robertson arrived on the campus in the fall of 1956. Over the next few years, Ms. Dosher Higgins would have the opportunity to see Oscar mature. Recently, she stated, in regard to Oscar, "from a shy freshman in 1956 to a national hero in 2014. I knew in those days I was watching history in the making."[4]

Dick Baker, who was the director of community relations at UC when Oscar Robertson arrived on the campus, took responsibility for giving him the nickname "The Big O." According to Baker, it was early in the '57–58 season when Lee Allen (late historian for the National Baseball Hall of Fame), who, writing for the Cincinnati Enquirer at the time, told him that he ought to get a nickname for Oscar. "How's "The Big O" strike you?" asked Baker. "That's a helluva good name," Allen replied.[5]

Despite all the ballyhoo over Robertson's arrival in Cincinnati, just a couple of blocks away from the Armory Fieldhouse in the neighborhoods of Corryville, Clifton, and Clifton Heights that bordered and surrounded the big campus, Oscar was persona non-grata and regarded by most neighborhood merchants as just another black man that posed a threat to their livelihood, especially in the places where white people socialized: the theatres, restaurants, and taverns. The feeling among the tavern owners and restaurateurs in the area at that time was that, although they loved the way Robertson played basketball and were big fans of his, they feared that if he came into their place of business, then perhaps he would return the following evening with a whole lot of black friends and drive away their white clientele.

So about all that was available to Robertson in the area was a take-out pizza and hamburgers—about the same fare that would have been available to him in the deep south.

In some areas, in close proximity to the campus, blatant rather than subtle segregation existed. In Corryville, on the east side of the UC campus, there was a weekly bingo game held in an old gymnasium run by a veteran's group that enforced a policy of seating bingo players in various halls in the facility according to race. Hence there were black halls and white halls for bingo players.

The feeling by black Bearcats players that they weren't welcome off the UC campus in the surrounding neighborhoods persisted for more than a decade after Oscar Robertson had graduated. Rick Roberson, a native of Memphis, Tennessee, who bypassed the opportunity to become the first black player to play at Memphis State by choosing Cincinnati instead, was one who openly expressed the feeling that he wasn't welcome in areas off-campus. Roberson, who played for the Bearcats from 1966 to 1969 and would become the school's fourth all-time best rebounder behind Oscar Robertson, Jack Twyman, and Connie Dierking, always felt uncomfortable only a few blocks away from the UC campus.

During Oscar Robertson's sophomore year, in one of the first road games of his collegiate career on December 21, 1957, he was confronted with a sickening episode of racism when the Cincinnati Bearcats went down to Texas to play the University of Houston Cougars.

In the years following World War Two into the early 1960s, the city of Houston, Texas went through a period of enormous economic, social, and cultural change. It was one of the largest municipal metamorphoses in American history. By 1958, Houston had become a modern boomtown. Between 1950 and 1960, the population of the city rose by 36%, from 596,163 to 938,219. By 1970, the city's population would exceed one million inhabitants and continues to grow today.

Entering the 1960s, with the space race between the United States and the Soviet Union in full throttle, Houston would become the headquarters of NASA, and with the expansion of the ship channel, the city was now coming under the spotlight of international attention and potential investors. The voters in the county of Morris had even approved a $20 million bond issue to build an air-conditioned, domed stadium, to be used by professional baseball, football, and basketball, to possibly be ready for use by 1962. In order to expedite the needed cultural change necessary to transform Houston from a sleepy southern town into a huge international city, quietly civic leaders, civil rights advocates, and influential business leaders in the community got together for a meeting of the minds at the "whites only" Rice Hotel and in just one day they would agree to end racial segregation in public accommodations in the city of Houston.

Houston, Texas had, for generations, been culturally on the cusp of the deep-south and its backward racial atmosphere had stunted the growth of the city. But, with forward-thinking leadership, by 1968, Houston would become a booming metropolis with gleaming skyscrapers and bustling suburbs.

The city's growth was a factor in prompting Eddie Einhorn, the future owner of the Chicago White Sox and ever the entrepreneur, to coordinate what is considered the first nationally televised college basketball game in 1968. Billed as the "Game of the Century," Einhorn put together a spectacular college basketball showdown featuring two of the most talented black athletes of the twentieth century: UCLA's Lew Alcindor and The University of Houston's Elvin Hayes playing in the Astrodome. The game was watched by millions of fans across the country.

But in late 1957, when the University of Cincinnati Bearcats were about to come to town, Houston was a cow town with skyscrapers just beginning to dot its landscape and its inhabitants' still clinging to its racially intolerant past. Oscar Robertson would become one of the many talented black people that Houston was not yet ready to embrace and seemed to take pride in insulting.

The Cincinnati Bearcats were staying at the Shamrock Hilton Hotel in Houston for their game with the University of Houston Cougars. Around 12 midnight, UC coach George Smith went to Robertson's room and informed him that the management of the hotel wanted him out. Robertson was taken across town to Texas Southern University where he was given a dorm room to spend the night, while his white teammates remained downtown at the Hilton.

In retrospect, looking at the insensitivity of George Smith's inaction when confronted with racial discrimination toward one of his players, reasonable minds would question why the coach didn't remove his entire squad from the hotel. The ignominious action of the hotel management just wasn't an insult to Oscar, it was a huge insult to the entire Bearcat team and to the University of Cincinnati.

But looking back at the incident through the prism of time, one needs to be reminded that in the 1950s and early 1960s, inequalities in accommodations for athletes of color, regardless of if they were amateur or professional, was a dirty little organizational sanctioned norm.

Nearly all the Major League Baseball teams of the era had segregated accommodations for white and black players in Florida during spring training. The policy advanced by the front offices was that their clubs were part-time residents in the state and they didn't really have the standing to question the local laws or social norms of the communities they trained in. It was, in fact, an endorsement by the teams' management of discrimination against their employees. It made hypocrites out of supposedly fair-minded baseball men such as August Bush, Branch Rickey, Bill Veeck, Jr., Gabe Paul, and others. George Smith was just as hypocritical when being faced with the discrimination aimed at Oscar Robertson in Houston by taking no action on his or the university's behalf.

The game was played and only about 2,000 fans saw it in Houston's small and narrow gym. The Bearcats defeated Houston 70–53 as The Big O scored 25 points.

Later, Oscar Robertson was to state in his biography that as much as it bothered him that he had been forced to leave the hotel, it bothered him a lot more that he had been the only person that was forced to leave. "All this talk about being a team and winning and losing together, staying together and doing things together—as a team. What just happened? I asked myself. I had forgotten momentarily that this was America."[6]

The racial insults experienced by Robertson in Houston had been proceeded by insults at Denton, Texas. In the game against North Texas State in Denton, when Robertson first entered the locker room, he found that a black cat had been let loose. Then, when the game began, the fans got on him pretty hard, but they didn't rattle Oscar as he scored 37 points.

It appeared that the whole affair, all of the indignities that confronted Oscar Robertson in Texas, were swept under the rug by George Smith, the University of Cincinnati, and the Cincinnati press.

The Cincinnati press acted as if they were oblivious to the racial insults that Robertson had suffered in Texas, and there was not even a hint of any of the episodes printed in the city's three major daily newspapers: *Cincinnati Enquirer, Cincinnati Post,* or *Cincinnati Times-Star.* In the *Enquirer,* on the page carrying the Houston game summary, there appeared a companion article highlighting the average day for Oscar Robertson on the

UC campus. Basketball and school at Cincinnati were portrayed as a rather warm and fuzzy experience for The Big O.

Such overt episodes of racial discrimination overwhelmed Oscar Robertson emotionally and led him on a perpetual thought process that life was unfair and that if you were black you were always going to be victimized. But this defense mechanism also protected Oscar and drove his fierce sense of competitiveness on the basketball court where he demonstrated with ease that he was superior to everyone, not just white players, but other black players, too. Going forward in the pros, Oscar's Cincinnati Royals teammates would be constantly held on the short lease of his intense scrutiny.

If Oscar Robertson as a sophomore had done nothing more than what he did on the night of January 9, 1958, at Madison Square Garden in New York, his legacy in college basketball and as a Cincinnati Bearcat would still have been assured for all time. At the time Robertson was averaging 30 points and 16 rebounds per game. Then, in the most fabled game of Robertson's college career, he scored 56 points (22 field goals on 32 shots and 12 straight foul shots) vs. Seton Hall at the Garden as the Bearcats defeated the Pirates 118–54. Oscar's 22 field goals had topped the previous record of 21 by George Mikan of DePaul in the 1945 NIT.

Robertson's epic 56-point performance at Madison Square Garden broke the arena's all-time scoring record of 54 points held jointly by Tony Jackson of Brooklyn's Thomas Jefferson High School in 1957 and St. John's University's Harry Boykoff in 1947.

The professional record for the Garden at that time was 49 points held by Neil Johnston of the Philadelphia Warriors. That total would eventually be surpassed by Wilt Chamberlain of the San Francisco Warriors who had 73 in 1962. The scoring record for the current Madison Square Garden that opened in 1968 is 62 points set by Carmelo Antony of the New York Knicks in 2014.

There were plenty of pro scouts watching the Holiday Tournament games at the Garden, and they were interested in one soon-to-be-available player in particular—the Bearcats senior 6'9" center Connie Dierking who had 19 points in the Seton Hall game.

The local Cincinnati Royals, who had territorial draft rights, were interested in Dierking. One of Les Harrison's scouts notified him that Dierking was a keeper due to his work under the glass and his ability to shoot from the corner. However, Connie Dierking would be drafted by the Syracuse Nationals in the 1958 NBA draft.

The Bearcats were now 8–2. The two losses to Bradley, 73–79, and Oklahoma State, 57–61, had occurred on the road and without an injured Connie Dierking on the floor.

Cincinnati's 118 points vs. Seton Hall broke the Madison Square Garden college scoring mark by two points that had been set the year before when Bradley beat Xavier 116–81 in the second round of the NIT.

January 9 had been quite a night for Queen City round ball in New York. Overshadowed by the performance of Oscar Robertson and the UC Bearcats in their victory over Seton Hall was the fact that in the opening game at the Garden that evening, Xavier, also from Cincinnati, had defeated a scrappy Iona squad 71–61. The Musketeers were now 5–1 on the season—their only loss was to Cincinnati, 68–79, a month ago.

At the time Robertson set the new Madison Garden scoring record, college basketball was still struggling in New York as a result of the point-shaving scandals of the early 1950s. Robertson's performance against Seton Hall in the Holiday Festival had resurrected Madison Square Garden as the basketball epicenter of the world.

Carried off the floor by his Bearcat teammates and then surrounded by the press, Robertson was asked by *Cincinnati Post* sportswriter Wally Forste if this was his biggest basketball thrill. Robertson replied, "No. My biggest thrill was helping win two state high school championships at Crispus Attucks in Indianapolis."[7]

Oscar Robertson's performance vs. Seton Hall was acknowledged as the greatest one-man show in Madison Square Garden basketball history. Joe Lapchick, the St. John's coach, witnessed the game and described Robertson as "merely wonderful." Fuzzy Levane, the New York Knicks scout, called Robertson, "the best sophomore player since Wilt Chamberlain."[8]

The New York Times, in its report on the game, stated, "The 56 points tallied by the 6-foot, 5-inch star from Indianapolis set an individual scoring mark for the Eighth Avenue arena, where basketball has been played since 1934. Robertson left the game with 2 minutes 46 seconds remaining. He left with the cheers of 4,615 spectators ringing in his ears and with the knowledge that he had scored more points than the entire Seton Hall squad."[9]

Although there had actually been less than five thousand people in Madison Square Garden that January night, for decades going forward it seemed that nearly everyone in New York had witnessed Robertson score 56 points. If you were in New York in the 1960s through the 1980s and mentioned to a waiter, cab driver, bartender, or just someone in a casual conversation that you were from Cincinnati, they would immediately tell you that they had witnessed the game in which Robertson broke the Garden scoring record. Historically, Robertson's performance against Seton Hall had become one of the most enduring Big Apple sports legends of the 1950s, right up there alongside Bobby Thompson's home run in the 1951 playoffs against the Brooklyn Dodgers and Don Larsen's no-hitter in the 1956 World Series.

Lost among all the hoopla surrounding Robertson's performance at Madison Square Garden that night was the fact that he had also broken two University of Cincinnati scoring records; the previous Bearcats single-game scoring record of 49 points had been held by Jack Twyman vs. Western Kentucky in 1955 and the previous field goal record of 19 had been set by Larry Imburgia vs. Cedarvale in 1950.

On Saturday evening, January 11, 1958, two nights after Robertson's scoring binge at Madison Square Garden and seven straight road games, the UC Bearcats returned home to the Armory Fieldhouse and defeated North Texas State, 127–57. The previous high game total for the Bearcats had been the 119 points that they dropped in against Morehead in January 1957.

Perhaps seeking some revenge for the black cat incident in Denton, Texas, Oscar Robertson scored 35 points against the Eagles, playing guard and forward.

Bob Cousy was due in town with the Boston Celtics the following evening but had he been at the Armory Fieldhouse to witness the UC vs. North Texas game he would have been shocked to see The Big O playing his game. It's likely that Cooz would have acknowledged that he was witnessing his successor-in-the-making as the best player in the NBA.

Robertson, who had 12 assists in the game to go along with his 35 points, dazzled the fans with some of his passing. On one occasion, Robertson intercepted a North Texas pass and quickly started down the court only to be confronted with a wall of Eagle defenders. Immediately, he began to dribble the ball behind his back until he found an open man in Mike Mendenhall, fed him the ball, and he scored. Another time, Oscar was blocked by the defense as he went by the side of the basket only to pass the ball behind his back to Spud Hornsby who scored.

For a brief moment on a cold early January weekend in 1958, it seemed like Cincinnati had become the world capital of basketball. The weekend of January 11–12 would turn out to be an exciting one for basketball in the Queen City with a total of 14,596 fans witnessing games. In the Bearcats' Saturday night game against North Texas State played on the UC campus, 7,275 fans had been present at the Armory Fieldhouse. That was a record attendance figure for a basketball game played on the University of Cincinnati campus in a program that began as a varsity sport in 1901, with home games played in a gym located in the basement of McMicken Hall.

Xavier was on the road and lost to St. Joseph of Indiana 66–70, but if they had been at home in Schmidt Fieldhouse, the arena would have also been packed.

Now, however, in the 1957–1958 season, besides basketball being played at UC and Xavier, in the city there was also a new kid in town with the NBA Cincinnati Royals. The night after the University of Cincinnati had drawn its record crowd for the North Texas State game, 7,321 fans were in attendance at Cincinnati Gardens to witness the Royals defeat the Boston Celtics, 115–97. The Royals were led by former Bearcat Jack Twyman with 26 points and Maurice Stokes with 21. For the Celtics, Bob Cousy was the leading scorer with 16 points.

The Royals fans were mesmerized by the brilliant play of Maurice Stokes. It just seemed like Stokes was everywhere on the court, grabbing rebounds, intercepting passes, feeding his teammates, and scoring. He was just everywhere the ball was. On one play, Mo drove towards the basket alone but was blocked by the Celtics' Tom Heinsohn who had timed his leap perfectly to match Stokes. But while in the air Stokes twisted his body away from Heinsohn, faked a shot, and followed up with a shot that went backward over his head and banked into the goal.

With no disrespect intended for The Big O, some Cincinnati basketball fans, because of Mo Stokes' hustling style of play, began to wonder if the best basketball player in the city was not playing at Armory Fieldhouse but rather at Cincinnati Gardens. It would have been magical to see these two gifted athletes play as teammates on the Royals.

After playing in his first twelve varsity games at Cincinnati, Oscar Robertson was narrowly the college scoring leader in the nation. Oscar had a slight edge over Kansas' behemoth 7'1" center Wilt Chamberlain. In 12 games Oscar had scored 388 points to Wilt's 322 in 10 games. That gave Oscar an average of 32.3 points per game as opposed to 32.2 for Chamberlain. The formula for deciding the college scoring leader at the time was based on average points per game rather than total points. So, although Chamberlain had missed two games, where his average may have shrunk, he was still on Robertson's heels because of the formula.

UC coach George Smith helped a little in getting Oscar an edge on Chamberlain by moving him from forward to guard in the North Texas game where he could shoot behind screens. Smith said after the game, "I wanted him to get ahead of Wilt and shifted him outside and he came through. He deserves to be in the lead."[10]

Two days later, on January 13, this time at home in the friendly confines of the Armory Fieldhouse, in front of 5,300 screaming fans, the UC Bearcats and "The Big O" defeated Houston again, 93–58. Robertson had 37 points.

On March 1, The Big O broke the Wichita Fieldhouse scoring record with 50 points against the Shockers in a 113–107 double-overtime win by Cincinnati. The previous scoring mark at the "Roundhouse" had been 36 points by Jim McLaughlin of St. Louis University in 1956. The victory clinched the Missouri Valley Conference Championship for the Bearcats giving them a berth in the NCAA Tournament.

On March 14, 1958, the University of Cincinnati Bearcats, riding a 16-game winning streak, traveled to Lawrence, Kansas to make the school's first appearance in the NCAA tournament playing against the Kansas State Wildcats led by forward Bob Boozer in the Midwest Regional Championship round.

A few hours before the game, legendary coach Hank Iba who would win nearly 800 games in his career at Oklahoma A&M (Oklahoma State), including two NCAA titles in the mid-1940s, was pontificating on the upcoming Cincinnati-Kansas game while sitting with a group of eager listeners in a small restaurant on the edge of Lawrence. While Iba felt that the Bearcats had plenty of firepower, he leaned toward Kansas coming out on top.

"That Oscar Robertson is great, no doubt of it," said Iba, "but I'll tell you who makes that ball club go—it's that Ralph Davis."[11]

Unbeknown to Iba, the father, Ralph Davis, Sr., was part of the group listening to him and had not been introduced to him.

Ralph Davis would go on to be named a second-team All-American in 1960 and close-out his college career at Cincinnati with 1,073 points. At the time, the total made him number six on the UC all-time scorers list. Davis was a very underrated player and his potential was eclipsed by the greatness of Oscar Robertson. Had Ralph Davis played his college career among less diverse, less intense, and less skilled players at an Ivy League school like Bill Bradley did, instead of playing in the Missouri-Valley Conference where every game was a barn-burner, his legacy would have been equal to that of Bradley in the annals of college basketball.

Allen Fieldhouse was named after former Kansas State coach, Phog Allen, who had helped to get basketball introduced into the Olympic Games in 1936.

When the game started, there were 17,000 fans in the stands at Allen Fieldhouse and the Bearcats got a lot of vocal support from the University of Kansas fans present that wanted to see their arch-rival, Kansas State, go down. But when the smoke had cleared, K-State, led by Bob Boozer with 24 points and 14 rebounds, had conquered the highly touted Bearcats and Oscar Robertson, 83–80, in overtime. It turned out to be a game in which The Big O showed that he was human after all. Although he led both squads in scoring with 30 points, he shot only 60% from the field. Then, with one second remaining in regulation time, Robertson was at the free-throw line with a one-and-one. The score was Kansas State 74, Cincinnati 73. Robertson hit the first free throw to tie the game 74–74 but missed on the second attempt sending the game into overtime.

Oscar's missed free throw was not without controversy. With the crowd extremely revved-up, The Big O sunk his first free throw. But feeling the pressure, he walked around, wiped his hands and finally stepped back up to the line. It was learned later that the referees were invoking the seldom-enforced ten-second rule where a player has ten seconds in which to shoot. As Robertson was nervously preparing for his second free throw, teammate Ron Dykes saw one of the refs counting and he was already up to eight; it is not known if it was Lou Batmale from San Francisco or Johnny Coe from Salem, Oregon. Consequently, Robertson put the ball up and it hit the back of the rim and rolled off, and the game went into overtime.

Entering the overtime session, the Bearcats were plagued by foul trouble, as Connie Dierking and Wayne Stevens fouled out. Then, 34 seconds into the overtime session, Robertson fouled out. The Wildcats then proceeded to outscore the Bearcats 9–6 in the five-minute OT.

The following evening, Cincinnati defeated Arkansas in the consolation game to finish the 1957–58 season with a 25–3 record, the best in the school's basketball history.

In his sophomore year, Oscar Robertson had established himself as the premier college player in the nation. He was chosen by consensus as a first-team All-American and named the UPI and Sporting News College Player of the Year. Robertson won the national scoring title with 35.1 points per game, besting Elgin Baylor of Seattle with 30.5 points per game and Wilt Chamberlain of Kansas with 30.1 points per game. All three players averaged more than 15 rebounds per game.

The UC Bearcats had failed to make it past the Midwest Regional Championship round in the NCAA tournament and the next afternoon, Sunday, March 16, at Cincinnati Gardens, with Maurice Stokes lying unconscious in a hospital bed after hitting his head in a freak fall against Minneapolis going up for a rebound, the Detroit Pistons eliminated the Cincinnati Royals from the NBA Western Division playoffs winning the second game of the series 124–104 to a complete a two-game sweep.

Still, the basketball fans in Cincinnati wound up with a champion. The Bearcats' cross-town rival, the Xavier University Musketeers, entered the NIT at Madison Square Garden in New York with a mediocre 15–11 season record and got hot, winning four straight games, while defeating St. Bonaventure, 72–53, in the semi-final round and then slipping past interstate rival, University of Dayton, 78–74, in the final to take home the trophy and finish the season with a 19–11 record.

The University of Cincinnati Bearcats would have another fine season in 1958–59 winning 28 games, but even with Oscar Robertson leading the charge once again, the Cats would come up short of winning a national championship.

On January 31, Cincinnati defeated Wichita State at home in the Armory Fieldhouse 95–87 with Oscar Robertson scoring 44 points, including dropping in 14 straight free throws. At one point in the first half, the Bearcats had a 22-point lead only to see the Shockers battle back in the second half and nearly catch the

Bearcats. With the scrappy effort put forth by Wichita, everyone was expecting the Bearcats to have their hands full when the two teams met again.

Three weeks later, the two teams met again at Wichita, and this time the Bearcats defeated the Shockers 88–74. But it has been suggested that Cincinnati may have had a little off-the-court help in defeating Wichita. While a fix of the game seems to border on myth more than direct evidence, here is what is alleged to have happened:

Somewhere out there, Jack Molinas had once again raised his ugly head. Since being banned from playing in the NBA in 1954, Molinas had remained active in gambling on both college and professional basketball games, while setting up a rather large and elaborate game-fixing network.

In Charley Rosen's book, *The Wizard of Odds—How Jack Molinas Almost Destroyed the Game of Basketball,* allegedly on February 21, 1959, the game between the University of Cincinnati and Wichita State was fixed for Cincinnati to win.

Dave Budin, a Brooklyn junior high school gym teacher and Coney Island, New York bookie, told another bookmaker that Joe Hackin and Jack Molinas had two Wichita players and one Cincinnati player in the bag. Those player's names—if they ever existed—are not known.

Rosen's book claims that Hackin and Molinas wanted to sell the forthcoming Cincinnati-Wichita game to Pittsburgh bookmaker Frank Cardone for the $9,000 front money needed to make the fix. However, Cardone couldn't raise the money alone, so he brought in a Cincinnati bookmaker by the name of Gil. Half of the money was to go to the players from Wichita and Cincinnati and the other half was to be split by Hackin, Molinas, and their associates. When the deal fell through, Molinas got a backer in Philadelphia to put up the $9,000 front money on the condition he would limit his wagers to $50,000 which would keep the betting line intact. Cincinnati, originally picked to lose in the fix, was now picked to win and the players were informed. Hackin and Molinas bet heavily on Cincinnati, favored by 5½ points to win, and supposedly cleaned up when Cincinnati defeated Wichita 88–74.

In the second half, the Bearcats were comfortably covering the point spread, having a 67–52 lead with eight minutes to go. Then, the Shockers fought back gallantly inspired by the crowd, but they just couldn't overcome the Cincinnati lead.

According to the *Cincinnati Enquirer*, "Inspired by the continual roaring of the crowd, the Shockers fought the Bearcats on almost even terms, but in vain in the final eight minutes. Paper cups, spitballs, and other debris showered down on the floor at the end as the disappointed Kansans left the roundhouse."[12] If the Wichita comeback was legitimate, then someone or something put the brakes on it during those final eight minutes.

Oscar Robertson scored 34 points in the game and Ralph Davis added 24 as the victory took Cincinnati a step closer to wrapping up its second consecutive Missouri Valley Conference championship.

According to Jack Molinas, he and Joe Hackin were confident after they had given Dave Budin $5,000 that his contacts were legitimate, so he would use them going forward to fix a lot of other college games during the 1958–59 season. Supposedly, even Lefty Rosenthall of Chicago, portrayed by Robert De Niro in the movie *Casino,* and his associates were eventually brought into the later action by Molinas through a contact by the name of Dave Goldberg in St. Louis.

It seems reasonable that if something wasn't on the up in the UC vs Wichita game it would have been noticed by Shockers coach Ralph Miller, an outstanding coach. In 1951 and 1964, Ralph Miller was named the Coach of the Year in the Missouri Valley Conference. In 1968, Miller would go on to become the coach of Iowa and later lead Oregon State to a PAC Ten Championship and later be elected to the College Basketball Hall of Fame.

Significant Wichita players who participated in the game were Dick Cassidy, Ron Heller, John Gates, Lanny Van Eman, and Virgil Brady. All appear to have played the game hard-nosed. So, if there was any deception in play by these players, it was very well concealed.

The 1958–1959 Cincinnati Bearcats roster, coached by George Smith, consisted of the following players: Oscar Robertson, Ralph Davis, Mike Mendenhall, Dave Tenwick, Carl Bouldin, Bill Whitaker, Larry Willey, John Bryant, Ron Dykes, Rod Nall, Mel Landfield, Dick Taylor, and Dick Cetrone. It's very doubtful that someone on the Bearcats squad was in the bag.

Robertson, Davis, Mendenhall, and Willey were all eventually drafted by NBA teams. From a historical perspective, all the lesser known Cincinnati players look clean as well. Dick Cetrone, a native of Pittsburgh, only averaged 1 point per game. After graduation, Cetrone was an assistant coach at Oak Hills High School (Cincinnati) for a year, then went back to Pittsburgh and coached a high school team for decades. Ron Dykes was from Middletown and had played with Jerry Lucas on the legendary Ohio state championship team. John Bryant, the only other black player on the Bearcats besides Oscar, went on to get a Ph.D. in Education. Dave Tenwick became a lawyer. Bill Whitaker from Hughes High School, the son of a legendary Cincinnati area high school principal (Finneytown), was as straight-laced as they come and wouldn't have known a bookmaker if one fell out of a tree on him. All of the reserves, such as Dykes, Taylor, Nall, and Landfield, played, but not enough to fix a game. So just who could have been the conspirator?

Following an appearance in the NCAA Tournament, the Cincinnati Bearcats would finish 1958–59 with a record of 26–4 (13–1 Missouri Valley Conference). Their only MVC loss was to Bradley, 66–84, at Peoria. Cincinnati's two non-conference losses were to North Carolina State and North Carolina in the Dixie Classic played in December 1958.

Once again, Oscar Robertson was Mr. Basketball as he led the nation in scoring with an average of 32.6 points per game and was named Player of the Year by *The Sporting News,* USBWA, UPI, and the Helms Foundation. Also, for the second straight year, Robertson was named a first-team All-American, along with Bailey Howell (Mississippi), Bob Boozer (Kansas State), Jerry West (West Virginia), and Johnny Cox (Kentucky).

The 21–3 Bearcats advanced to the NCAA Tournament without one of their leading playmakers, Mike Mendenhall, who was declared ineligible. Nonetheless, they defeated TCU 77–73 in the Midwest Regional Semi-Final and Kansas State 85–75 in the Midwest Regional Final. Now the Bearcats advanced to the Final Four, along with California, Louisville, and West Virginia, which would be played at Freedom Hall in Louisville.

College basketball fans across the country were hoping for a championship final between Cincinnati and West Virginia and a shootout between two of the greatest guards in college basketball history. While UC had All-American and Player of the Year Oscar Robertson, the Mountaineers had All-American Jerry West, who would finish the season with a scoring average of 26.6 points per game.

The Mountaineers did their part to advance to the championship final by defeating Louisville 94–79 as Jerry West had 38 points and 15 rebounds. Now it was up to the Bearcats.

In the Midwest Semi-Final, the Bearcats were opposed by the University of California Golden Bears coached by Pete Newell who had played college basketball in 1937–39 as a forward at Loyola of Los Angeles and then tried playing professional baseball as a farmhand with the Brooklyn Dodgers minor league team at Pine Bluff, Arkansas. However, after serving in the U.S. Navy in World War Two in the Pacific theatre, Newell returned to basketball at the University of San Francisco where his squad won the 1949 NIT.

At the time of the 1959 NCAA tournament, Newell's Golden Bears, ranked 11th in the final AP Top Twenty, had a record of 23–4 and were riding a 14-game winning streak into the tournament.

Pete Newell was a defensive-minded coach who used a balanced attack. Two years before, Newell's Golden Bears had almost beaten Kansas by cleverly pulling Wilt Chamberlain out of position. Now Newell knew that in order to defeat the Bearcats he would have to contain their one-man show Oscar Robertson. Newell had two quality players around the basket in 6'10" center Darrall Imhoff and 6'5" forward Bill McClintock. But the job of guarding the 6'5", 205-pound scoring machine Robertson was given to 6'3", 155-pound Bob Dalton, who was averaging 7.3 points per game. While Newell knew that Oscar Robertson was Mr. Everything, he was actually confident that Mr. Nothing Bob Dalton could do the job.

Newell and the Golden Bears decided to start off by using a little psychology on The Big O. So, when the players were introduced before the game, grinning from ear to ear, Bob Dalton shook Oscar Robertson's hand and said to him, "Hi, my name's Dalton—what's yours?"[13]

Robertson was momentarily stunned! At that point in his career, he had been on the cover of magazines as much as Marilyn Monroe and Mickey Mantle. The Big O was virtually a household name.

When the game started, Robertson was even more stunned by the pressing defenses and trappings the Golden Bears employed. In the end, California, led by the dominating performance of Darrall Imhoff who scored 22 points and grabbed 16 rebounds, defeated the Bearcats 64–58. California held Oscar Robertson to just 19 points. Also, California held the Cincinnati Bearcats to 26 points below their season average of 84 points per game.

Oscar Robertson now asserts that he doesn't remember the introduction incident or Bob Dalton doing a great job defending him. Nonetheless, the Dalton incident must have bothered The Big O. Pete Newell said Robertson cornered him a year later and said, "Coach, that guy knew what my name was, didn't he?"[14]

The following evening, The Big O would be back on his game scoring 39 points and grabbing 17 rebounds as Cincinnati defeated Louisville 98–85 in the consolation game to take third place in the tournament.

In the championship final, Jerry West finished with 28 points, but West Virginia blew a 13-point first-half lead to lose to California. The winning goal was scored by center Darrall Imhoff with 17 seconds left in the game. Although Imhoff was left-handed he tipped the ball in with his right hand. Jerry West says Imhoff's tip-in "was the ugliest play you could ever imagine."[15] West Virginia had one more chance to win the game when the Golden Bears missed a free throw with 2 seconds remaining; Jerry West grabbed the rebound but couldn't get a shot off. California won 71–70.

Following the 1959 NCAA Tournament, the Harlem Globetrotters offered Oscar Robertson a lot of money to forego his senior year at Cincinnati and join the team. But Robertson, a preseason pick for the 1960 All-American team along with Jerry West of West Virginia, Jim Hagan of Tennessee, Ron Johnson of Minnesota, and Tony Jackson of St. John's, decided to remain with the Bearcats.

On February 8, 1960, as Oscar Robertson neared the end of his collegiate career, he set another record. In a 123–74 Bearcats victory over North Texas State, Robertson scored 62 points, a school record.

The Bearcats won the Missouri Valley Conference Championship again in 1959–60 and entered the NCAA Tournament with a season record of 25–1 (13–1 MVC), their only loss coming on January 16 at the hands of Bradley 90–91. Out of a total of 40 MVC records, Oscar Robertson finished his college career holding 16 of them.

It was now the last chance for Oscar Robertson to win a National Championship with Cincinnati and the Bearcats entered the 1960 NCAA Tournament ranked number one in the final AP poll.

In the Midwest Regional Semi-Finals played in Manhattan, Kansas, Cincinnati quickly dispatched DePaul 99–59 with The Big O scoring 29 points and grabbing 9 rebounds.

Then, in the Midwest Finals, the Bearcats defeated Kansas 82–71 after being down 42–40 at half-time. Oscar Robertson scored 43 points and hauled in 14 rebounds. It was the Bearcats 27th win of the season.

The Bearcats then advanced to the Final Four in San Francisco along with California, Ohio State, and New York University.

In order to reach the championship game, Cincinnati had to get by California again. But the Golden Bears just seemed to have The Big O's number, holding him to 18 points and 10 rebounds, as they defeated the Bearcats 77–69. Cincinnati believed that this time they had the answer to containing Darrall Imhoff pairing him off against 6'9", 240-pound sophomore center Paul Hogue. While Hogue scored 14 points and had 11 rebounds, Imhoff scored 25 points and had 11 rebounds.

The following evening in the championship game, California was defeated by Ohio State 75–55. The key to the Buckeyes victory was a balanced attack, as they used twelve players in the game with All-American, 6'8" sophomore center Jerry Lucas scoring 16 points and hauling in 10 rebounds while holding Darrall Imhoff to just 8 points and 5 rebounds.

Ohio State coach Fred Taylor used his entire squad to defeat California. Besides Lucas with 16 points, Mel Nowell had 15 points; Larry Siegfried, 13; John Havlicek, 12; and Joe Roberts, 6. Even reserve Bobby Knight got in the game.

In the consolation game, Oscar Robertson closed out his collegiate career in true Big O style scoring 32 points with 14 rebounds as the Bearcats handled NYU with ease in a 95–71 triumph.

Although the University of Cincinnati Bearcats never won a National Championship during Oscar Robertson's years on the team, his individual performance had been overwhelming. He finished with 2,973 points and his averages for points per game in each of his collegiate career years were 35.1, 32.6, and 33.7. The Big O had become the all-time major college scoring leader by surpassing Dickie Hemric of Wake Forest who previously held the record with 2,587 career points. However, it had taken Hemric four years to accumulate his points.

The list of honors and awards that Robertson received during his college days were nearly as tall as his 6'5" frame: three-time consensus All-American, three-time *Sporting News* Player of the Year, three-time UPI Player of the Year, and on and on. When Robertson left the University of Cincinnati, he had replaced Jack Twyman as the all-time career leader in scoring. The Big O would remain the all-time major college scoring leader until 1970 when bested by "Pistol Pete" Maravich of LSU.

But going forward, Oscar Robertson would be more than just a basketball legend at the University of Cincinnati—he would become an ambassador of trust for the school. He would remain loyal to UC and promote not only its athletics program but also its academic programs.

It was because of The Big O that talented players, both black and white, future All-Americans such as Paul Hogue, Ron Bonham, and Tom Thacker, Tony Yates, and George Wilson enrolled at the University of Cincinnati. It was their presence that would result in the Bearcats winning two consecutive NCAA National Championships in 1961 and 1962, defeating Ohio State twice, then narrowly missing a third National Championship in 1963, losing the final game to Loyola of Chicago in a controversial double overtime. For decades following those championship years, Cincinnati fans were thanking coach Ed Jucker for the Bearcats success when they should have been thanking Oscar Robertson.

Future Michigan All-American Cazzie Russell out of Carver High School in Chicago had been courted by both Oscar Robertson for Cincinnati and John Wooden of UCLA. The reason Russell chose to enroll at Michigan rather Cincinnati was due to the personality differences between the coaches. Bearcats coach Ed Jucker had a propensity to be a sourpuss, whereas Wolverines coach Dave Strack was very charismatic.

Reflecting on his decision to enroll at Michigan, Russell stated, "The way Dave Strack treated me and my family was the key to my coming to Michigan. I loved Dave Strack and his family. His wife, Miss Ruth Ann, was special. And I babysat for some of their girls."[16]

Had Oscar Robertson had a little more help from Ed Jucker in recruiting Cazzie Russell, Cincinnati may have had a real dynasty in college basketball in the 1960s instead of a near-miss.

In the 1959 basketball World Championships, the United States finished third, losing in the final round to both Brazil, who won the title, and the Soviet Union. Going into the 1960 Olympic Games in Rome, the USA was bound and determined to reclaim its dominance in a sport native to the Stars and Stripes. To accomplish that feat, the United States put on the floor what is considered the greatest amateur basketball team ever assembled.

The U.S. team would be coached by California's Pete Newell, assisted by Warren Womble of Peoria who had coached the 1952 USA Olympic Championship Team.

The Olympic trials were held in Denver in April 1960, 96 players from the NCAA, AAU, and United States Military tried out for the squad and 12 players and 12 alternates were chosen.

Among those joining Oscar Robertson on the USA team from the NCAA were future NBA stars Jerry West, West Virginia; Jerry Lucas, Ohio State; Darrall Imhoff, California; Walt Bellamy, Indiana University; and Jay Arnett, Texas. Chosen from the AAU were Bob Boozer, Kansas State; Allen Kelley, Kansas; Lester Lane, Oklahoma; and Burdie Haldorson, the 6'8" star of the Bartlesville, Oklahoma Oilers, the champions of the National Industrial League. Chosen from the Armed Services team was Adrian Smith, who had played at Kentucky.

The pool of NCAA and AAU talented former and current college stars available for the 1960 Olympics Team was so deep that many players chosen as alternates would go on to have notable professional careers: Wayne Hightower, Kansas; Tom Meschery, St. Mary's of California; Thomas "Satch" Sanders, NYU; and John Havlicek and Larry Siegfried of Ohio State.

Oscar Robertson, who would be the first player taken in the 1960 NBA draft as the territorial pick by the Cincinnati Royals, and Jerry West, who would be the second player chosen by the Minneapolis Lakers about to move to Los Angeles, were named co-captains of the USA team.

Jerry West has always maintained that with him and Oscar Robertson on the 1960 USA Olympic team, the Russian team had no chance of winning the Gold Medal. "We both had chips on our shoulders," said West, "[Robertson's] had to do with race, beginning with the various struggles his Crispus Attucks High School team had in being recognized, whereas mine was fueled by anger toward a father who found fault with me at every turn, as well as a personal mission to fulfill a desire for perfection and a way of replacing my dead brother."[17] (West's older brother, David, had been killed in action in Korea in 1951).

The 1960 Olympic basketball competition was played between August 26 and September 10, and the Americans won all eight of their games, taking the Gold Medal. The Soviet Union took the Silver Medal and Brazil the Bronze.

The USA team overwhelmed its opponents by averaging 101.9 points per game as opposed to allowing only 59.9 points per game. Pete Newell used every player on his squad liberally in defeating in succession—Italy 88–54, Japan 125–66, Hungary 107–63, Yugoslavia 104–42, Uruguay 108–50, Soviet Union 107–63, Italy 88–54, and in the championship game Brazil 90–60.

Oscar Robertson was the leading scorer for the USA team with an average of 17.0 points per game followed by Jerry Lucas, 16.8; Jerry West, 14.5; Terry Dischinger, 11.5; and Adrian Smith, 10.9.

7

The Big O Comes to the NBA

& the ABL Folds

At the end of the 1959–60 season, the Cincinnati Royals exercised their territorial draft rights with the number one pick in the NBA draft to select Oscar Robertson, aka "The Big O," who had just completed his spectacular collegiate career at the University of Cincinnati and won a Gold Medal in the Olympics in Rome.

Jack Twyman remarked that before Oscar Robertson joined the Royals, the offense of the team depended on him. But in Oscar's rookie season he went from averaging 31 points to 24 points per game. "In effect, I became a supporting player to him. But you could see right away that Oscar was a franchise player."[1] Robertson would add a new competitive edge to the Royals, as the year before he was drafted, they had won only 19 games, but in his first two years with the team, they would win 33 and 43.

During the last three years, 1958–1960, the University of Cincinnati, with Oscar Robertson, had not won a national championship, but they had won three consecutive Missouri Valley Conference championships. During that period, Robertson had been a three-time All-American, three-time College Player of the Year, and won a Gold Medal in the Olympics.

During the same period, Bob Cousy and the Boston Celtics had reached the NBA Finals three times, losing to St. Louis in 1958 and then winning back-to-back NBA championships in 1959 and 1960. Cousy had been an All-Star each year and led the NBA in assists each of the last three years. In one game in 1959, Cousy had 19 assists in one half.

Now the time had come for the brilliant careers of Oscar Robertson, the 23-year-old rookie, and Bob Cousy, the 32-year-old veteran, two of the greatest guards in NBA history, to collide on the hardwood. A national sports magazine asked Bob Cousy about what he thought The Big O would do in the league. Cousy stated that "[Jerry] West could be the best. And Oscar could be a Royal letdown."[2]

Jerry West said that while Elgin Baylor was the player he studied when he first came into the league, Oscar Robertson was the player that he tried to emulate. While Robertson felt the press favored West, stating in his book, *The Big O—My Life, My Times, My Game*, "America looked at Jerry fondly,"[3] West asserts that "Oscar was never a rookie, not even close."[4]

In addition to Oscar Robertson, the Royals had also acquired the draft rights in a trade with the St. Louis Hawks to one of his 1960 Olympic Gold Medal team members: 6'8" forward Bob Boozer who had played his college ball at Kansas State. Also, the Royals had drafted Oscar's underrated teammate from the University of Cincinnati, 6'4" guard Ralph Davis.

One of the unique aspects of the 1960–61 Cincinnati Royals was the team's regional makeup. While it wasn't unusual for NBA teams of the time to have a few regionally known players, six of the twelve members of the Royals, fifty percent, had played on college teams located within fifty miles of Cincinnati. From the University of Cincinnati, there was Oscar Robertson, Jack Twyman, and Ralph Davis. From just across the Ohio River in northern Kentucky was Larry Staverman from Villa Madonna College (Thomas Moore College), Arlen Bockhorn had played at the University of Dayton, and Wayne Embry at Miami (of Ohio) in Oxford.

While the Royals' management and coach Charlie Wolf may have been catering to the house, hiring players with local connections, having the trio of Oscar Robertson, Jack Twyman, and Wayne Embry on the 1960–61 edition of the Cincinnati Royals looked to make them a much-improved team.

Of course, speculation was still being advanced in Cincinnati about what Maurice Stokes could have added to the team playing with Robertson, Twyman, and Embry rather than lying in a hospital bed in a horrible, hopeless, vegetating physical state. There is no doubt that a Robertson-Stokes combination would have been a considerable force to be reckoned with in the NBA for several years to come and would have been a major threat to the

Bob Cousy—and Bill Russell—led Boston Celtics dynasty of the early 1960s.

In 1960–61, the NBA was an eight-team league with two divisions. The Eastern Division consisted of Boston, Philadelphia, Syracuse, and New York. The Western Division consisted of St. Louis, Los Angeles, Detroit, and Cincinnati.

On October 19, 1960, The Big O made his NBA debut playing against the Lakers who had just relocated from Minneapolis to Los Angeles. The Lakers featured high scoring Elgin Baylor and rookie guard Jerry West.

When Bob Short moved the Lakers to LA, he wanted Bill Sharman of the Boston Celtics to coach the team. Sharman was still on the Celtics' active player list. Red Auerbach was willing to let Sharman go to the Lakers, but in exchange, he wanted Jerry West. Short quickly broke off negotiations and hired West Virginia coach Fred Schaus.

The Royals vs. Lakers game was played before 8,176 people at Cincinnati Gardens, the largest crowd to see the Royals play at home in their history at that time. To the absolute delight of those fans, the Royals won a shoot-out with the Lakers 140 to 123.

While veteran Jack Twyman led the Royals in scoring with 30 points and Arlen "Bucky" Bockhorn added 20, Oscar Robertson was spectacular in his first professional game finishing with a triple-double scoring 21 points with 12 rebounds and 10 assists.

For the LA Lakers, Elgin Baylor had 35 points, 17 rebounds, and 3 assists. It was also Jerry West's first game in the NBA, and he debuted with 20 points, 5 assists, and 2 rebounds.

The Cincinnati Royals' front office was all smiles about Oscar. In the previous season, the Royals' home attendance at Cincinnati Gardens for 31 games was 58,244 (1,879 per game). But just five home games into the 1960–61 season the Royals, with a record of 5–3, had drawn 35,241 (7,048 per game). It was no surprise that most of those fans had come to see The Big O.

In the 1960–61 season, the Cincinnati Royals and Boston Celtics would meet nine times. The first meeting of the clubs would be a three-game series with a single game played at Boston, Cincinnati, and New York over the course of six days, November 5–11, 1960.

The first of the three games between the Royals and Celtics would take place on November 5 at Boston Garden and be a huge media event in that it was the first meeting of Bob Cousy, the old pro, vs. Oscar Robertson, the rookie. The Big O was coming into the Cooz's town and there were plenty of doubting Thomases among the Celtics faithful that weren't sure the Royals rookie would be able to rise to the challenge. *Sports Illustrated* even did an article on the game titled "The New Kid on The Block Takes on The Champ," the "new kid" being Oscar Robertson and the "champ" referencing Bob Cousy.

The Cooz had been an NBA All-Star in Boston when The Big O was still in junior high school in Indianapolis. When William Leggett of *Sports Illustrated* asked Cousy if facing Robertson for the first time was about pride, he responded that he had thought about their meeting all week long and talked to himself, "Of course it's pride," said Cousy. "Better get yourself up, Bob. Better be at your best, Bob. Oscar's coming to town to play in your arena before your crowd for the first time."[5]

On the evening of November 5, 1960, fans were lined up outside Boston Garden hours before the game for tickets. The Garden had a seating capacity of 13,909; at game time, 13,258 of them would be occupied.

Bob Cousy arrived at Boston Garden from his home in the suburbs in a gray 1960 Cadillac. Then, he entered Boston Garden through a secure entrance that led to a tunnel to keep him safe from the throngs of admirers who wanted to shake his hand.

Oscar Robertson, still a little dewy-eyed by the NBA experience, grabbed his gym bag and walked unostentatiously to Boston Garden from his hotel.

When the game began, Cousy scored the first bucket to give the Celtics a 2–0 lead. Bill Sharman was assigned the job of guarding Oscar and fouled him almost immediately. After six minutes the score was 6–6. While Cousy and Bill Russell did their usual jobs, overall, the Celtics seemed taken by surprise by the Royals' tenacity. After Cincinnati took a commanding lead in the second quarter, the outcome of the game was never in doubt. At the buzzer, the Royals had defeated the Celtics 113–104.

In regard to "The Cooz vs. The Big O" hoopla: statistically, Bob Cousy played 45 minutes and scored 27 points, while Oscar Robertson played 46 minutes and scored 25 points. All that Cousy had at stake in the game was to save face, if he had only scored 16 or 17 points and had a handful of assists in the game, he would have been off the hook. Bob Cousy really did not have to prove anything that night—he had three NBA championship

Cincinnati Royals, circa 1962. Bottom L to R: Oscar Robertson, Arlen Bockhorn; Top L to R: Jack Tywman, Wayne Embry, Bob Boozer. (Courtesy of Cincinnati Museum Center.)

rings and that fact alone said everything there was to say about his ability to play the game.

On the other hand, the challenge for Oscar Robertson was much larger; he had to legitimize himself as a pro on the NBA's largest stage. He needed to demonstrate that he was a lot more than a college hot-shot and perhaps had the potential to be the next Cousy. He came through that evening on the court in Boston with flying colors.

Off the court, well that's another matter. In the *Sports Illustrated* account of the contest, it was stated that after the game Bob Cousy sat on a bench in the Celtics locker room, "physically exhausted and near tears." As for Oscar Robertson, he was tired and bothered by a sprained ankle he had incurred a week earlier. Also, The Big O, never one to be fan-friendly, was annoyed with "the teenagers clamoring outside the locker-room door."[6]

When Robertson left the Garden that evening to go back to the hotel, he plowed his way through a group of star-struck teenagers while Cousy stood outside Boston Garden under a light drizzle and signed autographs for his admiring Beantown fans.

The next stop for "The Cooz vs. The Big O" roadshow took place three days later on November 8 at Cincinnati Gardens. A near-capacity crowd witnessed the Celtics defeat the Royals 136–120. While Robertson scored 31 points and Cousy scored 30 points, neither player was the leading scorer for his team that night. Jack Twyman led the Royals with 32 points, while Tom Heinsohn led the Celtics with 33 points.

The three-game Royals-Celtics series was concluded on November 11 at Madison Square Garden in New York with an amazing 18,499 fans present. Once again, Boston prevailed, defeating Cincinnati 128–110. Neither Bob Cousy or Oscar Roberson was at the top of his game that evening in "The Big Apple" as Cousy scored only 6 points and Robertson was held to 17. Once again, Tom Heinsohn led the Celtics with 30 points, while Jack Twyman again led the Royals with 29.

The Boston Celtics vs. Cincinnati Royals, or Cousy vs. Robertson series, had been a huge box office success. The total attendance for the three games played in Boston, Cincinnati, and New York had been 40,959 (13,653 per game). The two teams would continue to be a considerable draw when facing each other throughout the 1960–1961 season and two other games were scheduled on neutral courts in Philadelphia and New York again. In the nine games between the Celtics and Royals, Boston would win six and Cincinnati three while attracting a total attendance of 85,715 fans or an average of 9,524 per game.

Oscar Robertson, without a doubt, had been one of the greatest college players of all time. Now he would show that he was one of the greatest professional basketball players of all time. Robertson was considered the complete player, one that could shoot, dribble, pass, rebound, and play defense.

Ever since Draft Day 1960, every player in the NBA had been wondering just how good Oscar Robertson was. They finally got their answer on January 19, 1961, at the NBA All-Star Game.

The game, played at Syracuse before a sparse crowd of 8,016, was the perfect opportunity for The Big O to showcase his talents while playing with and against the best players in the NBA, and he didn't disappoint.

The outcome of the game was actually settled in the first quarter as the West squad romped their way to 47–19 lead and at the final buzzer had defeated the East 153–131.

While playing just 34 minutes, The Big O had barely missed a triple-double with 23 points, 14 assists, and 9 rebounds and was named the game's MVP.

The old pro, Bob Cousy, played 33 minutes in the game, had 4 points, 8 assists, and 3 rebounds.

Oscar Robertson would be named the NBA Rookie of Year in 1961 coming close to averaging a triple-double for the season, finishing with 30.5 points per game, 10.1 rebounds, and 9.7 assists per game. Also, Jack Twyman would finish the season with a scoring average of 25.3 points per game. Despite the one-two scoring punch of Robertson and Twyman, the Cincinnati Royals would finish with a dismal record of 33–46, last in the Western Division, and come up short by one game of making the playoffs.

On the other hand, for Bob Cousy and the Boston Celtics, in 1960–61 it was the same old same old; they defeated the St. Louis Hawks four games to one in the finals to win their third consecutive NBA championship and fourth title in the past five years. Fans were starting to ask the question; can anyone beat these guys?

In being selected as the MVP, Oscar Robertson led the NBA in assists (690) and assists per game (9.7). Prior to 1960–61, Bob Cousy had been the league's assists leader for eight consecutive years. In 1960–61, Cousy, with 587 assists, 7.7 per game, finished third behind Robertson and Guy Rodgers (677 assists, 8.7 per game).

In scoring, Wilt Chamberlain became the first professional to score 3,000 points in a season as he led the league by a mile with 3,033 points/38.4 points per game. Elgin Baylor finished second with 2,538 points/34.8 per game, while Oscar Robertson finished third with 2,165 points/30.5 per game.

Bob Cousy had finished seventeenth in the league with 1,387 points/18.1 points per game just behind Jerry West in sixteenth place with 1,389 points/17.6 per game.

The fact was that Oscar Robertson was coming and Bob Cousy was going. The Big O, who would be just 24 years old in the coming season, had played 3,032 minutes in 1960–61, third most in the league. Bob Cousy, who would be 34 years old in the coming season, had played just 2,588 minutes in 1960–61 and didn't finish in the top twenty for minutes played. Still, Cousy had played for more minutes in 1960–61 than any other season since 1955–56 when he played 2,756 minutes. So, the Cooz still had some gas in his tank and was no pushover for opposing teams.

The NBA would expand to nine teams in 1961–62 by adding the Chicago Packers to the Western Division along with Cincinnati, Detroit, Los Angeles, and St. Louis.

After eleven years, professional basketball had returned to the Windy City but continued to be a failure. During the summer, the Cubs and White Sox ruled the Chicago sports scene. In the fall, the Bears and Cardinals took over, and the winter belonged to the Black Hawks. The Windy City was just not ready yet for professional basketball.

In their inaugural season playing in the International Amphitheatre, the Chicago Packers, despite the fact they had the 1962 Rookie of Year in 6'11" center Walt Bellamy out of Indiana University, had a hard time drawing 3,000 fans a game and would have one of the worst seasons in NBA history, finishing in last place with a record of 18–62. Bellamy, who would go on to have a Hall of Fame career, actually had the best year of his career for the hapless Packers, finishing with an average of 31.6 points per game and 19 rebounds.

But the 1961–62 NBA season would feature two of the most incredible individual players' performances in the still somewhat young, wild, and wooly history of the league.

On December 2, 1961, in a game played in Philly, Wilt Chamberlain scored 78 points and grabbed 43 rebounds in a three-overtime loss, 147–151, to the Los Angeles Lakers. For the Lakers, Elgin Baylor scored 63 points and Jerry West, 32.

Then on March 2, 1962, Chamberlain would score 100 points in a game against the New York Knicks played in Hershey, Pennsylvania. Chamberlain would finish the season with an astronomical average of 50.4 points per game and 25.7 rebounds.

Also, Oscar Robertson would finish the season averaging a triple-double. It was a feat that had never been accomplished before in the history of the NBA. The Big O averaged 30.1 points per game, along with 12.5 rebounds and 11.4 assists.

Nonetheless, neither Chamberlain nor Robertson was chosen as the league's MVP; the award went for a second straight year to Bill Russell of the Boston Celtics.

The 1961–62 Cincinnati Royals would be a greatly improved team. All five starting players, including Oscar Robertson (30.8), Jack Twyman (22.9), Wayne Embry (19.8), Arlen Bockhorn (15.8), and Bob Boozer (13.7), finished with points per game averages in double digits.

The Cincinnati Royals finished in second place in the NBA Western Division with a record of 43–37, eleven games behind the division champions, the Los Angeles Lakers, 54–26, and five games ahead of third-place Detroit with a record of 37–43. While they made the playoffs for the first time in four years, they were quickly dispatched by Detroit 3 games to 1.

But something didn't add up in Cincy. In 1961–62, the Royals made the playoffs, yet attendance was down by 25% compared to 1960–61 when the Royals finished last in the Western Division. In 1960–61, the Royals had drawn a season total at Cincinnati Gardens of 194,017 or an average of 6,258 per game. But a year later, with an improved team, season attendance had fallen off to 146,468 or 4,724 per game.

In the Eastern Division, despite the phenomenal scoring and rebounding of Wilt Chamberlain, the Boston Celtics would finish in first place with a record of 60–20, eleven games ahead of the Philadelphia Warriors with a 49–31 record.

Boston reached the finals and defeated the Los Angeles Lakers 4 games to 3 to win their fourth consecutive NBA championship and fifth title in six years. However, the Lakers gave the Celtics a battle with their one-two scoring punch of Elgin Baylor and Jerry West.

Los Angeles took the lead in the series 3 games to 2 after defeating Boston 126–121 in game five. Elgin Baylor burned the Celtics by scoring 61 points while Jerry West added 21. In game two, won by LA, West had scored 40 and Baylor, 36, in defeating the Celtics 129–122.

But the Celtics lineup was just too deep for the Lakers and they lost games six and seven. While Bob Cousy and Bill Russell played consistently in each game, others were stepping up their game night after night: Tom Heinsohn, Sam Jones, Frank Ramsey, and Satch Sanders. Boston won game seven 110–107 with Bill

Russel scoring 30 points, Sam Jones, 27, and Frank Ramsey, 23. Bob Cousy had played in all 14 playoff games and for the seventh consecutive year had been the playoffs leader in assists with 123, an average of 8.8 per game.

It should be noted, that in 1961–62, the NBA had some competition from a rival league, the American Basketball League. The league had been formed by Abe Saperstein who felt the NBA failed to honor a promise to him for obtaining a franchise in Los Angeles. Saperstein alleged that, in return for his years of supporting the NBA with doubleheader games featuring his Harlem Globetrotters, the league promised him a franchise in Los Angeles. But then, seemingly out of nowhere, Saperstein was blindsided when the NBA approved the transfer of Bob Short's Minneapolis Lakers to LA. Angry and feeling cheated, Saperstein approached National Alliance of Basketball Leagues (NABL) team owner Paul Cohen (Tuck Tapers) and the Armature Athletic Union (AAU) Champion, the Cleveland Pipers' owner and ship-builder George Steinbrenner, to take the top NABL and AAU teams and players and form a rival league. Saperstein, along with Cohen, then solicited various local promoters in the other cities to finance what would become an eight-team league with franchises in Los Angeles, Cleveland, Hawaii, Pittsburgh, Kansas City, San Francisco, Washington, and Chicago. Saperstein would operate the Los Angeles Jets to be in competition with the transplanted Lakers. Then, he hired former Boston Celtics star Bill Sharman as coach and signed former NBA players Larry Friend and George Yardley.

While no major stars from the NBA jumped ship to play for the ABL, there were a couple of established players who signed on, including the Syracuse Nationals' Dick Barnett, who joined the Cleveland Pipers, and the New York Knicks' Kenny Sears, who joined the San Francisco Saints. Some marginal former NBA players, such as Larry Staverman of the Cincinnati Royals, also joined the league, signing with Kansas City. Also, former Globetrotter and New York Knicks player Sweetwater Clifton returned to professional basketball to play for Chicago and former Syracuse and Ft. Wayne star George Yardley signed with the Los Angeles Jets.

The only notable draft choice who ignored the NBA to sign with an ABL team was Larry Siegfried of Ohio State who joined the Cleveland team.

But the ABL took a bold imitative when it permitted a lot of talented players who had been blacklisted by the NBA for transgressions while in college to come into the league. The group included Connie Hawkins of Iowa who went to Pittsburgh, Tony Jackson of St. John's who joined the Chicago team, and Bill Spivey of Kentucky who signed with the Hawaii team.

The ABL, trying to get its feet on the ground, had a rocky season. Before it was over, the Washington team had relocated to New York, and on January 10, 1962, Abe Saperstein's Los Angeles Jets folded due to financial problems.

When the LA Jets folded, Bill Sharman, at the request of George Steinbrenner, moved to Cleveland and replaced John McLendon as coach. According to Sharman, "The day after the team folded, I got a call from George offering me the Pipers job. He said he'd promoted John [McLendon] to the front office without giving a reason."[7] Later, McLendon would state he actually resigned as Pipers coach due to the interference of George Steinbrenner.

The Cleveland Pipers went on to win the ABL East Division with a record of 24–18 and the Kansas City Steers won the West Division with a record of 28–12.

On April 9, the Cleveland Pipers wrapped up the ABL championship when they defeated the Kansas City Steers in the finals to take the series three games to two.

In some ways, the ABL had been innovative introducing the three-point field goal, later adopted by the American Basketball Association (ABA) and the NBA, and by widening the free throw lane to the Olympic size key, also later adopted by the NBA.

Connie Hawkins of the Pittsburgh Rens had been voted MVP after winning the ABL scoring title with 27.5 points per game and 13.2 rebounds.

But a lot of the ABL owners weren't sure that there would be a second season for the league. One, in particular, George Steinbrenner, decided to take a preemptive strike. Steinbrenner, along with Howard Marks, a Cleveland advertising executive, went out and signed Ohio State three-time All-American, 1960 NCAA champion, and Olympic Gold Medal winner Jerry Lucas to a three-year $90,000 contract.

Jerry Lucas had just finished his eligibility in 1961–62 at Ohio State and the Cincinnati Royals of the NBA held the territorial draft rights to him. The Royals had been watching Lucas since his high school days in Middletown, Ohio and exercised their right to him in the 1962 NBA draft. But George Steinbrenner believed that by signing Lucas it would open the door for him to move his ABL champion Cleveland Pipers into the NBA when the ABL folded.

A secret meeting took place on NBA president Maurice Podoloff's yacht on Long Island Sound. George Steinbrenner was joined at the meeting by George McKean, the owner of the San Francisco Saints in the ABL who would be Steinbrenner's partner. The plan was now that Steinbrenner had signed Jerry Lucas, the NBA would take in the Cleveland Pipers and merge them with the Kansas City Steers as an expansion franchise and effectively kill the ABL.

A deal was struck where Steinbrenner's Cleveland Pipers would join the NBA in the 1963–64 season and a schedule was even printed that showed the Pipers opening the season playing the New York Knicks. The financial costs however to Steinbrenner and McKean for entering the NBA were substantial. The cost for entering the league was $400,000, of which $100,000 would be paid to the Cincinnati Royals as an indemnity payment for the release of Jerry Lucas.

The ABL was effectively DOA as it attempted to open for its second season as a six-team league. While three teams, Pittsburgh, Kansas City, and Chicago returned, the Cleveland Pipers, the league's champion, were gone. A court order forced Dick Barnett to return to Syracuse of the NBA and three franchises relocated. The New York Tapers became the Philadelphia Tapers, the San Francisco Saints the Oakland Saints, and the Hawaii Chiefs the Long Beach Chiefs.

On December 31, 1962, the ABL ceased operations claiming losses of $1 million in 1961–62 and $250,000 for the current season of 1962–63.

The Cleveland Pipers never made it to the NBA. First, George McKean turned out to be underfinanced having spent a lot of cash keeping the Saints afloat in the ABL. Then, he and Steinbrenner fell behind in their payment schedule with the NBA. At that point, Maurice Podoloff put the kibosh on the deal.

Some of the ABL's best players moved on to other teams. MVP Connie Hawkins, "persona non grata" in the NBA, joined the Harlem Globetrotters. Bill Bridges joined the St. Louis Hawks.

Jerry Lucas would never see any of the money from the contract he had signed with George Steinbrenner and the Cleveland Pipers. Lucas told author and sportswriter Bill Madden, "I signed with George because he offered me $40,000, which was $10,000 more than the Royals had offered me. But, in the end, I never got a nickel of the $40,000 because the league folded."[8]

Lucas had come under a great deal of criticism for signing with the Cleveland Pipers. A lot of sportswriters were charging that Lucas signed to play in the ABL rather than the NBA because the lesser league would not be as taxing on him. He would not have to play the brutal NBA schedule and face opponents such as Bill Russell, Wilt Chamberlain, Bob Pettit, and Walt Bellamy.

There was also growling out of Cincinnati Royals fans asserting that Jerry Lucas had snubbed the Royals and the city because he was still smarting from his Big Ten Ohio State Buckeyes losing the championship game in the NCAA tournament two years in a row (1961 and 1962) to the University of Cincinnati Bearcats from the Missouri Valley Conference.

It was a fact that The Ohio State University did hold a rather smug attitude toward the University of Cincinnati. The interstate athletic indifference of OSU toward UC was epitomized by an incident prior to the Bearcats and Buckeyes meeting in the champions game in the 1961 NCAA Tournament when an overzealous Buckeyes fan crept under the cover of darkness onto the University of Cincinnati campus and painted across the doors of the Armory Fieldhouse: "OSU EATS LITTLE SCHOOLS LIKE U.C."[9] Beginning in the early 1930s, an aura of athletic snobbery had begun to permeate the Ohio State University athletic department and to a degree, it still exists today. Although Cincinnati and Columbus are located about 90 miles apart, the Buckeyes refused to schedule football games with the Bearcats for 68 years between 1931 and 1999. Following a game played in Cincinnati in 1897, the two schools would not meet again on the gridiron in the Queen City until 2002.

Furthermore, through 2018 the two schools have only met in basketball six times since 1961 and three of those games came as a result of the two teams colliding in the NCAA tournament with the Bearcats defeating the Buckeyes twice for the national championship in 1961 and 1962, while Ohio State defeated Cincinnati in the 2012 NCAA Regional Semi-Finals. The most recent meeting between UC and OSU in basketball took place on November 7, 2018, at UC's Fifth Third Arena with the Buckeyes defeating the Bearcats 64–56.

The University of Cincinnati, with a current enrollment of 40,000, is not the only inter-state school that has been traditionally snubbed by the Buckeyes in athletics. OSU has had a dismal record over the past 80 years in scheduling Division I Ohio schools, such as Kent State, Bowling Green, Dayton, Xavier, Miami (O), and Ohio University, both in basketball and football. The lame excuse more often than not offered by OSU athletic directors is that the Buckeyes would rather play non-conference games against out-of-state schools. Translation: Ohio State, a charter Big Ten school, does not wish to give credibility to the American Conference, Atlantic 10 Conference, Mid-American Conference, or any other in which rival Ohio colleges and universities compete—all of which they consider collegiate bush leagues compared to the Big Ten.

But in the case of ex-Buckeye Jerry Lucas, all of this was unfounded. He harbored no prejudice toward the city of Cincinnati, the UC Bearcats, or the Royals. Jerry Lucas was a superior and gifted player. Arthur Daley of *The New York Times* described Lucas' skills as follows: "[Lucas] has hands with a feather touch. He even tips in rebounds delicately and he has the complete repertoire of hooks, jumpers and everything else. When two men guard him, he's untouched."[10]

With the Cleveland Pipers belly-up, Jerry Lucas would find himself on the basketball sidelines for the first time in fourteen years. So, while waiting for the 1963 NBA draft, he returned to school at Ohio State and finished his degree in marketing. While on the campus, he even helped out Woody Hayes get his Buckeyes football players prepared for exams.

George Steinbrenner had lost a considerable amount of money in his ABL venture and was embarrassed to walk around the streets of Cleveland. But he eventually paid off all the investors in the Pipers. Still interested in sports-team ownership, Steinbrenner would now turn his attention to acquiring a Major League Baseball team. In 1971, along with a group of local investors, Steinbrenner would attempt to buy the struggling Cleveland Indians franchise from frozen food magnate Vernon Stouffer. However, two years later, along with another group of investors, Steinbrenner would be successful in acquiring the New York Yankees from CBS.

8

The Royals Move to the Eastern Division

& Cooz Retires a Champion

In 1962–63, the Philadelphia Warriors with Wilt Chamberlain relocated to San Francisco. In a geographical re-alignment of the divisions, the Cincinnati Royals were moved from the Western Division to Eastern Division to allow the Warriors to play in the West. The move would be a disaster for the Cincinnati Royals. Just at the Royals were improving they suddenly found themselves confronted with an insurmountable obstacle in having to defeat the perennial champions, the Boston Celtics, in order to reach the NBA Finals.*

The Cincinnati Royals opened the 1962–63 season October 20 on the road with a 115–104 loss playing the Chicago Zephyrs who, over the summer, had swapped out the team name Packers which commemorated the Windy City's glory years of being the nation's primary butcher to a more modern identification.

While the Royals rebounded with a stunning 116–115 home opener win against the Los Angeles Lakers at Cincinnati Gardens, they were soon confronted with the reality of having been gerrymandered in the league's franchise shift to the Eastern Division with the Boston Celtics.

In his first few years in the NBA, Bob Cousy had felt that he was the best player in the league and took the floor game after game determined to prove it. But after twelve seasons, he

---

* In 1970–71, the NBA divided the teams in two conferences. Previously the league had two divisions but no conferences (with the exception of the 1949–50 when the NBA had three divisions).

recognized that he was slower and that it was possible, on occasion, for younger players to make him look bad. Cousy had become concerned that people were expecting him to do things that he could no longer do. His worst fear was that there would be a father sitting in the stands who might remark to his son, "'Look, there's Bob Cousy, the greatest player in the world,' and there I am tripping over my feet."[1]

So Cousy announced that 1962–63 would be his last season. The Cooz wanted to go out while the Celtics were on top, and he was bound and determined to give everything his 35-year-old body could give to accomplish his goal.

The Royals met the Celtics for the first time on November 12 in Boston and lost 137–126. Bob Cousy scored 17 points in the game while Oscar Robertson electrified the Boston Garden crowd in a losing effort with 42 points.

Then on November 17, the Royals lost to the Celtics at Cincinnati Gardens 106–105. Tom Heinsohn led the Celtics with 25 points while Bob Cousy and Sam Jones each scored 19. For the Royals, both The Big O and Jack Twyman each scored 26 points.

At this early juncture in the season, it was clear where things were headed. The Celtics were now 9–2 and playing in high gear while the Royals at 5–6 were struggling to reach .500.

The Boston Celtics starters were still Bob Cousy, Bill Russell, Sam Jones, Satch Sanders, and Tom Heinsohn with K.C. Jones, Clyde Lovellette, Frank Ramsey, and Jim Loscutoff coming off the bench. But now the Celtics had become even stronger as a result of the 1962 NBA draft when, having the seventh pick, Red Auerbach selected 6'5" forward John Havlicek from Ohio State and signed him for $15,000.

George Steinbrenner had offered John Havlicek $15,000 in cash and $10,000 worth of stock in the American Shipbuilding Company to sign with the Cleveland Pipers of the ABL. In addition, the Cleveland Browns were interested in Havlicek as a wide receiver; they gave him a new car and $15,000 and after a tryout, cut him.

Everyone was surprised by the Celtics' selection of Havlicek. Jerry Lucas, a teammate of Havlicek at Ohio State, remarked, "When John was drafted reporters were asking me 'do you think John Havlicek can make it in the pros?' They just didn't see him play enough in college to learn how good he really was." When asked to compare Havlicek with Bill Bradley, Lucas stated, "While I never had seen Bill Bradley play in college, I can say that John was a far better pro."[2]

John Havlicek turned out to be a great pro and fit right in the Celtics running game. He would go on to play sixteen years for the Boston Celtics, become a 13-time All-Star, score 26,395 points, have his number 17 jersey retired, and become the third winningest player of all time, behind Bill Russell and Sam Jones, winning eight NBA championships.

While the Celtics seemed to have the upper-hand playing against the Royals, the games between them were becoming more intense—there were no blowouts. Celtics coach Red Auerbach was convinced that the Royals were as good as the Syracuse Nationals in the Eastern Division, maybe even better.

The Celtics, 16–5, and Royals, 13–9, met for the fourth time in the season on Sunday afternoon, December 2, at Cincinnati Gardens in front of 8,719 fans that yelled themselves hoarse in a game that turned out to be a raucous affair.

The Celtics won 128–127 in overtime with Sam Jones scoring 27 points, Tom Heinsohn, 22, and Bill Russell, 20. Also, Bob Cousy had 14 points including going 6 for 7 from the free throw line. For the Royals, both Oscar Robertson and Jack Twyman had 29 points while Arlen Bockhorn had 22. Oscar Robertson was 7 for 8 at the free throw line.

The Royals had lost the game on a questionable call by referee Sid Borgia with 22 seconds left in the overtime period when Borgia called goal-tending on Tom Hawkins on a shot by Tom Heinsohn that gave the Celtics a 128 to 126 lead. Adrian Smith hit a free throw to make the score 128–127 Celtics. Then, Bob Cousy missed a shot and the Royals called timeout. They set up a shot for Oscar Robertson and he missed it with 5 seconds to go.

Royals coach Charlie Wolf was asking what it took to beat the Celtics. The Royals had taken more shots, made more field goals and out-rebounded the Celtics. The answer was that the Royals had lost the game at the free throw line where they hit 23 and the Celtics hit 30.

Boston coach Red Auerbach was angry at Royals officials for throwing him to fans and not providing enough police protection. Following the game, as the Celtics left the floor, Auerbach was attacked by a fan. Auerbach alleged that 32-year-old Edward Finke, a former Elder High School athlete in Cincinnati, had directed foul language at him and kicked him. So, Auerbach decked him with a punch in the jaw.

In the locker room, Red Auerbach was livid. "The guy cursed me and kicked me in the leg so I belted him. I'll tell you one thing I want when I come here and that's a little protection. We wouldn't treat them like this in Boston. At least we would have a few police around to keep them from being attacked."[3]

Edward Finke alleged that Red Auerbach had sucker-punched him; both parties filed charges and later warrants were filed, and Auerbach and Finke were arrested by Cincinnati Police.

On December 29, a peace accord was reached between Red Auerbach and Edward Finke in the Cincinnati Police Court of Judge Clarence Denning. Through their attorneys, both parties withdrew assault and battery charges and the matter was closed.

At the All-Star Game break in mid-January 1963, the NBA Eastern Division leader was the Boston Celtics with a record of 28–14, followed by the Syracuse Nationals with a record of 24–19, closely pursued by the Cincinnati Royals at 23–22, while the New York Knicks occupied last place with a record of 14–32.

The 1963 NBA All-Star Game, the thirteenth, would be played in Los Angeles. For Bob Cousy and Oscar Robertson, the game would provide a rare opportunity to be teammates playing on the Eastern Division squad coached by Red Auerbach.

The Western Division had won the previous two All-Star games. In 1963, the West team, coached by Fred Schaus, included such very tall and very talented players as 7'1" Wilt Chamberlain, 6'6" Elgin Baylor, 6'11" Walt Bellamy, and 6'9" Bob Pettit, and they were favored to make it three in a row.

Fred Schaus' strategy for the game was to move Walt Bellamy to forward with Bob Pettit where they both would tower over either Tom Heinsohn or Jack Twyman and then team Elgin Baylor at guard with Jerry West in order to counteract the slick passing and high scoring potential of the East's Oscar Robertson and Bob Cousy along with Richie Guerin coming off the bench. The 6'9" Bill Russell would have to contend with the behemoth Wilt Chamberlain.

At game time, 14,816 fans had packed the Los Angeles Sports Arena and 3,000 still seeking tickets were turned away. The game was to be televised on a special 19-city network. At that point in time, the networks did not yet act like they owned the NBA as they do today and the game was scheduled to start at 11:30 P.M.

EST, a time when a lot of fans in the eastern time zone would be fast asleep for the night.

Jack Nicholson, who later became a very visible Lakers fanatic sitting at courtside waving his arms spastically, was not in the building. In 1963, Nicholson was still a struggling actor and was probably walking the streets of Hollywood looking for roles to follow up on his 1960 film *The Little Shop of Horrors*.

Still, it was a true Hollywood affair, as Pat Boone sang the National Anthem and Doris Day, who was one of the official hostesses for the game, sat looking fresh and glamorous in a courtside seat.

East coach Red Auerbach started an all-Celtics/Royals lineup with Cousy, Heinsohn, Russell, Twyman, and Robertson and it paid off. At halftime, the East, playing racehorse basketball with Bill Russell controlling the boards, Oscar Robertson with 16 points, and Jack Twyman scoring 10 points in 6½ minutes, gave the West a 56–50 lead.

However, the East kept the pace going in the second half with Oscar Robertson and Bill Russell putting on quite a show as they beat the West 115–108. The Big O scored 21 points in the game, and it was clear that the torch had been passed by Bob Cousy—Oscar Robertson was now King of the Backcourt.

Fred Schaus' experiment of moving Elgin Baylor to guard to control Oscar Robertson lasted exactly six minutes before he called it off and sent Guy Rodgers into the game and moved Baylor back to forward. During that time Baylor never got a field goal.

But it was Bill Russell, who was named the game's MVP, that really made the East click, scoring 19 points and getting 24 of the East's 32 rebounds. Time after time Russell took the ball from Wilt Chamberlain, Bob Pettit, or Walt Bellamy and whipped it across the floor to Oscar Robertson or Bob Cousy who then started the East on a fast break and two more points.

For the West Bob Pettit was the scoring leader with 25 points while both Elgin Baylor and Wilt Chamberlain had 17.

The combination of Bob Cousy and Oscar Robertson had put on a dazzling display of dribbling and laser-like passes that thrilled the crowd. When both were not in the game together the East found it hard to operate successfully and the West would mount a comeback.

But it was Bob Cousy who, with two minutes to go, put the game out of reach of the West. Following three free throws by

Tom Heinsohn, Cooz had set up Richie Guerin underneath for an over-the-head pass and two-pointer, then suddenly swept in an underhanded layup to give the East a safe 108–93 lead.

After the game, Oscar Robertson remarked, “It was a thrill to play with Cousy.” Then, he added modestly, “I can’t say I was doing much to stop Baylor when I was on him. He’s gonna get his points off anybody.”[4]

In thirteen years in the NBA, Bob Cousy had played in all thirteen of the league’s All-Star Games. Oscar Robertson, in his third year in the league, had played in three All-Star Games and been on the winning team each year in addition to being named the game’s MVP in his rookie season.

The 1962–63 season was Bob Cousy’s last in the NBA. On March 17—St. Patrick’ Day—13,909 fans (many who were already highly emotionalized by celebrating the “wearing of the green” in Boston saloons) and the Celtics management provided Cooz with a memorable and highly emotional farewell ceremony at Boston Garden prior to the last regular season game in his career with the Syracuse Nationals. The game and retirement ceremony were also being carried on channel 5 in Boston as well as by television stations throughout New England. It was one of the most emotional events in Boston sports history.

As the ceremony proceeded, sports writers for the *Boston Globe* and *Boston Herald* pecked out asinine analogies on their typewriters for their morning papers comparing the farewell ceremony for Bob Cousy to Lou Gehrig, suffering from amyotrophic lateral sclerosis, addressing the crowd at Yankee Stadium on July 4, 1939, saying he was “the luckiest man on the face of the earth” and Babe Ruth diagnosed with terminal throat cancer standing on wobbly legs addressing fans at Yankee Stadium on April 27, 1947.

None of it made any sense. If there was any hidden meaning in the powerful display of emotion displayed by the Celtics fans toward Bob Cousy it should have been written that they were not just Celtics fans but Boston sports fans who may have been suffering the psychosocial effects of misplaced hero worship, unresolved from the rejection by narcissistic Boston Red Sox slugger Ted Williams in his uncaring farewell in 1960.

Maybe Boston needed to say goodbye to one of their sports legends. Frugal Tom Yawkey who owned the Boston Red Sox for several decades was never much on spending money for ceremonies. When Ted Williams played his last game at Fenway Park on September 28, 1960, there were only 10,454 fans in the stands. There was even confusion of whether it was William's last game or if he would accompany the team to New York for the season-ending three-game series at Yankee Stadium—which he did not. Nonetheless, there was a brief ceremony at home plate and the game began. When Williams hit a home run in the bottom of the eighth inning, he rounded the bases, sprinted to the dugout and refused to come out to tip his hat to the cheering crowd. The fans continued yelling, "We want Ted!" but although he was sitting on the end of the bench in his blue Red Sox jacket, in his mind Ted Williams had already left the building.

Two and a half years later, on March 17, 1963, many of those same fans came to say goodbye to another hero, and Boston Garden was dripping with love from the rafters to its parquetry floor as the fans showered Bob Cousy with their affection.

Even Cousy's father, Joseph, and mother, Juliette, who suffered from arthritis had flown in from New York—it was only the second time she had ever flown. She told Gloria Negri, a reporter from the *Boston Globe,* that after attending a farewell tribute for her son the previous week at Madison Square Garden she had spent all the emotion she had.

Boston Mayor John F. Collins read an emotional proclamation proclaiming "Bob Cousy Week," then walked off the court red-eyed.

Red Auerbach read a tribute from President John F. Kennedy to Cousy and then started to shake hands with Cousy, but suddenly dropped his hand and embraced him while weeping on his shoulder.

But the waterworks in the stands were really opened up when 12-year-old Martha Grady, the poster girl for the cystic fibrosis drive, came onto the court and gave Cousy a hug to the thunderous teary-eyed applause of the crowd.

Bill Russell and Red Auerbach were standing next to each other as the love fest ensued. Bill Russell was a complex, sometimes moody man, and he began thinking about the taunts he had received from the Boston fans in his early years with the Celtics. He felt that a lot of the abuse he had taken was because of his various stands on civil rights issues. Furthermore, he was of the opinion that the Boston fans had not endeared him with the same affection they had shown for some of his white teammates.

But the fact was that at various times, Bill Russell had made himself the center of controversy with his remarks that were contradictory and taken as an insult by Boston fans. Early in his career Russell publicly remarked, "I don't play for Boston, I play for the Celtics."[5]

On another occasion, Russell had publicly stated that he didn't like white people, although going forward in 1977 he married a white woman, Didi Anstett, Miss USA 1968. It was Russell's second of three marriages.

As the excitement and nostalgia over Cousy's retirement continued that night, Russell turned to Red Auerbach and told him that when he retired, he would never do this. He was not going to miss the Boston fans. Several years later, in 1972, Red Auerbach arranged for Russell's number to be retired. Bill Russell was immediately cold to the idea and maintained that he had played for the Celtics, not personal trophies. Nonetheless, Russell was in town doing color commentary as a broadcaster and half-heartedly agreed out of his respect for Red Auerbach to participate in his number retirement festivities by standing at center court with a few of his former teammates.

Eventually, Bill Russell would soften and be present when his number was re-retired in 1999 during a huge celebration attended by 10,000 fans at the Fleet Center, the Celtics new arena. The occasion was a benefit for the National Mentoring Partnership and the Massachusetts Mentoring Partnership, programs very dear to Russell's heart.

As Bob Cousy stepped up to the microphone, he stood holding on to the lectern at center court flanked by his daughter Mary, wife Marie and daughter Missie, all teary-eyed, Cousy found it hard to speak. Then, apologizing for reading from handwritten notes, he began. He thanked his parents, his teammates, Red Auerbach (whom he still called Arnold), the Celtics management, the kids that attended his basketball camp—he even thanked the visiting Syracuse Nationals.

When Cousy began to choke back tears and bury his face in a towel, his daughter Marie gave him a handkerchief and then covered her eyes. There were approximately ten seconds of silence in Boston Garden and then one of the most iconic tributes in sports history came ricocheting down from high in the stands and could be heard clearly throughout Boston Garden. From up in the

BOB COUSY DAY
BOSTON CELTICS
NATIONAL BASKETBALL ASSOCIATION
BOB COUSY
BOSTON GARDEN, MARCH 17, 1963
SOUVENIR PROGRAM 50¢

Bob Cousy Day Program – March 17, 1963. (Courtesy of The Sports Museum.)

balcony a man with a loud raspy baritone voice yelled out, "We Love Ya Cooz!"[6] Immediately, the capacity crowd rose to their feet and broke into a loud applause of affirmation. Later, the fan who had yelled the tribute was identified as Joseph Dillion, a 32-year-old city worker.

Cousy finally concluded his farewell speech by stating with a sob, "If I had to do it all over again, I can't imagine doing it any other

Bob Cousy farewell at Boston Gardens. (Courtesy of The Sports Museum.)

place than Boston."[7] His speech was scheduled for seven minutes but by the time Cousy finished twenty minutes had passed.

The ceremonies continued with Cousy receiving a boxcar load of gifts including a black Cadillac. Even Dolph Schayes presented Cousy with a set of chinaware from him and his Syracuse Nats teammates. Then, Schayes, Cousy's long-time contemporary and rival, only a few months older and also New York City raised, added a little St. Patrick's Day flavor to the occasion when he placed his hands on Cooz's shoulders and bellowed into a microphone, "To Bob O'Cousy from Dolph O'Schayes,"—"Erin go braugh" and "Mazel Tov"[8] (Hebrew for good luck).

Among all the tributes to Cousy, Celtics owner Walter Brown probably said it best. "If you fans have a sinking feeling in your stomach imagine how I feel," said Brown. "I'm the guy who didn't want Bob Cousy in the first place. What a genius."[9]

After 40-some minutes of tribute to Cousy, the game was eventually played and the Celtics defeated the Nationals 125–116 led by Tom Heinsohn's 28 points and 19 each by Bill Russell and John Havlicek.

Red Auerbach felt that Cousy was emotionally spent from the pre-game hoopla and played him only 18 minutes in which he scored 8 points. After the game, Cousy remarked, "It took so much out of me that when I had played a minute, I felt as though I had played ten."[10]

When Cousy was taken out of the game with two minutes remaining the crowd chanted a deafening continuous roar of "We want Cousy!"[11] as play on the court continued nearly unnoticed.

The Boston Celtics won the 1962–63 Eastern Division Championship in a landslide with a record of 58–22. The Syracuse Nationals finished second with a record of 48–32, ten games behind. The Cincinnati Royals finished in third place with a record of 42–38, 16 games behind, and the New York Knicks occupied the division cellar with a pitiful record of 21–59, 37 games behind.

The Royals' third-place finish qualified for the playoffs. The format for the postseason at that time was that three teams in each conference made the playoffs. The semi-final round was played between the second and third place team. The division champion or leader then played the winner in the second round to determine the teams that would meet in the NBA Finals.

As for the money, the league ran the playoffs and the players shares were determined long before the season ended. The players did not get a share of the gate receipts so it was to their advantage to win each series and get on to playing the next opponent.

Game one of the Eastern Division Semi-Finals was played on March 19 in Syracuse with the Nationals defeating the Royals 123–120. Hal Greer paced the Nats with 32 points while both Oscar Robertson and Jack Twyman scored 29 points for the Royals.

Game two moved to Cincinnati where the Royals, led by a triple-double performance by The Big O, 41 points, 18 rebounds, and 12 assists, defeated the Nationals 133–115 to even up the series.

Back at Syracuse for game three on March 23, the Nats got by the Royals 121–117 thanks to Hal Greer who scored 30 points while holding Oscar Robertson to just 16. Lee Shaffer, the Nationals 6'7" forward drafted out of the University of North Carolina, had 34 points.

The series returned to Cincinnati on March 24 with the Nationals holding a 2-games-to-1 advantage in the series needing just one more win to advance to the Eastern Division Finals. But the Royals, led by Oscar Robertson's 29 points, defeated the Nats 125–118 to even up the series 2 games each.

The deciding game in the 1963 NBA Eastern Division Semi-Finals was played on March 26 in Syracuse before 7,418 fans at the Onondaga War Memorial. While Lee Schaffer scored 45 points for the Nats, it wasn't enough as the Royals, led by The Big O with 32 points, won in overtime 131–127 to win the series.

Oscar Robertson had been the leading scorer in the series and for the Royals with a 29.9 points-per-game average. Jack Twyman averaged 25.2 points per game.

For the Nationals, Lee Schaffer was the leading scorer with 27.2 points per game followed by Hal Greer with 23.4 points per game. Aging superstar Dolph Schayes had contributed 10.2 points per game.

No one knew it at the time, but game five of the 1963 East Semi-Finals would be the last game in the history of the Syracuse Nationals. The Nats were averaging about 4,000 fans per game. Ticket prices were $5.00 and were the only major source of the team's revenue. Nats owner Danny Biasone, the man that had brought the 24-second shot clock to professional basketball, was unable to negotiate a new lease with a lower rent for Onondaga War Memorial, so he sold the team to two buyers from Philadelphia, Irv Kosloff and Ike Richman, for $500,000. Biasone had bought the franchise for $6,000.

On May 22, the NBA approved the franchise shift that would return professional basketball to Philadelphia, and on August 6, the team name was changed from Nationals to 76ers. With the franchise shift of Syracuse to Philly the last of the NBA's small cities that had been the genesis of the league would fade into history.

From that point forward, basketball fans in Syracuse would embrace the Syracuse University Orange, and college games played in the Carrier Dome would become legendary.

Now that the Cincinnati Royals had eliminated the Syracuse Nationals, by virtue of being transferred to the Eastern Division before the season began, they would have to face the daunting challenge of getting by the perennial champion, the Boston Celtics in the Eastern Division Finals, to make it to the NBA championship series.

The 1962–63 Celtics were a balanced team, no player had averaged more than 20 points a game, and they were not overly concerned with playing the Royals; they had met them eight times during the regular season winning seven games and losing one. The one Celtics loss to the Royals, 130–133, had come on December 3 while playing on a neutral court in Providence, Rhode Island. Red Auerbach and his players knew that Oscar Robertson or Jack Twyman could get hot and the Celtics could lose a game or even two in the series, but they really expected to dispatch the Royals in five games.

Maybe the Boston Celtics were overconfident. Maybe the Cincinnati Royals were eager for the challenge and perhaps underrated. But no one in basketball was ready for what almost happened. The 1963 Eastern Division Finals would turn out to be one of the NBA's best playoff series during the decade of the 1960s. The Royals starting five of Oscar Robertson, Jack Twyman, Wayne Embry, Bob Boozer, and Arlen Bockhorn supported by Tom Hawkins, Hub Reed, Dave Piontek, and Adrian Smith coming off the bench were a determined group. They played intensely, dragging a Boston Celtics team that included seven NBA future Hall of Fame players Bob Cousy, Bill Russell, John Havlicek, Sam Jones, K.C. Jones, Tom Heinsohn, and Frank Ramsey, and a future Hall of Fame coach Red Auerbach, to the full seven games before losing the series three games to four.

The first shockwave in the series came in the opening game of the series at Boston Garden on March 28 when the Royals, after being down by 22 points led by Oscar Robertson with 43 points, came back to defeat the Celtics 135–132 and stun the Garden crowd of 11,162. Red Auerbach, as he often did, blamed the loss on the officiating, and the fact that his team hadn't played a game in a week.

The second game played on Friday night, March 29, at Cincinnati Gardens was witnessed by 11,102, the largest crowd to ever watch a Royals game in Cincinnati. The game was very good for the Royals' management's bottom line with gross at the gate at $22,000. At that time, the financial arrangements were that the host team and the league split the playoff gates with the league paying the expenses. If the series went an odd game then there was a three-way split. The Royals had cut into the Syracuse Nationals gate in the fifth game of semi-finals but still didn't make enough to pay their expenses for the games in Cincinnati.

In game two, the Celtics took charge and, in a blowout, beat the Royals 125–102. Bill Russell with 26 points and 24 rebounds led the way. Tom Heinsohn added 22. Red Auerbach used his bench and it produced with John Havlicek scoring 17 points and Frank Ramsey, 15.

When Bob Cousy had been introduced prior to the game, the huge Cincinnati Gardens crowd booed him loudly. Even the Cincinnati Gardens organist got into the act blaring out a low-key cord when Cousy was introduced that enticed the rabid Royals rooters to extend a Bronx cheer. The Boston newspapers responded that the Royals fans booing of Bob Cousy was bush league. While it was surprising to some, others felt it was warranted for Cousy roughing up Royals reserve guard Adrian Smith with a hard foul in game one in Boston. Coach Charlie Wolf hadn't helped Cousy's popularity either by making a charge that he played dirty basketball.

Bob Cousy responded to the hazing by scoring just 4 points, but he also had 13 assists, which led both teams. He had asked Red Auerbach to play him more in game two. "I was afraid we'd stop running," said Cousy. "I wasn't shooting well. I knew that. But I felt my floor game could help the club."[12] Cousy had played 56 minutes in the two games in the series, scoring a total of 20 points with 22 assists. Only Bill Russell, 92 minutes, Sam Jones, 65, and Tom "Satch" Sanders, 63, had played more than Cousy.

With the Celtics and Royals knotted at one game each, the series returned to Boston Garden for game three, Sunday evening, March 31. Despite that fact that The Big O was the leading scorer in the first two games averaging 31.1 points per game, sportswriters covering the series were suggesting that the Royals had caught the Celtics napping in game one, but in game two they had stopped the Royals momentum and could now sweep the next three games to wrap-up the series.

That didn't happen. The Royals defeated the Celtics at home again, 121–116, to take a two-games-to-one lead. A huge sellout crowd of 13,909 turned out at Boston Garden and they witnessed the Bob Cousy of old playing 36 minutes scoring 26 points with 7 assists. It was his biggest offensive output of the year. Bill Russell played another great game scoring 19 points and grabbing 24 rebounds, while Sam Jones and Tom Heinsohn both added 21. The Celtics went down not because of The Big O, who scored 23 points, or Jack Twyman, who added 18, but because of the great performances of two Royals subs coming off the bench in the second period—Adrian Smith and Dave Piontek.

The Celtics came out running and raced to an 11–2 lead. But the Royals fought back and were trailing after the first period 27–26. Then, in the second period, Royals coach Charley Wolf sent Smith and Piontek into the game; they shot the ball as if it had just come out of a hot oven getting rid of it fast. Smith hit four of five shots in the period and had 11 points while Piontek hit four in a row and had 9 points during the period.

The Celtics were down 67–60 with seconds to go before the half when Bob Cousy arched a hook shot from midcourt to cut the Royals lead to 67–62.

Over the course of the game Smith wound up with 13 points and Piontek, 11, and the two grabbed 8 key rebounds. Wolf didn't stop the substitutions with Smith and Piontek, he also sent in Tom Hawkins and Hub Reed who scored 12 points each. Both helped the Royals out-rebound the Celtics 73–70. The Royals subs were performing so well that Wolf kept Jack Twyman out of the game for the final 15 minutes and 45 seconds.

Red Auerbach kept the door to the Celtics locker room locked for fifteen minutes following the game. The Celtics had only made 45 of 115 shots in the game and had 18 turnovers that resulted in 15 points for the Royals. The Royals' bench, considered by some the worst in the league, had beat the Celtics, scoring 48 points, 21 rebounds, and 4 assists.

Bob Cousy's analysis of the Celtics' current circumstances in the series was, "we just relax too much at home. We think all we have to do is put on our uniforms and go out there and play. On the road we're worried and play better."[13]

The Royals seemed to be in the driver's seat with a 2–1 advantage coming home for game four. But the Royals were about to lose home-court advantage as a result of a faux pas by the Cincinnati Gardens management.

The Royals' majority stockholder, Thomas E. Wood, had died in 1961. Since that time, the team had been run by the Thomas E. Wood Estate. In the spring of 1963, the Wood Estate sold its 56% interest in the team and 40% ownership of Cincinnati Gardens to Louis "Louie" Jacobs, the multi-millionaire concessions czar and president of Emprise Corporation in Buffalo, New York which operated Sportservice, the concessionaire to many professional baseball, football, hockey, and basketball stadiums and arenas. Louis Jacobs had already owned 40% of Cincinnati Gardens, now he owned 80%.

Jacobs immediately named Tom Grace, who was serving as executive vice president of both the Cincinnati Gardens and the Cincinnati Royals, to remain in his position as well as to continue to represent the Royals on the NBA Board of Governors.

Immediately, Louie Jacobs got a quick lesson in absentee ownership when it was revealed that it was never considered that the Royals might still be playing in early April. Tom Grace had booked the Shrine Circus into Cincinnati Gardens for April 3 and it was impossible to change the dates or cancel the performances. Consequently, game four of the NBA Eastern Division Finals was scheduled to be played in Xavier University's small 3,000-seat facility, Schmidt Fieldhouse.

The Royals returned to Cincinnati with a four-day break to rest and practice their plays. Oscar Robertson remarked, "We wasted no time. The day after we got home, our team walked onto the floor of the Cincinnati Gardens for practice. The floor was covered with sawdust and hay, and we had to step over giant piles of elephant shit."[14]

The Royals practices were moved to Schmidt Fieldhouse, but the team wasn't happy about it. They were all saying that it was the hardest court they had ever been on. Tom Hawkins said there was no spring to the court. "A guy like Bill Russell with those long legs of his could come down with a bad case of shin splints," said Hawkins.[15] Nonetheless, a couple of the Royals did have experience on the Schmidt Fieldhouse floor. Dave Piontek had played at Xavier and Wayne Embry, as a member of the Miami Redskins, had also played some road games at Schmidt.

The Cincinnati Royals, who had finished the season 16 games behind the Boston Celtics, were now leading the Celtics 2–1 in the Eastern Division playoffs. At that time, the Boston Celtics were arguably the best basketball team ever assembled. The NBA playoffs should have held considerable national media attention, but national television wasn't interested at all. On Sunday, when the Royals beat the Celtics in Boston, the Los Angeles Lakers, sparked by Jerry West's 27 points, had defeated the St. Louis Hawks in game one of the Western Division playoffs, played in LA. But neither game was carried on national television. Instead, the networks carried bowling with "Whispering Joe" Wilson doing the dull commentary, golf, ski-jumping in Norway, college wrestling, and an interview with racecar driver Sterling Moss. The NBA was still lightyears behind baseball and football in national media coverage.

On April 2, as the Royals and Celtics held practice sessions at Schmidt Fieldhouse in preparation for game four, news broke that after owning the Cincinnati Royals for less than one week,

Emprise Corporation and Louis Jacobs were going to sell the Royals. The new owner was going to be Warren Hensel, a local businessman who claimed that he had a verbal agreement with Jacobs to sell him the Royals. Hensel had been captain of the University of Cincinnati basketball team in 1937, he was a huge fan and booster of Bearcats sports and had helped recruit Oscar Robertson and was also a personal friend of Jack Twyman's.

Hensel's interest in buying the Royals had both a positive and negative effect on the current team's morale. Hensel pledged to keep the team in Cincinnati and announced that he was in hot pursuit of signing Jerry Lucas for the Royals. But he was also announcing his intention to fire coach Charley Wolf and replace him with Cincinnati Bearcats coach Ed Jucker.

Almost totally ignoring the fact that Royals were currently leading the reigning NBA champion Boston Celtics 2 games to 1 in the Eastern Division playoffs, Hensel was already talking about the next season, how he felt the addition of Jerry Lucas would strengthen the team. He also wanted the Royals to draft Tom Thacker, who had just completed his college eligibility at the University of Cincinnati.

In regard to Lucas, Hensel told the press, "My thoughts as far as Jerry Lucas is concerned are that he's one of the greatest players that ever lived. Jerry's been a personal friend of mine since he's been in high school. I've always felt he would be a tremendous asset to the Royals."[16] To that end, Hensel began to wine and dine Lucas and his wife Treva, inviting them to come to Cincinnati, have dinner with him, and watch the Royals' playoff games with the Celtics.

Notwithstanding the Royals team, their fans, and the press, the news of the pending sale of the Royals by Louie Jacobs to Warren Hensel was big news to a lot of people.

Congressman Carl Rich, who was president of the Royals, didn't know about the sale. When Tom Grace, executive vice president of the Cincinnati Royals, was asked about the sale he denied any knowledge of it.

Pepper Wilson, the Royals general manager, was greatly annoyed at the timing of the announcement, regardless if it was true or not—it was a distraction that the Royals didn't need. "There's nothing like keeping a ball club upset," said Wilson. "There have been a lot of things going on lately—but our main concern has been with the ball club and winning in the playoffs."[17]

Coach Charley Wolf, who had coached the Royals to two winning seasons in three years, said the team was not doing anything but concentrating on beating the Celtics. But suddenly Wolf was in Warren Hensel's doghouse for benching Jack Twyman for a good part of the fourth period in game three. Wolf liked coaching but he was not held hostage by it in order to make a living as he had a thriving insurance business.

When contacted, Cincinnati Bearcats coach Ed Jucker said he would listen if the Royals made him an offer. However, at the moment, Jucker was getting ready to coach the American team in the Pan-American Games in Sao Paulo, Brazil later in the month.

Lame duck NBA commissioner Maurice Podoloff, who was going to be replaced following the current season, was contacted in Baltimore where he was providing executive oversight to the signing of a five-year deal to move the failed Chicago Zephyrs franchise to play in that city's Civic Arena beginning in 1963–64.

Podoloff stated that the sale of the Royals to Warren Hensel couldn't be considered because the sale of the Royals to Louis Jacobs by the Thomas E. Wood Estate had not yet been approved by the NBA Board of Governors. "The sale to Louis Jacobs has never been formally submitted and formally approved by the board," said Podoloff. "Until that is approved, no action by Jacobs has any validity."[18]

The entire situation was enormous in its magnitude of stupidity. But the most amazing aspect of it all was that such an experienced businessman as Warren Hensel had so little regard for due diligence. It was a gross display of incompetence by a man who wanted to be the CEO of an NBA team.

Amidst all the confusion of not really knowing who was signing their paychecks, over at Schmidt Fieldhouse the Royals were getting ready for game four with the Celtics. Jim Schottelkotte, the *Cincinnati Enquirer's* beat writer for the Royals wrote, "Never has one basketball team had so many bosses in so short a period of time."[19]

Game four was finally played at Schmidt Fieldhouse on April 3 with 3,498 fans in attendance and the game televised locally on channel 9. The crowd was probably larger than announced as every nook and cranny in the small facility had somebody standing in it. Of course, the would-be Royals owner, Warren Hensel, was there as well.

The Celtics, looking totally rejuvenated, beat the Royals handily, 128–110, to tie the series at 2 games each. The Celtics were led by the playmaking of Bob Cousy, who in the first period scored 15 of his 20 points for the game that gave them a 34–25 lead. Then, the dominating play of Bill Russell in the second period, who scored 14 of his 26 points for the night, put the Celtics in a commanding lead over Royals, 70–55 at halftime. Although the Royals tried desperately to catch-up in the second half, led by Oscar Robertson who scored 25 points in the game, the Celtics kept wearing The Big O down by sending in new defenders causing him to hit only 8 of 23 from the field. Other key Royals were having problems scoring as well. Jack Twyman had 14 points but only made 3 out of 13 from the field, while Bob Boozer had 9 points but was just 3 for 9 from the field, and Arlen Bockhorn scored 10 points but was only 4 for 10 from the field.

In the end, it was not just a case of the Royals not making shots but the incredibly tight defense played by the Celtics who clogged-up all the openings. Once again, Bill Russell was dominating with nine blocked shots and 21 rebounds.

Thirty years later, Jack Twyman, reminiscing on the Xavier fieldhouse game, remarked, "I remember it to be a turning-point—the unfamiliarity with the court, the smaller crowd, the frustration we had. We were disappointed in the lack of confidence they showed in the team by booking a circus for that date."[20]

Game five was played back in Boston in front of another packed house and the Celtics put the Royals on the ropes with a hard-fought 125–120 victory. The Celtics fought back from being behind, 34–32 after the first period, to take a 65–59 halftime lead. From that point on, with Bob Cousy leading the fast break, the Celtics pulled away, at one point leading the Royals by 18 points.

The work of Tom Heinsohn and John Havlicek was the key to the Celtics victory. Heinsohn led the Celtics with 34 points and Havlicek had 23. Tom Heinsohn had been dominating the Royals' Bob Boozer on both defense and offense in games three and four. Coach Charley Wolf came to the conclusion that the reason Boozer was shooting so poorly was because of the stress he was experiencing attempting to guard Heinsohn.

So, in game five Wolf assigned Jack Twyman to guard Tom Heinsohn. But Twyman only hit 3 of 16 from the field. However, the switch apparently helped the performance of Bob Boozer, who after two poorly played games attempting to contain Heinsohn, finally got his jump shot working, scoring 21 points.

Another contributing factor to the Royals loss was that they had allowed the Celtics to out-rebound them by 13 on the defensive boards. Bill Russell had 24 points and 26 rebounds.

Oscar Robertson had a cold first half, hitting only 3 of 12 from the field, but he came on strong in the second half scoring 17 points in the fourth period to finish the game with 36 points, which led both teams.

While the Royals were now trailing the Celtics 3–2 in the series, no one on either team was counting Cincinnati out. Bob Cousy was predicting that the Royals would be fired up for game six in Cincinnati.

Royals coach Charley Wolf, still dodging questions about whether or not he would be retained if Warren Hensel acquired control of the Royals, was advancing the opinion that his team had recently been in the same position in the semi-finals with Syracuse and that they would win game six and put the pressure back on the Celtics.

On Sunday, April 7, at Cincinnati Gardens, the enthusiasm of 7,745 screaming fans and 36 points by The Big O led the Royals to 109–99 victory over the Celtics in game six to set-up a do-or-die game seven in Boston.

It was the first time that the Royals had held the Celtics to under 100 points all season long. The game was a rough and tumble affair from the opening whistle to the final buzzer. At halftime, the Royals led 51–48 and the Celtics were having a tough time getting their fast break working. Charley Wolf was so certain that the Royals were going to win, that during the halftime break he told trainer Ray Baldwin to pack the team's blue uniforms—the Royals road uniforms.

For a change, the Royals owned the offensive boards and worked well on the defensive boards, out-rebounding the Celtics 80–67. Cincinnati's Wayne Embry, the Royals 6'8", 255-pound center, worked feverishly off the boards nearly out-rebounding Bill Russell 22–23. When Embry fouled-out with 59 seconds remaining in the game, he received a standing ovation from the Royals fans.

While Jack Twyman allowed Tom Heinsohn to score 20 points, he had his best game of the series. Twyman found his shooting range again, scoring 24 points, and grabbed 13 rebounds with 2 assists.

But once again, it was Oscar Robertson who led the charge for the Royals. At one point in the third period, Robertson hit five shots in a row and added a free throw before being interrupted by a two-pointer scored by Arlen Bockhorn. The Big O scored 16 of the Royals last 18 points in the period.

After six games, Robertson was leading all scorers in the series with an average of 31.8 points per game. Tom Heinsohn was second with 25.0 points per game and Bill Russell was third with 20.7.

In regard to The Big O's performance in game six, the *Boston Herald* stated, "Robertson was simply superlative the last five minutes with a ripped sole on the edge of his sneakers. He twisted, dibbled, dodged and drove through Boston defenders to score 36 points, assisted on 14 other baskets and hauled down 13 rebounds in the greatest one-man show of the series."[21]

It was apparent that the Celtics had expected to wrap up the series in game six and they expressed a lot of frustration in the locker room following the game.

Both Bill Russell and coach Red Auerbach were bitter about the officiating and blasted Sid Borgia and Norm Drucker. Red Auerbach quickly pointed out that either Borgia or Drucker had been an official in 14 of the Celtics 22 losses during the season. Drucker had worked in all five home-court loses in Boston.

Auerbach accused Borgia and Drucker of being one-sided, saying that the Royals had been climbing all over the Celtics backs but when his guys started to do it to the Royals, Borgia and Drucker called fouls. Furthermore, Auerbach alleged that Bill Russell couldn't move because the Royals had their hands all over him.

Red Auerbach and Sid Borgia had been having differences for years. "Sid was working the series out in the West between the St. Louis team and Los Angeles," said Auerbach. "There comes this beef from St. Louis they don't want Sid working. So what happens? He gets off the series and comes here to louse up our series."[22]

Throughout the game, Auerbach, assisted by Clyde Lovellette, stood on the sidelines heckling Sid Borgia. When Bob Cousy protested a call, he had a technical called on him. Then, in the second quarter, when Arlen Bockhorn loudly protested a foul call on him by Borgia that gave Bob Cousy two free throws, Red Auerbach protested that a technical should have been called. When Borgia ignored his ranting, Auerbach yelled for nearly all to hear in the arena, "You're a gutless son-of-a-bitch."[23] Then followed up by asking Borgia if he was chicken.

Auerbach went as far as to suggest that Sid Borgia was showing partiality toward the Royals. "It's Borgia's ambition to see us lose," said Auerbach. "There's no question in my mind that he's got it in for me and Bob Cousy."[24]

Bill Russell's domination under the boards during the series had been spectacular. After six games, he had 146 rebounds and an average of 24.3 per game. The second-best total was that of Oscar Robertson with 81 for an average of 13.5 per game.

But Russell also had issues with the way game six had been officiated. He was stating that he had been in the game for seven years and had always tried to believe that the officials did the best they could. "But tonight," he said, "tonight it was too much. Those guys let the game go mad. It was a wild scene."[25] In fact, on one occasion, Russell had been knocked to the floor and no foul was called.

In a most uncustomary move, in the third period, Auerbach had removed Bob Cousy from the game and he never came back in. When asked about the unusual move Auerbach simply replied that Cousy was not playing well. The fact was that Arlen Bockhorn was doing an extraordinary defensive job on him.

Bob Cousy had only 5 points, going one for eight from the field, playing 16 minutes in the first half. Because of his poor performance, Cousy was more conciliatory toward the referees saying that while Borgia and Drucker let everything go, he shouldn't have played as long as he did.

But overall, Cousy was having a very good playoff series. For six games, Cooz had played 170 minutes was averaging 14.8 points per game and his 49 assists were second best in the series to Oscar Robertson who had 54 at that point.

The evening before game six, Jerry Lucas and his wife had been entertained by Warren Hensel and his wife for dinner at the Hyde Park Country Club in Cincinnati. At Cincinnati Gardens the following evening Lucas was present, sitting center court with Hensel. Prior to the game, Lucas posed for pictures with his former Ohio State teammate John Havlicek and Hensel. When

Hensel was asked if he was going to sign Lucas, he replied as if he finally got it. "We can't talk contract," said Hensel, "because I'm not really the owner yet."[26]

There had been rumors circulating that the current Royals management and GM Pepper Wilson had been having trouble signing Jerry Lucas and were negotiating a trade with the New York Knicks that would have sent the territorial rights for him to the Knicks in exchange for Duke All-American Art Heyman. But when asked about the possibility of going to New York, Lucas indicated that he would prefer to play for the Royals adding, "Yes I believe I will sign if things work out," referring to the Hensel ownership.[27]

On April 10, the Eastern Division Championship was on the line and so was the money. "This is the money game," said Celtics guard Frank Ramsey. "We don't intend to lie down and let them grab the winner's share."[28] The oddsmakers had the Celtics as 9-point favorites. Each winning player would receive $1,400 and each losing player, $1,250. The losing shares included money from the semi-final series. The team moving on to the championship series could get as much $14,000 for each player.

Tip-off for the deciding seventh game of the series was scheduled in Boston for 8:00 P.M. But fans watching the game on station WCPO television in Cincinnati would have to catch the game in progress at 8:30 P.M. as airtime by the network couldn't be cleared.

It wasn't just professional basketball in 1963 that was still not taken seriously by the television networks but also college basketball. In 1961, Eddie Einhorn, future co-owner of the Chicago White Sox, bought the television rights to the NCAA basketball tournament for just $6,000. However, when he attempted to find stations interested in carrying the championship game between Ohio State and the University of Cincinnati, Einhorn couldn't find any stations outside of Ohio and Kentucky that were interested in showing the game.

In game seven, the Cincinnati Royals' Cinderella post-season came to an end as they lost to the Celtics 142–131. The Eastern Division Championship remained in Boston where it had been residing since 1957—seven straight East titles. But the Celtics were aware of the fact that they had not beaten the Cincinnati Royals, they had survived them. Bob Cousy later wrote in *The Last Loud Roar* that the Royals gave the Celtics everything they could handle.

Game seven had been another rough and tumble affair with two Celtics, John Havlicek and Tom Sanders fouling out, along with Tom Hawkins of the Royals. Red Auerbach had two technicals called on him and three Royals had five fouls called on them: Bob Boozer, Jack Twyman, and Wayne Embry.

The Royals made a game out of it in the first two periods, trailing at the half 68–64. But playing in front of the third capacity crowd in a row of 13,909 at Boston Garden, the Celtics were all business in the second half as they blazed their way to a 25-point lead, 123–98, in the third quarter. However, the Royals didn't quit. Led again by players coming off the bench, Adrian Smith and rookie Bud Olsen, the Royals fought back to within 9 points, 126–117, forcing Red Auerbach to send Bob Cousy back into the game. From that point on, Sam Jones, who scored 47 points, and Tom Heinsohn, who scored 31, took charge with a four-point string.

Red Auerbach lit his victory cigar with 1 minute 50 seconds left in the game, and at the final buzzer was carried off the court by the jubilant Celtics fans extremely relieved that the Celtics had finally laid the Royals to rest.

The game included a shootout between Sam Jones and Oscar Robertson. Jones hit 47 points while Robertson scored 43.

It was actually a very difficult night for The Big O. He wasn't sharp from the floor hitting only 11 of 24 shots. But at the free-throw line, he was deadly, hitting 21 out of 22 foul shots. Robertson didn't think too much of the officiating done by Mendy Rudolph and Earl Strom, acting like a crybaby each time a foul was called on him. In the third period, Robertson was held scoreless until the final 10 seconds. Despite cold shooting and dissatisfaction with the referees, in the end, the stat sheet showed that Robertson had scored 43 points. Not too shabby for having a bad night.

While the Celtics game-scoring record still remained with Bob Cousy, who had 50 points in a four-overtime effort in 1953, Sam Jones' 47 points were the most ever scored by a Celtics player in a non-overtime, 48-minute game.

On various occasions during the series, Jones had looked bad playing against Oscar Robertson, but in game seven he took the spotlight away from him. After the game, Sam Jones told the press in regard to The Big O, "Man I'm glad I'm through with him."[29]

Jones had been so worried about having to play against Robertson that on game day, he left his home at 11:30 A.M. People started calling his home at 9:00 A.M. asking for tickets. After a couple of hours, he told his wife Gladys, "'When those folks call, tell them I'm gone please.' 'Gone where Sam,' asked Gladys? 'Just gone,' he said. 'I'll see you at the Garden. Gotta see a movie, and stop thinking about Oscar.'"[30] Two hours before the game, Jones arrived at Boston Garden and had a private shooting practice.

Bob Cousy had gone into the showdown game with the Royals facing the possibility that it was his last game. But the Cooz played brilliantly, finishing with 21 points and 16 assists. The *Boston Herald* claimed that Cousy "delivered the coup de resistance at 3:45 of the [fourth] quarter when he fed a blind backward pass to Frank Ramsey for a layup that made it 123–98 and went out amid an ovation at the four-minute mark."[31]

Following the game, Walter Brown, owner of the Celtics, walked up to Charley Wolf and told him he would see him next year. Wolf replied, "I don't think so. I won't be back."[32] Brown believed that the showing of the Royals in the playoffs would give professional basketball in Cincinnati a big boost. He told Charley Wolf, "And we owe it all to you. You have done a tremendous job."[33]

When asked if he would vote to approve the sale of the Royals to Warren Hensel, Brown replied, "Actually I have an open mind about it. I've heard nothing adverse."[34]

If Warren Hensel was paying attention to the Royals gate receipts for the series, he would have noticed that a little over 7,000 fans were in the stands for the critical game six at Cincinnati Gardens in which the Royals grossed about $16,500 for the home game. The Celtics were averaging over 13,000 fans per home game for the Cincinnati series. In the Western Division series, the Los Angeles Lakers playing the St. Louis Hawks were attracting crowds of 15,000 at their arena, while St. Louis was averaging about 8,000 fans per home game. If Hensel was thinking the addition of Jerry Lucas would bolster the Royals' gate, he was dreaming.

Cincinnati's interest in professional basketball would peak in 1963–64. That's four years before the Cincinnati Bengals began playing in the Queen City. While it is a fact that the arrival of professional football in Cincinnati was a factor in Xavier University dropping its football program in the early 1970s and nearly causing the University of Cincinnati to do the same, professional basketball was in trouble in Cincinnati long before professional football came to town.

Nonetheless, at that moment, a lot of sportswriters were starting to speculate about what the Royals might do next season with Jerry Lucas and Tom Thacker, if they got both, playing with The Big O, Jack Twyman, Arlen Bockhorn, Bob Boozer, Adrian Smith, Wayne Embry, and Tom Hawkins. Some sportswriters were so bold as to suggest that the Celtics might be trying to upset the Royals next year. The current Royals management, with Tom Grace, Pepper Wilson, and Charley Wolf, would be responsible for the 1963 NBA draft as it occurred before the NBA Board of Governors met on April 30 to approve any change in ownership for the team.

A day after the Eastern Division playoffs ended, the first hurdle for Warren Hensel gaining control of the Cincinnati Royals was crossed. Louis Jacobs and Emprise Corporation of Buffalo, New York gained formal control of the Royals and Cincinnati Gardens from the Thomas E. Wood Estate. Jacobs' lawyer, Ambrose Lindhorst, met with Alfred M. Cohen, the attorney representing the Wood Estate, and reached an agreement that was believed to be worth $500,000.

Led by Elgin Baylor, 31.6 points per game, and Jerry West, 26.4 points per game, the Los Angeles Lakers defeated the defiant St. Louis Hawks in the Western Division playoffs, 4 games to 3.

But the Lakers were exhausted after having been dragged through the mill by a couple of the St. Louis veteran players, 30-year-old Bob Pettit, who averaged 29.4 points per game, and 31-year-old Cliff Hagan, who averaged 20 points per game, kept the pressure on Los Angeles in every game of the series.

The Boston Celtics had won four consecutive NBA titles and five titles in six years. While Boston was favored to whip the Los Angeles Lakers again, Red Auerbach was very aware of the fact that Lakers had almost dethroned the Celtics in the 1962 Finals when, in game seven, a jump shot by Frank Selvy just missed going through the hoop. Still, Auerbach was confident that, with a couple of breaks, the Celtics could wrap-up another title in less than seven games.

Game one of the finals was played in Boston and the Celtics beat the Lakers 117–114. In game two, also played in Boston, the Celtics went ahead two games to none defeating Los Angeles 113–106.

The finals moved to Los Angeles for game three, and the Lakers finally won, defeating the Celtics 119–99. In game four,

Boston Celtics – 1963 NBA Champions. (Courtesy of The Sports Museum.)

also played in LA, the Celtics moved out to a 3-games-to-1 lead, with a 108–105 win over the Lakers.

Back at Boston Garden for game five, the Lakers were facing elimination but took command after Tom Heinsohn, who had scored 23 points, was ejected and Bob Cousy, who had scored 12, fouled out. Led by Elgin Baylor with 43 points, and Jerry West with 32, the Lakers took command of the game and defeated the Celtics 126–112. In the losing effort, Sam Jones had scored 36 points and Bill Russell, 24, for Boston.

So the finals returned to Los Angeles for game six with the Celtics up 3 games to 2. Bob Cousy had a premonition that this would be the final game in his career with the Boston Celtics. He later wrote in his book, *The Killer Instinct,* that when the Celtics arrived in LA, he walked into his hotel and locked the door. Cousy wanted to be alone, he didn't answer the telephone and ordered all his meals via room service. Then, he sort of a went into a trance, fixated on the upcoming game. "I talked to no one," said Cousy. "I thought so long and so intensely about Frank Selvy, the Laker guard I would be playing against, that if he had walked into that room I might have leaped at his throat and tried to strangle him."[35]

In game six, Bob Cousy sprained an ankle and was helped to the bench. But when the Lakers went ahead by one point, he came back into the game. The Celtics were leading 104–102 with 2:48 left when Tom Heinsohn stole a Jerry West pass intended for Rudy La Russo, drove and scored. From that point on, Bob Cousy worked the clock as he had done in the old days, fancy dribbling as the final seconds on the clock ticked off and his career came to an end. When the buzzer sounded, Cousy threw the ball high into the air and raced to embrace Red Auerbach.

The Celtics won the game 112–109, winning their sixth NBA championship and fifth in a row. Bob Cousy had scored 18 points in the game while holding Frank Selvy to just 3. His heir apparent, Sam Jones, scored 36 points.

For thirteen years with the Boston Celtics, Bob Cousy had played on six NBA championship teams playing 30,131 minutes, scoring 16,955 points (18.5 points per game), and having 6,945 assists (7.6 assists per game). He had led the NBA in assists eight years in a row (1952–53 to 1959–60) and been a 13-time All-Star.

There have been many sports dynasties, but the mystique of the Boston Celtics of the 1950s and 1960s has been enduring in its legacy in that it defined a professional sport for a couple of generations of fans. It also had a deep psychological effect on those who competed against the Celtics.

1963 Boston Celtics with President John F. Kennedy at the White House. (Courtesy of The Sports Museum.)

Oscar Robertson stated, in regard to the 1963 NBA Semi-Finals series against the Celtics, by the Cincinnati Royals he was dejected. "Afterwards, the reporters, fans, and players alike blamed our loss on the circus debacle and the ownership chaos. The truth is we had the opportunity to beat Boston. We couldn't do it. A lot of the Royals were gun-shy about playing them; it was almost as if they couldn't go forward and play aggressively against the green-and-white Celtics uniforms."[36]

Jerry West played his heart out in the 1963 NBA Finals against the Boston Celtics, averaging 29.5 points per game, and felt the sting of defeat everlasting.

"During the 1960s, we [the LA Lakers] lost to the Boston Celtics six times in the Finals," said West. "If it had been six different teams we'd lost to, perhaps the pain of those losses would be diluted. But the same team over and over? Those losses scarred me, scars that remain embedded in my psyche to this day."[37] Even later, when West became the general manager of the Los Angeles Lakers, he tried to avoid going to Boston Garden—he didn't like it there and the memories of playing there were too painful.

9

Cousy Takes Over at Boston College

& Jerry Lucas Joins the Royals

Since enrolling at Holy Cross eighteen years ago, Bob Cousy had lived in Worcester, Massachusetts. He had become a partner in an insurance company in Worcester, and following his playing days with the Boston Celtics, he planned to continue living in the town with his wife, Missie, and two daughters. But upon hanging up his black Chuck Taylor All-Star high-top sneakers, Cousy was presented with several other options for a career and signed contracts with three companies to do public relations and sales.

But basketball had been his life, and Cousy didn't want to completely separate himself from the game. As luck would have it, in early summer of 1963, Boston College offered him the head coaching job for its basketball program with a salary of $12,000 a year. As Boston College was located in Chestnut Hill, about an hour's drive from Worcester, it was a perfect fit for both his work and domestic life.

In 1962–63, the Boston College Eagles had finished the season with a record of 10–16 under interim-coach Frank Powers, a BC professor, who had agreed to take the job. When Cousy took over, Powers agreed to stay on as an assistant and coach the freshman squad.

Cousy knew that Boston College was primarily a football school, but it was his goal not just to rebuild the Golden Eagles basketball program but to put it on the map. He believed that he had an ace in the hole for recruiting by just being Bob Cousy. He wanted to recruit players that had similar backgrounds and goals like him. In other words, Cousy wanted players from a poor economic background with a hunger to succeed.

Cousy's first blue-chip recruit was John Austin, a 6'0" guard from Washington, D.C.

Red Auerbach had told Cousy about Austin, and he helped recruit him for Boston College while still playing for the Celtics.

John Austin had begun playing basketball in Washington at the Boy's Club, competing against Dave Bing and John Thompson. As a sophomore, he played at Bishop Carroll High School in D.C. and then transferred to DeMatha High in Hyattsville, Maryland. Austin's teams won championships at both schools.

As for enrolling at Boston College, Austin remarked, "I enjoyed Catholic high school so much, I wanted to continue in a Catholic College. I also wanted to take advantage of the tremendous academic atmosphere of Boston, and thirdly, I knew Red Auerbach of the Boston Celtics and he told me Bob Cousy would be BC's new coach. I felt that I could learn a lot from him and also be seen by the Celtics at the same time."[1]

As a sophomore in 1963–64, John Austin was the only black player on the Boston College team. Playing three years of varsity ball, 1963–66, John Austin would become the Boston College all-time scoring leader for a three-year varsity career finishing with an average of 27.1 points per game.

Bob Cousy's first game as Boston College coach, December 12, 1963, would be a 74–93 loss to Massachusetts. It would be rough going for the Golden Eagles as they would ultimately lose the first five games of the season to Massachusetts, Connecticut, St. Bonaventure, Temple, and Canisius before giving Cousy his first win defeating Dartmouth.

But there was hope for BC, a few days after defeating Dartmouth, they defeated Georgetown 107–97 with John Austin scoring 49 points.

In his first year as coach, Bob Cousy's Boston College Golden Eagles would finish unranked and undistinguished with a record of 10–11, including two losses to arch-rival Holy Cross. Cousy could not remember any team of his ever finishing with a record below .500, and he knew that he had his work cut out for him in elevating the status of the Boston College basketball program. But John Austin finished the year with a scoring average of 29.2 points per game, and Cousy knew there was a player that he could build his team around.

In Cincinnati, by August 1963, local businessman Warren Hensel had still not completed his purchase of the Cincinnati

Royals. By early October, Hensel would still be waiting to complete the verbal agreement he had with Louis Jacobs and Emprise Corporation to complete the sale.

While there has been substantial speculation that Warren Hensel could not come up with the cash to buy the Royals, the fact was that Louis Jacobs, after carefully considering the deal, had decided to renege on his promise to sell the team to Hensel. On October 3, Ambrose “Bro” Lindhorst, attorney for Jacobs, announced that the Royals were not for sale.

“I just don’t understand it,” remarked Hensel. “I’ve been at a complete loss. I haven’t been able to talk to the man [Jacobs] in several months. My only contact has been with Bro Lindhorst.”[2]

According to Oscar Robertson, the Royals players considered the front office situation bizarre, but they had to concentrate on preparing for the coming season.

Bizarre was an understatement. Since the end of the 1962–63 playoffs, while deciding what he wanted to do with the Royals, Louie Jacobs had been using Warren Hensel as an unpaid front office pawn, allowing him broad discretion in making decisions for the Royals. To that end, Hensel hired Jack McMahon as the Royals new coach replacing Charlie Wolf. Then, in mid-August, Hensel convinced Jerry Lucas to sign with the Royals after courting him for months.

Warren Hensel was no doubt a decent and honest man with good intentions in attempting to buy the Royals, but he was also naïve in dealing with a man like Louis Jacobs.

In 1972, *Sports Illustrated* proclaimed Louie Jacobs, “The Godfather of Sports.” Warren Hensel didn’t realize that, in dealing with Louie Jacobs, he was scraping along the dark side of sports. Jacobs never cared about the character of the people he did business with. Louis Jacobs’ modus operandi in making deals was driven by his penchant for being pragmatic, *quid pro quo.* His deals didn’t always involve a formal contract, and instead of developing business plans, Louie relied on rational action or intuition as his guiding force.

Louis Jacobs, Louie, or L. M., as his friends called him, was a self-made man—a real Horatio Alger story. Born into poverty on Delancey Street on New York’s Lower East Side, he, along with his two brothers Marvin and Charley, sons of a Polish immigrant tailor, built a sports concession empire.

Louie started it all after the family, by then numbering six, moved to Buffalo around the turn of the twentieth century. Louie Jacobs got his introduction into the sports concession business by selling peanuts in the Buffalo ballpark and popcorn at the Gayety Theatre, a local burlesque house. Meanwhile, Louie's siblings shined shoes and rented canoes at Delaware Park Lake. The three learned how to accumulate capital and put it to use opening concession booths.

At the age of 15, Louie Jacobs was arrested in Buffalo for hiring boys to run cabs for him. Under existing laws, Jacobs was too young to be an employer.

By 1927, the Jacobs brothers had got their first big league contract to provide concessions for the Detroit Tigers at Navin Field.

Louie went to Detroit and personally managed the employees and every aspect of the contract. At the end of the 1927 season, Jacobs took a check for $12,500 to Tigers owner Frank Navin and presented it to him. The stunned Navin inquired, "'What's this for?' 'You made a bad contract,' said Louie. 'You deserve more than you guaranteed.'"[3]

Frank Navin spread the word, and soon the Jacobs brothers were running concessions in several major league parks. The business known as Jacobs Brothers, beginning in 1915, evolved into what is known as Sportservice in 1948. Later in 1961, the business expanded into Emprise Corporation, and Sportservice became a subsidiary. With the passing of his brothers, Louie Jacobs restructured the Emprise Corporation ownership so that he became an employee of his sons, Jeremy and Max.

In 1960, Sportservice was the concessionaire to the Rome Olympics. By the early 1970s, Sportservice was the concessionaire for seven Major League Baseball teams (Baltimore Orioles, Chicago White Sox, Cincinnati Reds, Detroit Tigers, Montreal Expos, Milwaukee Brewers, and St. Louis Cardinals), eight NFL professional football teams, four NHL hockey teams, and five NBA teams located in Baltimore, Buffalo, Chicago, Milwaukee, and Cincinnati. In addition, Sportservice had contracts with fifty horse and dog tracks in the USA and Canada, plus ten more in England and Puerto Rico, while also doing various golf tournaments.

By the early 1970s, Emprise had 70,000 employees working in 39 states, Canada, England, and Puerto Rico and was a hundred million dollar a year operation, selling five million bags of peanuts annually, thirty million soft drinks, twenty million hot dogs, and twenty-five million containers of beer.

Along the way, Louie Jacobs and his brothers did business with many solid citizens and sports icons. Bill Veeck signed contracts with Sportservice for every major league franchise that he owned, the St. Louis Browns, Cleveland Indians, and Chicago White Sox, and the minor league Milwaukee Brewers.

In regard to the company's cash flow, it was Louis Jacobs' belief that money should go out of the company as fast as it came in to sustain growth.

When Connie Mack's Philadelphia Athletics franchise was on the verge of collapse in 1951, he came to see Louie. Louie gave Mack a $250,000 interest-free loan. Rational action dictated to Louie Jacobs that he couldn't sell hot dogs and peanuts if the Athletics weren't playing. A couple of years later, Jacobs helped Mack sell the Athletics to Charles Finley who moved the team to Kansas City.

Danny Menendez, the owner of the AAA Toledo Mud Hens, had placed a frantic call to Louie telling him that his franchise was in deep financial trouble and about to fold. Louie told Menendez that he would be on the evening train from Buffalo to Chicago which stopped in Toledo at 4 A.M.—so be sure that he was at the train station to meet him. Menendez was on the platform pacing frantically back and forth when the train pulled in to Toledo early in the morning. Louie got off in his pajamas and slippers and handed Menendez a check, then got back on the train. With the money Jacobs had advanced Menendez, the Toledo franchise survived. What Louie got out of the deal was an extended contract to sell hot dogs.

Sportservice even loaned the City of St. Louis $12 million in the early 1960s (a guarantee of $400,000 a year) to help secure the financing for Busch Memorial Stadium. In return, Louie Jacobs got a 25-year concession contract. Then, after Emprise invested another $1.2 million in concession booths and equipment, the contract was extended to 30 years.

While Louis Jacobs and his brothers saved a lot of sports franchises from financial disaster and collaborated with some men of impeccable character, there was also a dark side to their business relationships. While Louie was considered to be an honest, hard-working man, he did business with a lot of unsavory characters, and some of those deals raised eyebrows and also got the attention of Congress.

Rumors persist that during prohibition, Louie Jacobs bought speed boats to bring illegal liquor from Canada to Buffalo. Also, it is alleged that as far back as 1937, the Jacobses were loaning money to Cleveland mobster Moe Dalitz. History shows that later, Dalitz would be instrumental in bringing syndicate gambling to Las Vegas when he acquired the Stardust Casino. Federal investigators did uncover one loan of $250,000 to the Stardust from Louie.

Giacomo "Jack" Tocco, who died in 2014 at the age of 87, had a business degree from Detroit University and operated a linen business in the Motor City. Jack Tocco was also a *capo* in the Detroit Mafia. Tocco was an associate of Emprise in the Hazel Park Racetrack. Emprise owned 12% in the track. Tocco, executive vice-president of Hazel Park, along with two other members of the board of directors, Anthony J. Zerilli, the son of a Mafia don and Dominic "Fats" Corrado, had been named by the McClellan Committee as members of the Detroit Mafia.*

Later, Anthony Zerilli was convicted with Emprise in a casino conspiracy. Three months before the *Sports Illustrated* article appeared in May 1972, a federal jury in Los Angeles found Louie and his eldest son Max guilty of conspiring to help conceal the identity of two purchasers of a Las Vegas casino.

After Howard Hughes had bought Las Vegas' Frontier Hotel and Casino in 1972, a jury in Los Angeles federal court concluded that the casino's real ownership had been illegally concealed. The real owners had been Detroit mobsters Anthony J. Zerilli and Michael S. Polizzi. The jury found that Emprise had made substantial loans to front men for the allegedly mob-related owners.

Both Zerilli and Polizzi received five-year prison sentences in the scam. Emprise was fined $10,000 and Louie Jacobs and his son, Max, were named as unindicted co-conspirators, but neither received a prison sentence and by the time the case was heard, Louie had died three years earlier in 1968 from a heart attack.

In the mid-1970s, Anthony Zerilli's name would surface again as he would be a suspect in the killing of Teamster union leader

* The McClellan Committee, AKA the United Sates Senate Select Committee on Improper Activities in Labor and Management, was created on November 30, 1957, and dissolved on March 31, 1960. Robert F. Kennedy was Chief Counsel of the Committee until he resigned on September 11, 1959, to assist his brother Senator John F. Kennedy in his presidential campaign.

Jimmy Hoffa. Zerilli died in 2015 at that the age of 87 of natural causes.

On several occasions, according to the *Sports Illustrated* article, Raymond Patriarca, the don of the New England Mafia, had helped associates connect with Louie. One, in particular, was an Eastern Pennsylvania mobster by the name of Russell Bufalino. In 1959, Louie had helped Bufalino arrange the financing for four amusement parks in the Pittsburgh area.

Louie Jacobs had also financed James Plumeri, a New York labor racketeer, who would be killed in a mob hit in 1971, in various boxing ventures ran by Frankie Carbo in the 1950s. During the 1940s and 1950s, Carbo and his crime associates controlled Madison Square Garden and several high-profile boxers including Jake LaMotta, Rocky Graziano, and Sonny Liston. In addition, it had been rumored that Plumeri and Carbo had controlled Floyd Patterson. It was alleged that the working relationship that Louie Jacobs had with Plumeri was that he was to use his labor clout with another mobster Johnny Dio to head-off strikes at sports sites where Sportservice had concessionaire contracts.

Jerry Catena would be the successor to Vito Genovese as the don in the New York crime family of the same name. When Jerry Catena came into a million dollars, Louie helped him invest it. Catena wanted to buy Lion Manufacturing, which made slot machines.

Tony Corallo was a Lucchese crime family member who reportedly controlled the majority of the loan sharking and illegal gambling in Newark, New Jersey. According to Corallo, Jerry Catena couldn't use the million dollars cold cash he had to buy Lion Manufacturing because if he used the cash, he could face prosecution for tax evasion, so Louie Jacobs stepped forward to assist Catena.

The finance plan put in place by Louie was that Emprise would be a major stockholder in Lion Manufacturing by virtue of a voting trust agreement from a million-dollar loan to Lion in 1962. Later, Louie's son Max Jacobs said that his father wanted to buy into Lion because they made a great coffee machine, but when he learned the true nature of Catena's intentions for the company to make slot machines, he sold out his interest in the company.

In the *Sports Illustrated* article, Louie's two sons, Max and Jeremy Jacobs, admitted that there were Emprise dealings with some of the people named above. In regards to Anthony Zerilli,

Max Jacobs said, "Indeed there had been a loan, a big one—$256,000—in 1956. Sportservice had become the concessionaire at Hazel Park in 1949. When stock was made available seven years later, Zerilli and Tocco came to Louie Jacobs for financial backing—just as [Bill] Veeck and [Connie] Mack had. For every two shares they purchased with Jacobs money, Louie was allowed to purchase one. Emprise wound-up with 12% of the stock. The loan was paid off in December 1960."[4]

Perhaps mob-related people just came with the territory in such sports venues as horse racing, dog racing, jai-alai, and boxing, but Louie Jacobs seemed to work cordially with members of the criminal element and always seemed to be in control of their common interest. Mafia dons respected Louie and honored his boundaries.

Buying into the Cincinnati Royals was not an unusual investment for Emprise and the Jacobses. At various times, Emprise had owned stock in other sports teams, such as the Buffalo Bisons baseball team of the International League and the Buffalo hockey franchise in the American Hockey League. But as things stood in 1963, the Cincinnati Royals were per se the only known professional sports franchise with mob connections.

Louie Jacobs had taken part in the building of Cincinnati Gardens. When the building project had run into financial trouble, he invested in it and wound up owning 40% of the stock.

In the fall of 1963, after forking over $400,000 to the Wood Foundation, Louis Jacobs owned 56% of the Cincinnati Royals stock and 80% of Cincinnati Gardens. The Royals had lost $25,000 in 1962–63 and had a carry-over loss of $150,000. But the franchise, which had been purchased by the Wood Estate and other local investors in 1958 for $200,000, had increased significantly in value in recent years—the same for the market value of Cincinnati Gardens. The signing of Jerry Lucas was expected to significantly increase the Cincinnati Royals' gate receipts in the coming 1963–64 season. It is highly possible that Louie Jacobs had come to the conclusion that, with the addition of Jerry Lucas, he had acquired a franchise with huge growth potential on the bottom line.

As for Warren Hensel, what was he going to do? Sue Louie Jacobs for breach of contract? There was no contract, and Louie had more lawyers than Hensel and was well connected to the NBA Board of Governors.

After sitting out the 1962–63 season, Jerry Lucas was ready to get back to playing basketball. The Cincinnati Royals had exercised their territorial draft rights to Lucas, and Warren Hensel had been the driving force in signing him for the Royals.

Jerry Ray Lucas was born on March 30, 1940, in Middletown, Ohio, a little steel mill town with approximately 50,000 residents located halfway between Cincinnati and Columbus.

Lucas became nationally known during his high school days playing at Middletown High School under legendary basketball coach Paul Walker where he scored 2,466 points, shattering the high school scoring record set by Wilt Chamberlain of 2,252 at Philadelphia's Overbrook High School. Lucas led the Middletown Middies to two consecutive Ohio State high school basketball championships in 1956 and 1957 and was named the Ohio Player of the Year in both 1957 and 1958. In state championships play, Lucas averaged 44 points per game. In a tournament his sophomore year, Lucas scored 55 and 44 points on consecutive nights. After the Middies won the 1957 state title, for a week Middletown called itself Lucasville.

On the night of January 17, 1958, with Jerry Lucas rewriting the Ohio high school basketball record book, two undefeated teams from southwest Ohio, Middletown and Hamilton, met at the Cincinnati Gardens in front of 13,646 spectators, the 17th largest crowd in the arena's history.

Middletown won the game 64–49 as Jerry Lucas scored 31 points and guard Tom Sizer, 22. However, the game was no breather for the Middies as the Hamilton Big Blue had rallied to make the score 43–40 at the end of the third period. Then, Tom Sizer poured in 9 points to spark the Middies to a 60–41 lead with two minutes remaining. It was Middletown's 64th consecutive victory.

That year the Royals had just moved to Cincinnati from Rochester and average attendance for their home games at Cincinnati Gardens was 3,641. So, the Jerry Lucas/Tom Sizer-led Middletown Middies, a high school basketball team, had a gate draw that was over three and half times that of an NBA team in Cincinnati.

Going into the final game of the Ohio State high school tournament in 1958, the Middletown Middies, led by Jerry Lucas, had won 76 straight games. Then, Middletown lost the championship game to Columbus North, 63–62.

Jerry Lucas – Ohio State Buckeyes.

For decades following the loss to Columbus North, the loyal Middletown fans have suspected that something was wrong with Jerry Lucas in that game. On March 12, 2008, Rob Oiler wrote a column in *The Columbus Dispatch* raising the question that maybe Jerry Lucas had held back in the championship game because of hurt feelings. The record showed that he only scored 25 points on 17 attempts.

In his column, Oiler resurrects the issue that during the week before the championship game, the mother of Lucas's teammate—guard Tom Sizer—was complaining that Lucas was getting too much attention. The speculation is that Lucas, who was always an unselfish player, became emotionally scared and shut down his game vs. Columbus North. Apparently, the issue was well-known by both Lucas and Sizer and both have denied anything like that ever happened.

Tom Sizer went on to play for the University of Cincinnati on two NCAA National Championship teams in 1961 and 1962, coached by future Royals coach Ed Jucker, that would defeat the Ohio State Buckeyes featuring his former high school teammate Jerry Lucas on the squad.

By the time that Jerry Lucas graduated from Middletown High, he stood 6 feet 8 with a reach of 12 feet three inches above the floor. He had been a straight-A student, president of the senior class, and a member of the National Scholastic Honor Society, and received offers from 160 colleges and universities.

According to Jerry's mother, "We were told by an alumnus from one school in the East that if Jerry enrolled there my husband would get $15,000-a-year job [the husband, Mark Lucas was making $6,500-a-year as a pressman], that the mortgage on our home would be paid off, that Roy [Jerry's 16-year-old brother who stood 6'3", weighed 180, and was a fine football player] would also get a scholarship to the same school."[5] Also, Jerry would have a new car and expense account.

What Jerry Lucas wanted was an academic scholarship to study business administration with no strings attached. He also wanted to go to school within 200 miles of Middletown so his parents could see him play. That encompassed some very elite college basketball territory. Located within those boundaries are Cincinnati, Xavier, Ohio State, Dayton, Western Kentucky, Miami (OH), Kentucky, West Virginia, Indiana, and Louisville.

Lucas chose Ohio State and entered in the fall of 1958. An All-American for three varsity years, he led the Buckeyes to three Big Ten Championships, three NCAA tournament finals, and the 1960 NCAA championship defeating California in the finals, 75–55.

Had California not defeated Cincinnati to reach the finals, Jerry Lucas would have played his one and only game of his college career against Oscar Robertson.

In 1961 and 1962, despite having star-studded rosters that in addition to Jerry Lucas included John Havlicek, Larry Siegfried, Bobby Knight, and Mel Nowell, the Ohio State Buckeyes teams lost the NCAA tournament in consecutive years to the University of Cincinnati Bearcats.

Regardless of the failure of the Buckeyes to defeat the Bearcats, Jerry Lucas was named MVP of the Holiday Tournament at Madison Square Garden in 1961, College Player of the Year in both 1961 and 1962, and Sportsman of Year for 1961 by *Sports Illustrated*.

In the summer of 1960, Jerry Lucas played on the Gold Medal-winning USA Olympic basketball team in Rome. The team included future NBA stars Oscar Robertson, Bob Boozer, Adrian Smith (all future Royals teammates), Jerry West, Darrell Imhoff, Terry Dischinger, and Walt Bellamy. Another future Royals teammate chosen for the Olympic team, Jay Arnett of Texas, elected not to participate.

Prior to the start of the 1963–64 season, Maurice Podoloff stepped down as president, although some maintain that he was forced out.

Podoloff was replaced by Walter Kennedy, a public relations man and politician. Walter Kennedy had done some public relations work for the Harlem Globetrotters. At the time, he was voted in as the NBA's second president, he was in his second term as mayor of Stamford, Connecticut. In 1962, Kennedy had been the campaign manager for U.S. Senator Abraham Ribicoff.

As the mid-1960s were fast approaching, the NBA was still in a state of structural metamorphosis; it had, in effect, little more than a trial national television contract with ABC and labor unrest with the players was on the horizon. Walter Kennedy would have to oversee it all.

Kennedy quickly demonstrated that he was going to be a no-nonsense president when he fined Red Auerbach $500 for rowdy behavior in a pre-season game. He also indicated that he was going to continue his predecessor's tough stance against the players union, an issue that would reach a crisis level during the All-Star Game that year.

Beginning in 1963–64, the Syracuse Nationals relocated to Philadelphia and became the 76ers. Also, the Chicago Zephyrs, who had been added as the expansion team Chicago Packers in 1961–62, were transferred to Baltimore and became the Baltimore Bullets.

Chicago had been in the Western Division, but rather than properly realign the Eastern and Western Divisions, the NBA created a geographical travesty, leaving the Baltimore team in the Western Division and Cincinnati in the Eastern Division.

The failure by the NBA to realign the conferences properly in accordance with geography has not gone unnoticed. Over the ensuing decades, pro-basketball historians have more often than not advanced the opinion that the failure of the NBA to return the Cincinnati Royals to the Western Division had a dramatic effect on the history of the team. Simply stated, with the transfer of Chicago to Baltimore, it is the belief of many that if the Royals had been returned to the Western Division, they might have appeared in five straight NBA Finals. The record shows that between the seasons of 1962–63 and 1966–67, the Royals peaked. But being in the Eastern Division, they were confronted with the monumental obstacle every season of getting by the Boston Celtics to reach the finals.

Jerry Lucas played his first NBA game on October 10, 1963, in St. Louis as the Royals defeated the Hawks 112–93. In his professional debut, Lucas scored 23 points. Wayne Embry led the Royals with 25 points and Oscar Robertson added 22.

The following evening, Lucas played his first game at Cincinnati Gardens as the Royals lost to the Boston Celtics 92–93. Lucas had 13 points and Robertson, 20.

As expected, the presence of Jerry Lucas playing with Oscar Robertson not only elevated the Royals in competitiveness but also temporarily in gate attraction. On December 27, 1963, the Royals defeated the Boston Celtics 91–87 at Cincinnati Gardens with a packed house of 14,163 fans for the post-Christmas shootout.

By the All-Star Game break on January 12, the Royals had a record of 30–15 and were putting plenty of pressure on the Boston Celtics.

Besides having Lucas and Robertson, the Royals also had a new coach, Jack McMahon, who had been hired by Warren Hensel. Jack McMahon had played college ball at St. John's University and captained the team in his senior year, 1952, that lost to Kansas, 80–63, in the NCAA Finals. He was then drafted by Rochester and played eight years in the NBA with the Royals and St. Louis Hawks. Prior to coming to Cincinnati, McMahon had been coach of the Chicago Zephyrs.

In regard to McMahon's coaching style, Oscar Robertson remarked, "Jack McMahon was like a lot of coaches of that era, he was fiery. On the sidelines, he would yell and moan until he was red in the face. He also came in and, like many coaches, immediately decided we needed to play better defense and try to run more."[6]

In 1954, an NBA players union had been started by Bob Cousy. Dissatisfied with the indifference of the team owners to players economic circumstances, Cousy began writing to an established player from each of the league's teams (Paul Arizin, Philadelphia Warriors; Carl Braun, New York Knicks; Bob Davies, Rochester Royals; Paul Hoffman, Baltimore Bullets; Andy Phillip, Fort Wayne Pistons; Jim Pollard, Minneapolis Lakers; Dolph Schayes, Syracuse Nationals; and Don Sunderlage of Milwaukee) encouraging solidarity among the players. The only player that didn't respond was Andy Phillip, who was not going to attempt to bite the hand that fed him. Pistons owner Fred Zollner, who owned a machine works plant, was very anti-union and this prevented the Pistons players from participating.

At the NBA All-Star Game in January 1955, Cousy went to NBA President Maurice Podoloff with a list of concerns that included payment of back salaries to the members of the defunct Baltimore Bullets, establishment of a twenty-game limit on exhibition games, after which the players should share in the profits, abolition of the $15 "whispering fine"* which referees could impose on a player during a game, payment of $25 expenses for public appearances other than radio, television or certain charitable functions, establishment of an impartial board of arbitration to settle player-owner disputes, moving expenses for traded players, payment of player salaries in ten installments rather than twelve to provide more money to players cut during the season, and an increase in meal money from $5 a day to $7 a day.

There was some accord reached as Podoloff agreed to the payment of two weeks' salary to six players who had played for the Baltimore Bullets before the franchise folded, agreed to a meeting with the player representatives within two weeks over their concerns, and the raise in meal money.

While the modest raise in meal money only came to about $200 a year, the players felt like they had won a substantial victory.

But Podoloff and the team owners continued to delay meeting with the players until Bob Cousy met with AFL-CIO officials over possible union affiliation in January of 1957. At that point, the league agreed to bargain in good faith with the players union following the season. In April, the NBA Board of Governors formally recognized the NBPA and agreed to their terms.

* A whispering fine meant that referees had the authority to leverage an in-game fine for criticism of a ref or their call.

Cousy continued to be the union president until 1958 when he became frustrated with players ignoring their $10 annual union dues. Boston Celtics teammate Tom Heinsohn replaced him.

The 1964 All-Star Game, played at Boston Garden, almost didn't happen. The NBA's nine owners and its president, Maurice Podoloff, had been, for the most part, once again ignoring the players union and its president, Tom Heinsohn.

When Walter Kennedy became NBA president, Tom Heinsohn, president, and vice president Lenny Wilkens of the NBA Players Association (NBPA) had attempted to tell him what the players wanted but were ignored. The players wanted a pension plan, athletic trainers on every team, and a ban on playing Sunday afternoon games after playing on Saturday nights. In 1964, the NBA was nothing like it is today. The minimum salary was $8,000 and most players had off-season jobs to make ends meet.

There had been a major snowstorm in the northeast prior to the All-Star Game date that made all transportation between New York and Boston nearly impossible, so players were arriving any way they could to get to Boston. The three Cincinnati Royals players selected to play in the game, Oscar Robertson, Wayne Embry, and Jerry Lucas, were diverted from Cincinnati to Minneapolis where they caught a plane for Washington then took a train to Boston.

As the players trickled into Boston Garden, Tom Heinsohn was there with a paper for them to sign stating that they would support a strike. There had been a Board of Governors meeting that day and no one would talk to Heinsohn and the player representatives that were on hand.

So Heinsohn, the son of a labor leader, took matters into his own hands with the All-Star team. "We relayed what we wanted to do and they all signed the paper that they would support this thing," said Heinsohn. "We went down and talked to the commissioner [president] about 5 o'clock and told him that because they hadn't met us, we were not going to play unless they met our demands."[7]

Game time was still a few hours away, and suddenly everyone wondered what was going to happen, including ABC that was supposed to televise the game nationally for the first time.

Things were getting heated, too! Bob Short, the owner of the Los Angeles Lakers, burst into the trainer's room and began screaming at Jerry West and Elgin Baker that if they didn't play in the game, he would personally see that they didn't play again.

Red Auerbach, who was the East team coach, caught up with Tom Heinsohn in the hall and told him "he was the biggest heel in sports."[8]

The players, most concerned about their livelihood, took a vote. The count was 11–9 in favor of playing. They voted again and the vote was reversed; now it was 11–9 against playing.

Tom Heinsohn had put his great relationship with Celtics owner Walter Brown on the line to push the union's agenda and was not about to back down.

Someone had to blink—as it turned out, it was Walter Kennedy. He assured the players that by summer he would come up with an acceptable pension plan. The players knew that Kennedy was negotiating a new TV contract and began to consider what effect a strike might have on those negotiations. The players had won.

Oscar Robertson would replace Tom Heinsohn as president of the NBPA in 1966 and spearhead a drive that would eliminate the reserve clause in the NBA.

In the end, 13,464 fans braved the weather to pack Boston Garden and the game was delayed only 15 minutes. The East beat the West, 111–107, in front of a national audience of millions, showcasing its biggest stars.

Oscar Robertson led the East scoring with 26 points and 8 assists. Bill Russell had 21 rebounds. Rookie Jerry Lucas had 11 points and 8 rebounds.

Ageless Bob Pettit led the West with 19 points and 17 rebounds. Wilt Chamberlain had 19 points and 20 rebounds. Jerry West had 17 points and 5 assists.

On the night of February 29 in Philadelphia, Jerry Lucas showed the NBA and anybody who doubted him just how good he really was. In a 117 to 114 victory by the Royals over the Warriors, Oscar Robertson was the leading scorer with 43 points while Jerry Lucas scored 28 points and pulled down 40 rebounds.

Lucas' 40 rebounds in a game broke the club record of 38 set by Maurice Stokes vs. Syracuse on January 14, 1956. Jerry Lucas' second-best rebound effort would come on November 20, 1965, when he grabbed 37 rebounds vs. the Detroit Pistons.

Jerry Lucas' 40 rebounds put him in some very elite company in the NBA records book. Throughout the 2017–18 season, only four players have ever had 40 or more rebounds in an NBA game. "Wilt the Stilt" Chamberlain pulled down 40 or more rebounds in a game fifteen times in his career. Chamberlain's best effort was 55 rebounds vs. the Boston Celtics on November 24, 1960. Bill Russell had 40 or more rebounds in eight games, his best being 51 rebounds against the Syracuse Nationals on February 5, 1960. The last player to do it was Nate Thurmond who had 42 rebounds vs. the Detroit Pistons on November 9, 1965.

Since 1978, the highest rebound total in an NBA game is 37 by Moses Malone vs. the New Orleans Jazz on February 29, 1979. The great Kareem Abdul Jabbar's best effort was 34 rebounds vs. Detroit on December 14, 1975.

The 1963–64 Cincinnati Royals finished with a record of 55–25, four games behind the Eastern Division champion, the Boston Celtics, who finished at 59–21. But unlike the previous season, with Robertson and Lucas in the lineup, the Royals made every game with the Celtics a battle as the two teams split the season series at 5–5.

Oscar Robertson had a remarkable season just missing a triple-double year with averages of 31.4 points per game, 9.9 rebounds, and 11.0 assists and was named MVP.

Jerry Lucas also had a great year averaging 17.7 points per game, 17.4 rebounds, and 2.6 assists and was named Rookie of the Year.

In Buffalo, Louie Jacobs was all smiles; his Royals had averaged 6,909 paid admissions per home game at Cincinnati Gardens. It was the highest home attendance figure in the history of the Royals franchise.

In the 1963–64 Eastern Division Semi-Finals, the Royals defeated the Philadelphia 76ers 3 games to 2 in a very close series. Each team won all their home games. Cincinnati had a slight edge in the series by having three home games.

The series with the 76ers had been stressful and closely played, and now the Royals were confronted with taking on a rested Boston Celtics team in the Eastern Division Finals. There was no repeat of the exciting series that the two teams had played the year before as the Celtics defeated the Royals 4 games to 1.

It has long been speculated that the loss of reserve forward Bob Boozer was a huge contributing factor to the Royals loss to the Celtics. With the addition of Jerry Lucas, Royals coach Jack McMahon determined that Boozer was expendable and at midseason traded him to the New York Knicks. With limited bench strength in the playoffs, the Royals were handicapped.

But a larger contributing problem was the Royals lack of offense. The Cincinnati Royals had finished first in offense during the season, averaging 98.9 points per game, but the Boston Celtics did a magnificent job in containing the Royals, holding them to 93.2 points per game while allowing them to score above 100 points in just one game.

The Boston Celtics then went on to defeat Wilt Chamberlain and the San Francisco Warriors for the 1963–64 NBA championship. For the Boston Celtics, it was their sixth straight NBA championship since 1959.

Oscar Robertson had been slow in acknowledging the contributions of Jerry Lucas in the Royals lineup in 1963–64. He even went so far in his biography, *The Big O—My Life, My Times, My Game,* to point out that the year before, without Lucas, the Royals had taken the Celtics to a deciding seventh game because they were a better-balanced squad. According to Wayne Embry, Oscar Robertson wasn't close to Jerry Lucas and wanted the Royals to draft George Wilson, a 6'8" forward who had just graduated from the University of Cincinnati and had played on the Bearcats 1962 national championship team and the 1963 runner-up team.

George Wilson was drafted by the Cincinnati Royals in 1964 as a territorial draft pick. Prior to joining the Royals, Wilson was a member of the 1964 United States Olympic Team that won the Gold Medal in basketball at the games held in Tokyo, Japan.*

On Labor Day, September 7, 1964, Celtics majority owner Walter Brown was vacationing with his family at his summer home in Hyannis, Massachusetts when he suffered a heart attack and died shortly after. Brown was 59 years old. At his funeral, Brown's wife, Marjorie, gave Red Auerbach his St. Christopher Medal. Auerbach would keep the medal in his pocket during all the Celtics games in the coming season.

At the All-Star break on January 10, 1965, the Royals had a record of 24–13, but once again were having trouble beating Boston with a mid-season record of 0–5 against the Celtics. The Royals would finish 2–7 against the Celtics.

Then, a further obstacle was put in the Royals' way at the All-Star Game break when Wilt Chamberlain returned to Philadelphia and the Eastern Division. The San Francisco Warriors were in dire straits financially and needed to reduce costs and get a cash infusion, so they traded Chamberlain to the Philadelphia

* Following the 1965 season, the NBA discontinued the territorial draft pick and began a using a coin-flip method of allowing last place teams in each division to select a quality draft pick. The coin flip system would remain in effect until 1985 when a lottery system was introduced.

76ers for three players, Paul Neumann, Connie Dierking, and Lee Shaffer (who retired rather than report) and $150,000 in cash. Chamberlain, now combined on the 76ers with future Hall of Famer Hal Greer, would form a considerable offensive force.

The Royals finished in 1964–65 with a record of 48–32 and were promptly dispatched in the Eastern Division Semi-Finals by Wilt Chamberlain and the Philadelphia 76ers, 3 games to 1.

In the 1965 NBA Finals, it was the same old song—the Boston Celtics defeated the Los Angeles Lakers 4 games to 1 to win their seventh title in a row and eighth in the past nine years.

Following the finals, Marjorie Brown and minority owner Lou Pieri sold the Boston Celtics to Marvin Kratter and National Equities for $3 million. Walter Brown had bequeathed 11.6 percent of the Celtics' stock to Red Auerbach, and when the team was sold, he made nearly $350,000. National Equities would own the Celtics from 1965 to 1968, then sell the team to the Ballantine Brewery.

In Chestnut Hill, Bob Cousy had just finished his second year as head coach of the Boston College Golden Eagles. At a farewell dinner for the seniors on his 1963–64 squad that went 10–11, he told the team that he was resolved that as long he was coach, Boston College would never again lose two games in a season to Holy Cross and that they would never again lose more games than they won.

In practices, Cousy set his plan in motion to improve the Golden Eagles. On offense, they worked on developing a fast break. On defense, he made the team be more aggressive by working on close man-to-man patterns and special pressure defenses to harass poor ball handlers.

With John Austin again leading the Golden Eagles in scoring with an average of 26.9 points per game and sophomore center Willie Wolters coming up with rebounds, Bob Cousy achieved all the goals he had set for his team in 1964–65. The team was greatly improved over the one Cousy had inherited the year before and finished with a record of 21–7. Furthermore, Boston College beat Holy Cross twice, 95–94 and 111–89, and just for good measure, the Golden Eagles thumped Boston University, 90–85, and Harvard, 83–72, to make them king-of-the-hill in Beantown college round-ball. In recognition of their record, Boston College received an invitation to the 1965 NIT where they lost in the first round 97–114 to St. Johns, the eventual tournament winner.

Prior to the 1965–66 season, Red Auerbach informed Cousy that he intended to retire as Boston Celtics coach at the end of the year and wanted to know if he was interested in replacing him. Although the Celtics job would pay three or four times what he was making at Boston College, Cousy turned it down. The Rodgers Center, which held about 3,000 people, was now packed for every BC home game. Despite the rigors of recruiting, Cousy was happy where he was and looking forward to the coming season.

Cousy's 1965–66 Golden Eagles finished with 21–5 record. It was John Austin's senior year, and he averaged 27.1 points per game.

Boston College was again selected to play in the NIT at Madison Square Garden. In the first round, BC defeated Louisville, led by All-American center Wes Unseld, 96–90, in three overtimes. The game entered the first OT in a very dramatic fashion. Guard Ed Hockenbury, the Golden Eagles captain, drove the lane and took a hook-shot with one second remaining. The ball seemed to hang on the rim forever then, as the buzzer sounded, fell through to tie the game.

Advancing to the quarterfinals, BC lost a hard-fought game to Villanova 85–86.

While John Austin finished his career at Boston College as the school's all-time scoring leader, his legacy was larger in that his achievements paved the way for Bob Cousy and future BC coaches to begin recruiting talented players for the school.

Unfortunately, John Austin's professional basketball career was a short one, just two years. Drafted in the fourth round in 1966 by the Boston Celtics, Austin played in 1966–67 for Baltimore in the NBA, then the following year, he was a member of the New Jersey Americans in the ABA.

While Bob Cousy was steadily increasing the competitiveness of the Golden Eagles, he was quickly becoming dismayed with the rigors of college recruiting. In the nearly twenty years since he had left Holy Cross, college basketball had started to become big business. He felt as if he had to kiss the feet of 18-year-old players to encourage them to come to Boston College.

Cousy said he was talking to a recruiter from a school in the Southwest who filled him in on what they did to get a recruit to commit to the school. "We send them across the border into Mexico to shack up for a few days. Every one of those kids signs on the dotted line when he gets back."[9]

The NCAA Tournament, the billion-dollar television extravaganza now known as "March Madness," was only a few years away from becoming an integral part of American sports culture, and in its wake was the supplanting of academic integrity in college sports.

While by the middle 1960s cash, clothes, cars, rides in jets, jobs for parents, and sometimes sex were becoming common recruiting tools on lots of campuses, Bob Cousy kept his distance from such practices. Cousy knew that he had some tough barriers to get over in recruiting. Boston College had strict and somewhat difficult entrance requirements, and the school did not accept junior college transfers. When a recruit came to Chestnut Hill, Cousy had dinner with him, then had another player show him around the campus, perhaps arrange a meeting with a dean or professor in the recruit's field of interest, then wind up the campus visit by attending a movie or hockey game.

Cousy decided to sell recruits on the school by emphasizing the quality of education they would receive, and he rarely spoke with a potential recruit that he wasn't sure was serious about coming to Boston College. He began to put an emphasis on recruiting locally, using his experience in the game and the chance for recruits to have their parents and friends see them play as primary selling points.

Cousy still made the occasional recruiting trip to Pennsylvania, Maryland, or back home to New York, but he began to recruit some very talented players from a 100-mile radius or less around Chestnut Hill. They included Billy Evans, a 6'0" guard from New Haven, Connecticut; Terry Driscoll, a 6'7" forward from Winthrop, Massachusetts; Steve Adelman, a 6'6" forward from Worcester Academy; and Jim Kissane, a 6'7" forward from Hyde Park, New York. All of these players would be instrumental in making Boston College the premier college basketball team in New England during the late 1960s.

10

The Royals Continue to Struggle in the Eastern Division

& Cousy is Accused of Associating with Gamblers

In Cincinnati, Oscar Robertson continued to make the Royals a formidable force. For his first five years in the NBA, The Big O had averaged 30.3 points, 10.4 rebounds, and 10.6 assists per game. He had finished in the top five for assists and points five straight years while making the All-NBA Team five straight years and winning an MVP award in 1964 when Wilt Chamberlain and Bill Russell were in their prime. But his brilliant career was counterbalanced by a reputation that he had acquired that he was indifferent to his coaches, had disdain for referees, and constantly criticized them. While he cold-shouldered his fans and often the media, everybody in Cincy still loved Oscar.

With the addition of Wilt Chamberlain, the Philadelphia 76ers instantly became a force in the NBA Eastern Division. In 1965–66 Philadelphia, led by Chamberlain's league-leading 33.5 points per game and 24.6 rebounds, dethroned the Boston Celtics as perennial division champions, winning the East title by one game over the Celtics 55–25 to 54–26.

The Cincinnati Royals finished in third place with a record of 45–35 and attracted an average of 6,329 fans per game at Cincinnati Gardens which would be the second-highest season total for their years playing in Cincinnati.

The 1965–66 Royals were, of course, led again by The Big O, who averaged 30.4 points per game along with 9 rebounds and a league-leading 11.5 assists. It was the fifth time in six years that he had led the league in assists.

Jerry Lucas had another fine season, averaging 21.5 points and 19.1 rebounds per game. Happy Hairston, who the Royals selected in the 1964 draft out of NYU, also had a good season, averaging 14.1 points per game. In addition, the Royals had acquired veteran center Connie Dierking who, coming off the bench, had a solid season and being a former Cincinnati Bearcat, attracted a lot of fans.

The 1966 NBA All-Star Game, played at Cincinnati Gardens on January 11 and witnessed by a sell-out crowd of 13,625, was won handily by the East over the West, 137–94. Royals guard Adrian Smith was named MVP of the All-Star Game after coming off the bench and scoring 24 points for the East. There really wasn't much left for Wilt Chamberlain to do for the East, although, he scored 21 points and had 9 rebounds. To the delight of the fans, the game had a distinct Cincinnati Royals flavor to it as, in addition to the play of Smith, Oscar Robertson scored 17 points, had 10 rebounds, and 8 assists, while Jerry Lucas had 10 points and 10 rebounds.

The Royals were a much better team than their record and third place finish indicated. In the Eastern Division Semi-Finals, they had a shot at dethroning the Boston Celtics in the five-game series. The Royals won two of the first three games then came up short, losing the last two games to lose the series to Boston, 3–2.

Boston then beat the Philadelphia Warriors 3 games to 2 in the Eastern Division Finals.

On April 28, 1966, Red Auerbach lit up his final victory cigar as the Celtics defeated the Lakers, 98–93, to take their seventh NBA title in a row. It was Auerbach's ninth NBA title in 16 seasons.

Red Auerbach would now become general manager of the Celtics and five-time NBA MVP Bill Russell would become player-coach, signing a contract calling for $125,000 a year.

In the 1966 playoffs, once again Bill Russell had been an overwhelming force in leading the Celtics to the title. For 17 games Russell had played an average of 47.9 minutes per game while averaging 19.1 points, 25.2 rebounds, and 8 assists.

While both Wilt Chamberlain and Bill Russell were immense obstacles on the court for every NBA opponent to deal with, it was Russell who was the larger problem of the two.

Bill Russell was such a dominant player that his game-by-game performance left an indelible mark etched into the psyche of almost every player that ever played against him.

1966 Los Angeles Lakers. Left to Right: Elgin Baylor, Jerry Chambers, Jerry West.

Jerry Lucas remarked, “Bill Russell was the best player I ever played against. He made you think. I used to see where he was at before I shot the ball.”[1]

Jack Twyman stated the thing that made Bill Russell so dominant was that if you got by Bob Cousy and Tom Heinsohn, then there was Russell standing at the basket waiting to block your shot. “No one ever dominated a sport the way Russell did with the Celtics,” said Twyman.[2]

During the 1960s, the Los Angeles Lakers lost to the Boston Celtics six times in the NBA Finals. The defense of Bill Russell had a lot to do with that. More than forty years after the fact, Bill Russell still haunts Jerry West. “One block by Russell still embarrasses me even now, partly because anyone, including my kids, can see it on YouTube."[3]

Bill Russell would immediately become a great player-coach for the Celtics while remaining a superior floor leader. Russell's biggest problem would be Wilt Chamberlain, the prolific scorer, and Chamberlain's biggest problem would be Russell, the defensive wizard, and the two would continue to stage many brilliant duels over the next few years, but only once would Chamberlain's Philadelphia 76ers beat Russell's Boston Celtics for the NBA title and that was about to happen.

No one knew it at the time, but 1965–66 had been the high-water mark season for the Royals franchise in Cincinnati. Going forward, there would be a slow decline in the team's performance and fan interest in professional basketball in The Queen City would begin to wane.

Prior to the 1966–67 season, the Royals traded five-time All-Star center Wayne Embry to the Boston Celtics for a future third-round draft choice and Jack Twyman retired. Both Embry and Twyman had been dissatisfied with their playing time in 1965–66.

Jack Twyman had been a six-time All-Star and played his entire 11-year NBA career with the Royals in Rochester and Cincinnati. In 1960, he and Wilt Chamberlain were the first players to average over thirty points per game in a season. Chamberlain averaged 37.6 and Twyman, 31.2. Twyman would become a color commentator for NBA games on ABC and continue to serve as the brain-injured Maurice Stokes' legal guardian.

With the departure of Embry, coach Jack McMahon promoted Connie Dierking to starting center with draft pick 6'11" Walt Wesley out of the University of Kansas backing him up.

The 1966–67 Royals immediately dug themselves into a hole, losing nine out of the first fourteen games. But they picked up steam at the end of the season winning seven out of the last ten games to finish in third place in the Eastern Division with a record of 39–42, a record good enough to make the playoffs. But in the Eastern Division Semi-Finals, the Philadelphia Warriors defeated the Royals 3 games to 1. It would be the last time that the Cincinnati Royals would make the playoffs.

While Oscar Robertson averaged 30.5 points per game, it would be the last season in his spectacular career that he would finish with a scoring average of over 30 points per game.

The Royals had drawn 4,755 fans per home game in the season, a 25% decline below the previous season, but their home schedule was limited. Before the season had begun, Louie Jacobs had arranged for some of the Royals' home games to be played in other cities. Cleveland Browns owner Art Modell agreed to sponsor nine Royals home games at the Cleveland Arena. The crowds at Royals games in Cleveland were consistently among the largest in the season and the NBA took notice. In addition to Cleveland, the barnstorming Royals also played games on neutral courts in Dayton, Kansas City, Pittsburgh, Memphis, Syracuse, and New York at Madison Square Garden vs. the Detroit Pistons.

On March 19, 1967, Jack McMahon resigned as coach of the Royals and was hired as coach and general manager of the expansion San Diego Rockets scheduled to join the NBA in 1967–68 along with the Seattle Supersonics.

As he stepped out the door, Jack McMahon didn't burn any bridges and said that everyone had been nice to him in the Royals organization and let him run the team. But no doubt he had felt tremendous pressure in coaching the Royals with the constant rumors that he would be fired.

"Every year here it was the same story," said McMahon. "Even in the first year when we set every kind of record, there were rumors I was out." In regard to his difficulties with veteran players such as Jack Twyman and Wayne Embry, he remarked that being a coach is not a friendship business, "Somebody had to be the boss and make decisions. Jack [Twyman] felt he could play 40 to 45 minutes effectively at both ends and I didn't. Everybody thinks they can play 48 minutes, and if they didn't feel that way, they wouldn't be a great player."[4]

Prior to the 1966–67 season, the Baltimore Bullets moved to the Eastern Division as the NBA returned to Chicago for a third try and the expansion Chicago Bulls were placed in the Western Division. With ten teams now in the NBA, the playoff format was changed to include eight teams playing two semi-finals in each division, a division final with the winners, and the championship final between the two division final winners.

In the Eastern Division Semi-Finals, Philadelphia had defeated Cincinnati, and then the Boston Celtics defeated the New York Knicks who had finished in 4th place in the East and after a seven-year absence made it back to the playoffs.

In the Eastern Division Finals, Philadelphia dethroned Boston as perennial champions, knocking off the Celtics 4 games to 1, making it the first time they had not made it to the championship finals since 1957.

By 1967, NBA playoffs games were still getting bumped. The first game of the series in Philadelphia had to be moved to the Palestra because a circus had been booked in Convention Hall. Nonetheless, the 76ers went on to take a commanding 3 games to 0 lead in the series. Beating the Celtics and Bill Russell had been Wilt Chamberlain's goal since he began to play in the NBA, and now he was just one game away.

After the Celtics finally rebounded to win game four in Boston, they returned to Philadelphia and were quickly beaten by the 76ers 140–116 and their over-zealous fans who, in the 4th period, pelted them with eggs, fruit, and coins while shouting, "Boston is dead!"

Following the game, after spending a few minutes in the Celtics locker room, Bill Russell, gracious in defeat, went to the 76ers locker room and offered his congratulations to Wilt Chamberlain.

The 76ers then defeated the San Francisco Warriors, 4 games to 1, despite a high scoring effort by Rick Barry, to take the 1967 NBA title.

In the 1966–67 collegiate season, Bob Cousy's Boston College team was ranked number 9 in the nation by AP. This was a tough bunch of Golden Eagles that went to the Sugar Bowl Classic in New Orleans and after narrowly losing to Utah 90–88, beat Tennessee 68–61 to leave town 9–1. Leading the way for BC was senior and team captain Willie Wolters, who would finish his career at BC as the all-time leading rebounder, along with Steve Adelman, scoring 18.9 points per game, and Terry Driscoll, 13.7, both who were being set up by Billy Evans on his way to becoming BC's all-time assists leader.

Boston College finished the regular season with a record of 19–2 and received a bid to the NCAA tournament. In the opening round, they defeated Connecticut, 48–42, and then moved on to the Eastern Regional Finals in College Park, Maryland and defeated St. Johns 63–62. But the next night Cousy attempted to have his team run against a bigger and faster North Carolina team, and BC was defeated 90–86 to finish the season with a record of 21–3. If Boston College had won, they would have reached the 1967 Final Four, along with UCLA, Dayton, and Houston, playing for the National Championship.

In 1952, Bob Cousy had bought half ownership in 500 acres of woodland called Camp Graylag in Pittsfield, New Hampshire. The property was converted into a basketball camp that Cousy continued to successfully operate until 1971.

During the summer of 1967, Cousy was at his basketball camp when he got a call from a writer from *LIFE* magazine by the name of Sandy Smith. He told Cousy he was doing an article on basketball and wanted to interview him. So Cousy told Smith to come on up to Graylag.

But when Smith arrived, he revealed a hidden agenda; he wasn't there to interview Cousy about basketball, but rather his alleged associations with gamblers. Rather than show Smith the door Cousy spoke to him in generalizations of how he had always attempted to avoid gamblers. In his book, *The Killer Instinct,* Cousy said he told Smith that one year he and Red Auerbach had tried a mock gambling exercise attempting to pick the winner of each game on the NBA schedule. As it turned out, they were wrong much more than right and if they had actually been placing bets, they would have lost their shirts.

On September 8, 1967, *LIFE* was on the newsstands with the article that Smith had contributed to: "The Mob—Part 2, $7 Billion from Illegal Bets and a Blight on Sports." Cousy nearly had a nervous breakdown when he saw it! The article accused him of having close friendships with an organized crime figure and a gambler.

The article stated that on January 8, 1966, the FBI had arrested Gilbert Beckley of Miami, and on that day, he had handled bets of $250,000 and made a profit of $129,000. Beckley had kept a black book, and when police began to peruse it, they found next to a telephone number the word "Skiball," the nickname for Francesco Scibelli, a Genovese Crime Family member that ran a gambling syndicate in Springfield, Massachusetts. Scribbled next to "Skiball" was the name of Bob Cousy.

LIFE stated that when Cousy had been interviewed he denied knowing Beckley, but admitted that Scibelli was a friend whom he met through an even closer friend, Andrew Pradella. It was further stated in the article that Pradella was Scibelli's partner in bookmaking, and the two were known in gambling circles in the northeast to always have very good information—earning their name in gambling circles as the "Scholar Group."

It was alleged by *LIFE* that Cousy admitted that he knew the two were gamblers. He often talked to them about both professional and college basketball teams and their chances of winning. The article quoted Cousy as saying, "I'd be having dinner with Pradella when Scibelli would come over. They [Pradella and Scibelli] got together each night to balance the books or something." But he never considered that the two were using what he told them to fix betting lines and make smart bets on their own. "I thought they figured the betting line with mathematics. But it doesn't surprise me. I'm pretty cynical. I think most people who approach me want to use me in some way."[5]

The article even went as far to state that Pradella had invited Cousy to a banquet in Hartford that turned out to be a gangster conclave and that was being watched closely by the police.

In his book, Cousy states that he never told Sandy Smith that the mob was at the banquet that he described as a gangster conclave. According to Cousy, the event had been for a retired fighter who had been active in youth work in Hartford. He stated, "I had sat at the head table with two well-known 'gangsters', Willie Pep [former featherweight champion] and the late Rocky Marciano [retired heavyweight champion]."[6] Later, Howard Cosell told Cousy that he, too, had been invited to the banquet.

Lastly, Cousy was quoted in the article as saying the whole thing was hypocritical, "I don't see why I should stop seeing my friends just because they are gamblers. What should I tell Andy when he calls and asks about a team? That I won't talk to him about that?"[7]

Bob Cousy wasn't the only athlete mentioned in the *LIFE* article. It was also mentioned that Boston (New England) Patriots quarterback Babe Parilli and other members of the team frequented a store called Arthur's Farm in Revere, Massachusetts, allegedly visited by mafia types. Later, Bob Cousy's name would surface as also having frequented Arthur's Farm in a U.S. House Committee hearing.

More on that allegation would come to light through the testimony of Joseph Barboza (AKA Joe Baron) on May 24, 1972, in front of the U.S. House of Representatives Select Committee on Crime. Barboza was a former member of the Patriarca mob in Rhode Island and Massachusetts. As a result of a mob hit on one of his friends, Barboza broke with the mob and testified against racketeers.

During the House hearings, Associate Counsel Chris Nolde inquired of Barboza what Arthur's Farm was. Barboza stated that it was a meeting place for Mafia types and an outlet for stolen merchandise. "It was a vegetable store. Primarily a vegetable store," stated Barboza. "He also had clothes in there that were hot clothes." Then, Nolde asked what kind of people went there. Barboza replied, "Henry Tameleo [New England Mafia underboss] hung out a lot when he wasn't at the Ebb Tide and conducted a lot of business in there with a lot of racket guys he would meet in there. I was there one time when Bob Cousy from the Celtics came in, and Babe Parilli came in, and Gene Conley [Boston/ Milwaukee Braves, Philadelphia Phillies, Boston Red Sox pitcher, and Boston Celtics player], and went in back of the vegetable store, in the clothes section."[8] According to Barboza, half the Boston Patriots team frequented the place.

The *LIFE* article had devastated Cousy. He wasn't naïve. He had been playing professional basketball when the college point-shaving scandals broke in the early 1950s and when Jack Molinas of the Ft. Wayne Pistons was banned by the NBA for consorting with gamblers. He knew a gambler when he saw one. It boggles the mind that he could be so totally unaware of the company he was keeping.

Dave Anderson, a long-time sports columnist for the *New York Times* and a Holy Cross graduate, class of 1951, was a friend of Cousy's. According to Anderson,

Off the court, Bob always had a sense of who he is and where he is. Late in his Celtics career, I remember visiting him in the old Paramount Hotel in midtown Manhattan before a game against the Knicks. He had a sore leg that was limiting his playing time, and as we walked to the Garden that evening, several men huddled in Eighth Avenue doorways recognized him and asked, "How you feeling, Cooz?" or "You gonna play, Cooz?" He never even looked at them, much less answered them.

"Don't you say hello to your fans?" I asked.

"They're not fans," he said. "They're bettors."

The Cooz wasn't about to tip street-corner bettors to how his leg felt, good or bad.[9]

Against the advice of friends, who told him to ignore the *LIFE* article, Cousy immediately called a press conference in hopes of setting the record straight.

On September 8, Cousy held an emotional, tear-filled, seventy-minute news conference. Sobbing at times, Cousy said he had met Andrew Pradella when his son attended his summer basketball camp from 1954 to 1964. He and Pradella had played golf together, and he had no evidence he was a gambler. Cousy said that Pradella never tried to capitalize on their friendship in any way. Still, he acknowledged that he had been told four years ago by Edward McNamara, Boston Police Commissioner, that an investigation of gambling in Massachusetts was underway. He was told Pradella was involved in the investigation. "I suppose I'm guilty of indiscretion," Cousy admitted. "But I'm not guilty of anything else. If you're guilty of something or have something to hide, you're evasive, and I don't sneak around."[10]

When Cousy got home to Worcester that evening he was so distraught that a doctor gave him a sedative.

Meanwhile, at Boston College, Athletic Director Bill Flynn was standing behind his man. "We feel the same as we always have about Bob Cousy," said Flynn. "This is a very unfortunate situation. I can't speak for everyone at the college, but I believe in him."[11]

What was done was done. Cousy was still the Boston College coach and his reputation and his team's reputation had to be kept squeaky clean, he had to operate in the game without a hint of corruption and there was no longer any room for mistakes that would impinge on his character.

At that time, everything was on the up in Boston College basketball and would remain that way through Bob Cousy's tenure as coach, however, just a little over a decade later, a point-shaving scandal would take place at BC.

In Nicolas Pileggi's book, *Wise Guy,* published in the mid-1980s, it was brought to light that Henry Hill, a Lucchese crime family associate, had bought Golden Eagles players to fix games in 1978–79. In 1990, the movie *Goodfellas* with Ray Liotta playing the part of Henry Hill, based on Pileggi's book, was released and became one of the most popular mob pictures of all time.

Regardless of the controversy that had surrounded Coach Cousy, the 1967–68 Boston College Golden Eagles finished with a record of 17–8. Although they failed to win 20 games for the first time in four years, the Golden Eagles ware still considered the best team in New England, and at one time during the season were ranked 6th in the nation in the AP poll. Terry Driscoll, now a junior, had another fine season, finishing with an average of 17.8 points per game. Boston College was invited to play in the 1968 NCAA Tournament but lost in the first round to St. Bonaventure, 102–93.

On May 2, 1967, the Cincinnati Royals hired former University of Cincinnati head basketball coach Ed Jucker as their new coach at a salary of $22,000 a year, replacing Jack McMahon.

Ed Jucker had served seven years as an assistant coach at the University of Cincinnati, his alma mater. He became head coach of the Bearcats beginning in 1960–61, a year after Oscar Robertson had graduated.

Jucker abandoned the successful racehorse offense employed by his predecessor George Smith for an emphasis on defense. His first Bearcat team started with a 5–3 record. Then, they won 22 consecutive games, culminating with a 70–65 overtime victory over Ohio State and Jerry Lucas in the National Championship Final. The next season, UC extended its winning streak to 37 games and went on to defeat Ohio State again, 71–59, in the 1962 NCAA Tournament for their second consecutive national title.

The following season, Cincinnati, ranked No. 1 in the nation in defense and the final AP poll, met Loyola of Chicago in the NCAA Final. The Bearcats led Loyola by 15 points with 14 minutes left in the game, only to lose in overtime, 60–58.

After two more seasons, Ed Jucker resigned, saying the pressure of being the Bearcats head coach was affecting his health and his family.

A lesser known fact about Ed Jucker's tenure at the University of Cincinnati is that he was both Sandy Koufax's college basketball coach and baseball coach. After graduating from Lafayette High School in Brooklyn, Sandy Koufax came to the University of Cincinnati on a basketball scholarship in the fall of 1953. At the time, Ed Jucker was coach of the freshman basketball team at UC. So, Koufax played freshman basketball for him in the 1953–54 season.

Jucker was also the head coach of the Cincinnati Bearcats baseball team and invited Koufax to try out for the squad. "I didn't even know he could pitch," said Jucker. "At the end of the basketball season, he told me to come over to the gym to take a look at him. I was amazed. It was almost like the wonder man. It struck me in such a fashion. The way he could throw—the speed and the curve—you just didn't see that."[12]

Koufax threw so hard that only one teammate could catch him: Danny Gilbert. That spring, Koufax had a record of 3–1 and in a game against Louisville, he had 18 strikeouts. For the season, he had 51 strikeouts in 31 innings.

While Koufax was having some trouble getting the ball over the plate, that did not preclude major league scouts from pursuing him. Ed Jucker recommended Koufax to the hometown Cincinnati Reds, but they turned him down. But scouts knew his potential with his 90 mph plus fastball, and the Brooklyn Dodgers and Pittsburgh Pirates wanted him. Bill Zinser, a Cincinnati native working for Brooklyn as a scout, signed Koufax to a $14,000 bonus contract with his hometown Dodgers.

The unfortunate aspect of this situation is that while the sporting world would find out how great a pitcher Sandy Koufax was, winning three Cy Young Awards and throwing four no-hitters on his way to the National Baseball Hall of Fame, we will never know how good a basketball player he may have become.

In the coming 1967–68 season, the NBA was about to be confronted with some serious competition from a start-up rival, the newly formed American Basketball Association (ABA). The league consisted of ten teams in two divisions. In the East were the Pittsburgh Pipers, Minnesota Muskies, Indiana Pacers, Kentucky Colonels, and New Jersey Americans. The West Division consisted of the New Orleans Buccaneers, Dallas Chaparrals, Houston Mavericks, Anaheim Amigos, and Oakland Oaks.

The new league had tried to lure away many of the NBA's biggest stars. In fact, the Indiana Pacers, who were going to be coached by former Cincinnati Royals and Villa Madonna College (Thomas Moore) player Larry Staverman, attempted to sign Oscar Robertson. Nonetheless, the Royals number one draft pick, Mel Daniels, was signed by the Minnesota Muskies.

The NBA would counter the ABA by adding two new expansion teams for 1967–68, the San Diego Rockets and the Seattle Supersonics.

The only coaching Ed Jucker had done since resigning at the University of Cincinnati in 1965 had been during the previous summer when he coached the Spanish national team. But he had been offered the head coaching job of both the Oakland Oaks and Indiana Pacers in the ABA.

During his time at Cincinnati, Jucker had developed his style of play to compliment the skills of his players, deliberately slowing the pace of the game down, and it worked. But the NBA game was fast-paced and everyone felt it was going to be interesting to see how Jucker would adapt to coaching in the pros.

As it turned out, the Royals under Ed Jucker were a running team averaging 116.6 points per game. The Royals scored over 130 points in 13 games. On November 28, the Royals defeated the Seattle Supersonics, 153–133.

Oscar Robertson led the NBA in scoring with an average of 29.2 points per game and assists with 9.7 per game, despite the fact he had missed part of training camp due to a contract dispute, then pulled a hamstring the first week of the season that continued to flare up all season long, taking him in and out of the lineup.

Jerry Lucas had a fine season, too, averaging 21.5 points and 19 rebounds per game.

But the Royals were not a winning team, finishing in fifth place in the Eastern Division with a record of 39–43, not good enough for a playoff berth.

Missing the playoffs bothered the players and they were not satisfied with Ed Jucker as coach.

According to Jerry Lucas, "Ed Jucker was out of his element."[13]

Oscar Robertson had a broader view of Jucker. "Ed Jucker was a college coach at heart, but that rah-rah stuff doesn't work in the pros. He used to tell us to go out and make things hurt a little bit," said Robertson. "He regularly forgot names in the huddle. He once forgot Wilt Chamberlain's name, instead telling us to stop the big kid."[14]

After a one-year absence, the 1967–68 NBA championship returned Boston after the Celtics defeated the Los Angeles Lakers 4 games to 2 in the finals. Bill Russell became the first black head coach to lead a major professional sports team to a title.

Cincinnati Royals owner Louie Jacobs was a workaholic. He never took vacations. He often told people the same sun that shines in Rome shines in Buffalo. Louie had told Cincinnati Reds owner Bill DeWitt, Sr. that he intended to die at his desk. At 10 A.M. one day in early 1968, that is exactly what happened.

With Louie's demise, the torch of the Emprise holdings was passed to his two sons. Jeremy, 28 years old, became president of Emprise and his son Max, 31 years old, became executive vice-president and chairman of the board of the Cincinnati Royals.

Prior to 1968–69, the NBA again added two more expansion teams, the Milwaukee Bucks in the East and the Phoenix Suns in the West, and the league now consisted of 14 teams.

On July 9, the Philadelphia Warriors traded Wilt Chamberlain to the Los Angeles Lakers for Darrall Imhoff, Jerry Chambers, and Archie Clark.

The ABA wouldn't go away, and prior the 1968–69 season, the Anaheim Amigos moved to Los Angeles and changed their name to the Stars. When the Stars learned that Wilt Chamberlain was coming back to the west coast, they attempted to sign him, but when he asked for a contract calling for a million dollars, they declined. Chamberlain signed a four-year contract with the Lakers calling for $250,000 a year.

So, with Chamberlain back in the Western Division, conceivably the Royals had one less obstacle in their way in making the playoffs in the Eastern Division in 1968–69.

Once again Oscar Robertson had a fine season. He finished fifth in the league in scoring with an average of 24.7 points per game and once again led the league in assists with 9.8 per game.

On the evening of February 17, at Cincinnati Gardens a sparse crowd of 3,922 fans saw The Big O break Bob Cousy's career assists record in a 125–113 loss to the Phoenix Suns. Robertson had 8 assists in the game which pushed his career total for nine seasons to 6,955. Bob Cousy had 6,949 assists for thirteen seasons with the Boston Celtics.

Jerry Lucas had another stellar season, finishing fourth in rebounds with 18.4 per game and averaged 18.3 points per game.

But for the second straight year, the Cincinnati Royals missed the playoffs and once again finished fifth in the Eastern Division with a record of 41–41.

While the Royals' points per game were slightly down from the previous season (116.6 to 114.5), there was a pretty good cast of players supporting Robertson and Lucas. Tom Van Arsdale averaged 19.4 points per game and aging center Connie Dierking contributed 16.2. Overall, the Royals had seven players that finished in double digits in points per game and Adrian Smith missed finishing in double digits by a fraction of a percentage point.

The Royals had only won half of their games and it seemed to most observers that with two future Hall of Fame players, The Big O and Jerry Lucas, playing great ball, the two could have won that many games surrounded by a roster made up of a bunch of college benchwarmers. So what went wrong?

The fact was that the NBA Eastern Division was getting stronger. The Boston Celtics had basically the same team they won the championship with the year before but finished in fourth place in 1968–69.

The Baltimore Bullets, led by NBA MVP Wes Unseld, Earl Monroe, Bob Quick, and Gus Johnson, won the Eastern Division. The Philadelphia 76ers, without Wilt Chamberlain, finished second. The New York Knicks, who were steadily building a formidable roster player by player in the late 1960s with Willis Reed, Dave Debusschere, Phil Jackson, Cazzie Russell, Walt Frazier, and Bill Bradley, finished in third place.

But the Boston Celtics surprised everyone when they eliminated the Knicks 4 games to 2 in the Division Semi-Finals, then downed the 76ers 4 games to 1 in the Division Finals.

Boston then met the Los Angeles Lakers in the championship series. The series was hard fought and went to a seventh game in Los Angeles. Then, the Celtics got a little extra motivation from Lakers owner Jack Kent Cooke who was so sure of winning the championship that he had balloons suspended from the ceiling of the Forum. Then he issued a memo detailing a victory celebration that would follow Game 7. When Bill Russell and John Havlicek got hold of a copy of the memo, they used it to rally the Celtics.

The Celtics defeated the Lakers 108–106 in Game 7 and the balloons were confined to the rafters of the Forum as Boston won the 1969 NBA championship 4 games to 3.

While Jerry West scored 42 points, had 13 rebounds, and 12 assists in Game 7, the Lakers beat themselves hitting only 28 of 47 free throws. Wilt Chamberlain, who had a huge reputation for being a poor free throw shooter, hit only 4 of 13 shots from the charity stripe.

Jerry West was named the series MVP, the first and only time a player on the championship finals losing team has been honored as such. But the balloon folly upset Jerry West greatly and damaged the relationship between Cooke and himself. A couple of years later, Jerry West's relationship with the Lakers' owner would deteriorate further when he discovered that Cooke had lied to him when he said that he and Wilt Chamberlain were making the same salary—$250,000. The fact was that there was a side agreement between Cooke and Chamberlain where he was getting his money tax free.

For the Boston Celtics, it was their eleventh NBA championship in thirteen years. Bill Russell, with more championship rings than fingers, retired and like Bob Cousy went out on top.

Another odd twist of fate in the final game of the 1969 championship series was that it would result in a split in the longstanding friendship between Bill Russell and Wilt Chamberlain. Most persons familiar with the circumstances surrounding the split blame it on Russell.

Often when the Celtics would play Wilt's team, whether it be the Warriors, 76ers, or Lakers, Russell would have dinner with Chamberlain prior to the game. He did the same with Oscar Robertson. In fact, when the Celtics were in Cincinnati, often The Big O's wife, Yvonne, would cook dinner for them. Then, Russell and Chamberlain or Russell and Robertson would take the court and try to exhaust each other. Bill Russell never liked the term rival, preferring instead to refer to opposing players as competitors. What Russell liked about Wilt Chamberlain was that he pushed him to the hilt when he played against him.

Russell became upset with Chamberlain when he sat out the final five minutes of game seven of the 1969 NBA Finals—his last game in the NBA. Albeit no one knew that this was Bill Russell's last game; he hadn't even told Red Auerbach. What happened was that Chamberlain had mentioned to Lakers coach Butch van Breda Kolff that he had sustained an injury. While Chamberlain wanted to go back in the game, van Breda Kolff was totally against it and as competitive or masochistic as it may appear, Bill Russell never forgave Wilt Chamberlain for not taking it to him on the court until the end.

For the record, when Chamberlain left the game, he had 27 rebounds. Bill Russell played five minutes longer in the game than Chamberlain and finished with 21 rebounds.

In Cincinnati, Ed Jucker was feeling the heat from the press, fans, and front office for the Royals' dismal season—so on May 9, he resigned as head coach.

Ed Jucker would eventually return to the college ranks in 1972, becoming head coach at Rollins College in Winter Park, Florida. In Jucker's second year, the Rollins College Tars finished 18–9 and received their first-ever berth in the NCAA Tournament.

Before the 1968–69 college season began, Bob Cousy quietly informed Boston College Athletic Director Bill Flynn that this would be his last season. On the record, Cousy was stating that he had enjoyed his time at Boston College, but he had other options and had begun to consider them.

But off the record, Cousy felt that at some point in time coaching had become a dehumanizing process. Like Ed Jucker, Cousy was starting to feel the pressure of college coaching and the need to win every game. Cousy had lost a recruit because the player had attended his basketball camp between his junior and senior years in high school which, in the wisdom of the NCAA, constituted a violation because it gave Boston College an unfair advantage in signing him. Cousy was frustrated with the NCAA that enforced minuscule regulations while turning a blind eye to academic standards. He was proud that every player he had recruited for BC had earned their degree, and that after they left school, he maintained relationships with them. On the other hand, it bothered him that a lot of players at other schools finished their eligibility and were immediately forgotten by those that had recruited them.

It was also very apparent that the *LIFE* magazine article accusing Cousy of associating with Mafia members and point-spreads in basketball had greatly influenced his decision to quit.

Cousy's resignation was kept under wraps until January 20, 1969. At the time, the Golden Eagles were 10–3 and going forward they didn't lose another game in the regular season. At that point, Cousy's record at BC for 5½ years was 101–37, and the Golden Eagles had participated in four post-season tournaments.

In his official announcement, Bob Cousy said he was leaving Boston College to devote his time primarily to his boys' basketball camp and the public relations work he had been doing for three companies, including the one that manufactured his basketball shoes. He was also modeling sports clothes.

But Cousy also approached the press with some bitterness about leaving coaching. "You get a kid to come to your school nowadays by licking his boots," said Cousy. "It's an unhealthy situation. Once you have committed yourself to begging him to come, there can never be a player-coach relationship. The kid is the boss."[15] He added that fortunately for him, coaching at Boston College had been a part-time job. He didn't need the money to support his family.

Still, Cousy kept the door slightly ajar, indicating that he expected to be back in basketball in some capacity. While only a few years ago he had turned down the Boston Celtics head coaching job, he suggested he would reconsider a professional coaching job if the offer was substantial, but not at the expense of displacing an existing coach.

BC athletic director Bill Flynn told the press, "Cousy's departure would mark the end of the finest basketball era ever at the heights."[16]

In the last home game that Bob Cousy would coach, before a packed house of 4,500, Terry Driscoll scored 28 points and grabbed 17 rebounds as Boston College upset NCAA-bound and 9th ranked Duquesne, 93–72. It was BC's 16th straight victory.

Senior forward Terry Driscoll was having the best year in his Boston College career averaging 23.3 points per game and was the third leading rebounder in the nation.

Boston College finished the regular season 21–3, ranked 16th in the final AP poll. Now Bob Cousy would close out his college coaching career in the NIT at Madison Square Garden in his hometown of New York.

Boston College was a fine fast-break team and played reasonably well on defense, but the tallest player on the squad was 6'7" Terry Driscoll. The three losses that BC had during the season where against St. Johns, Villanova, and Northwestern, all three which had very big, bruising players up front.

In the first round of the NIT, Boston College faced Kansas. Going up against the Jayhawks, the Golden Eagles were at a distinct disadvantage in height. The Jayhawks' front line consisted of 6'10" center Roger Brown, 6'8" forward Gregg Douglas, and 6'9" forward Dave Robisch. In addition, they had 6'3" guard JoJo White, who averaged 18.1 points per game.

But the Golden Eagles were determined to give Bob Cousy a glorious send-off. BC quickly discovered that while Kansas was taller and stronger, they were slower. So Cousy used a fast-break offense to take a 58–44 lead with 12 minutes left in the game. But when Terry Driscoll fouled out, it left BC completely vulnerable underneath the basket, and Cousy pulled a page out of Ed Jucker's playbook that he had used at Cincinnati to defeat Ohio State twice for the NCAA championship, telling his players to stall the ball and force the Jayhawks to come out and get it.

But Kansas didn't budge, and as BC guards Billy Evans and Jim O'Brien dribbled away minutes on the clock, the crowd at Madison Square Garden began to boo. With the clock running down, Kansas finally went after the ball and began to foul. It was too late, and Boston College won the game 78–62.

Bob Cousy had been a fast-break player and coach during his entire basketball life and his use of the stall really annoyed some people, including the Jayhawks' coach Ted Owens who immediately advocated a 30-second shot clock for college basketball.

Next up for Boston College in the quarterfinals was Louisville who they had beat in a memorable triple-overtime game in the 1966 NIT. The game turned out to be a wild one with two ejections and a fight. The Gardens crowd of 12,605 screamed and yelled and loved every moment of it. The tempo of the game had been fast-paced and very determined by both teams.

With 16 minutes left to go, the score was tied at 50–50 when two reserves, Ed Lionis of Louisville and Vince Costello of Boston College, started slugging it out under the basket after a fast-break play. Both players were ejected, and each team was awarded two technical free throws.

With 22 seconds left, the winner was still in doubt with Boston College leading 83–79. But thanks to a great game by Terry Driscoll, who had 29 points and 22 rebounds, the Golden Eagles survived to defeat the Cardinals 88–83.

The game had been such an emotional affair for Billy Evans, who had tied an NIT assists record with 13, that at the final buzzer he broke down in tears. It was the 18th straight victory for Boston College.

Bob Cousy was very aware that both Kansas and Louisville, the two teams his Golden Eagles had just beaten, were superior to his team and the driving force behind the Boston College team's hyper-motivation was, "let's win for Cooz and send him out in a blaze of glory." Cousy's team wanted to do for him what St. Johns had done for legendary coach Joe Lapchick, giving him a going away present by defeating Villanova in the 1965 NIT.

Boston College moved on to the semi-finals against Army, coached by future iconic Indiana coach Bobby Knight, who had defeated South Carolina 59–45.

Cousy decided to scrap his man-to-man defense and use a zone defense and, in effect, play Army's game. After leading at halftime, 42–40, Boston College shot an incredible 80% in the second half, led by Ray LaGace, who came off the BC bench and scored four crucial shots to defeat Army 73–61. Once again, Terry Driscoll led the Golden Eagles in scoring with 28 points, and he now had a three-game total in the tournament of 78.

In the other semi-final, Temple, coached the last 17 years by silvered-haired Harry Litwack, overcame a five-point deficit with six minutes left to defeat Tennessee 63–58 to set up the first all-Eastern NIT Final in four years.

A huge crowd of 17,437 was present for the NIT Final and to give Bob Cousy his send-off, and millions of others watched on TV. But it was Temple that played like their coach Harry Litwack was retiring as the Owls spoiled the Garden party for Cousy, defeating Boston College 89–76 and ending their 19-game winning streak while forcing 13 BC turnovers.

It was 6'5" senior John Baum, who had been recruited by Harry Litwack after he saw him play for a business college in Philadelphia, that led the way for Temple, scoring 30 points as the Owls dominated the Golden Eagles under the basket.

Terry Driscoll scored 18 points and had 16 rebounds for Boston College. Driscoll had scored 96 points in the tournament and was named MVP. Following the game, Driscoll sat in the Boston College dressing room with a towel over his head with tears in his eyes.

Terry Driscoll would be taken in the first round of the 1969 NBA draft by the Detroit Pistons and subsequently play seven years in the league with Detroit, Baltimore, and Milwaukee, then play one year in the ABA with St. Louis and close out his career by playing one year in Italy.

At the final buzzer, there were tears everywhere in Madison Square Garden, tears for the Temple Owls and Harry Litwack, tears for Boston College, and tears for Bob Cousy. When Cousy was called out to center court to accept the NIT second place award, the crowd gave him one last huge roar and Cousy began to weep. Even BC cheerleading captain Jane Egan was crying. “We wanted so much to win for Cooz,” she said.[17]

In the middle of the postgame awards ceremony, the entire Temple Owls team walked over to the Boston College bench and shook hands with Bob Cousy.

Then, Cousy walked to the Boston College dressing room and stood outside the entrance addressing reporters. He praised his team and commented on Terry Driscoll’s future in pro basketball. When asked if he might coach a professional team next season, he stated that he doubted it. But he added, “I have two NBA appointments and one with Arthur Brown who owns the New York Nets in the other league. I’ll have lunch with all of them and there will probably be luncheon dates with plenty more people in pro basketball. I never turn down a free lunch.”[18]

Bob Cousy was followed by Chuck Daly as coach at Boston College, but immediately the program began to experience a downturn in winning. After two unsuccessful seasons, Daly left to accept the head coaching position at the University of Pennsylvania.

11

No Room in Cincy for Cooz and The Big O

After starting 20–9, the 1968–69 Cincinnati Royals finished with a record of 41–41. Ed Jucker had used a laissez-faire approach to coaching the Royals. Players had a lot of freedom to do want they wanted. They voted on what time practice would start and, on the road, moved from city to city separately or in small groups. Often, players cut by Jucker were informed by the team trainer. There were cliques among the players, and around the league, the Royals' scouting and draft procedures were considered laughable.

In Buffalo, Max Jacobs was getting antsy. Unlike his late father Louis, Max Jacobs was just as interested in winning as he was in selling hotdogs in Cincinnati Gardens. With more money coming in from the deal the NBA had signed with ABC in 1964, player's salaries were increasing and so was fan interest, and the value of NBA franchises was on the rise. Jacobs was keenly aware of the fact that in 1965 Bob Short had sold the Los Angeles Lakers to Jack Kent Cooke for $5,175,000, and more recently, Marjorie Brown and minority owner Lou Pieri had sold the Boston Celtics for $3,000,000.

In 1968–69, the Royals had drawn an average of 4,065 fans per home game. Max Jacobs was confronted with a team that was underachieving with fan interest slipping year-by-year in the Queen City and facing a challenge from the ABA that was not to be taken lightly. The ABA Indiana Pacers, located 100 miles west from Cincinnati, were outdrawing the Royals, Jacobs needed to make changes.

In early May 1969, although he had a year remaining on his three-year contract, Ed Jucker, under pressure from owner Max Jacobs, resigned as coach of the Cincinnati Royals.

About the same time, Bob Cousy, who had resigned as coach at Boston College, entered into a cloak and dagger scenario using the code name "Emil Vudak" to negotiate with Max Jacobs for the vacant coaching job of the Cincinnati Royals.

In late March, while Bob Cousy was in New York coaching Boston College in the NIT, he received a telephone call from George Mikan, then commissioner of the ABA, asking if he would be interested in coaching the New York Nets. Cousy met with the Nets and they made an offer to him which he turned down.

Then, Cousy got a call from an editor for the *Boston Record-American* telling him to call Max Jacobs. At the time, he didn't know who Jacobs was, but when he learned that Max Jacobs, along with his brother Jeremy Jacobs, were the owners of the multi-million-dollar Emprise Corporation and also owned the Cincinnati Royals, he contacted him. Max met with Cousy in New York and Worcester, and at each meeting, he offered him more to take the Royals job. When Max raised the total of the compensation package to $100,000 a year for three years with the money being invested for him, Cousy came to the conclusion that if the market went up, he would be set financially for life.

Nonetheless, Cousy went to see Red Auerbach who advised him to wait as he thought Bill Russell might retire after the season, then he could have the Celtics job. But Cousy knew that in taking the Boston job there was only one place to go—down. The press would have been harsh in their criticism and the Celtics didn't need a "name coach." They already had all the prestige they could handle. Cousy thanked Red but decided he had to seriously consider the offer from Max Jacobs. He had a $100,000 offer and didn't have to make an immediate commitment, but after a few weeks of ruminating on the matter, Cousy contacted Jacobs and said yes.

Although Cousy and Jacobs had attempted to keep their negotiations secret, reporters were starting to follow up on leads. The day before Max Jacobs hired Cousy, he told a reporter from the *Cincinnati Post* that he had never met with Cousy and he anticipated that Ed Jucker would return as coach of the Royals.

On May 9, at a quickly arranged press conference in the Cincinnati Club ballroom with about fifty members of the media in attendance, Max Jacobs announced that Bob Cousy would be the new coach of the Cincinnati Royals. Max also apologized to the reporter he had misled saying that he was under pressure to get the negotiations completed.

Bob Cousy, along with his wife Missie and their youngest daughter Tricia, had flown into Cincinnati the night before and were all present for the formal announcement by Max Jacobs that Cousy had been hired.

Max Jacobs stated that hiring Bob Cousy was part of the program designed to revamp the Royals' image. When Jacobs was asked if trades were possible, he replied, "That as it applies to the players, is the business of Bob Cousy. That as it applies to the front office, is the business of Joe Axelson. I'm going to step back and get back to the rest of my business."[1]

In addition to Cousy, Jacobs also hired Joe Axelson to replace Pepper Wilson as Royals vice president and general manager. Axelson was born on Christmas Day, 1927, in Peoria, Illinois. He earned a bachelor's degree from Northwestern University in 1949, then joined the Army, serving in the Signal Corps, where he did some coaching. For the past ten years, Axelson had been employed at the collegiate level administering athletic programs for the National Association of Intercollegiate Athletics (NAIA).

Although Joe Axelson had no professional basketball experience, and Cousy, while one of the all-time great professional players, had no professional administrative experience, Max Jacobs granted them autonomy in making all decisions for the team.

It was a move by Max Jacobs that clearly exposed his lack of knowledge in running a professional sports team. At the very least, the Cousy-Axelson administration would require a learning curve, and that meant that major mistakes were highly possible.

Bob Cousy had maintained that when he retired from coaching at Boston College, he had no intention of returning to coaching. But when he started receiving offers from ABA and NBA teams, he reconsidered. That was his story and he was sticking to it. What Cousy failed to mention was that Max Jacobs had just made him the highest paid coach in professional basketball. While Cousy said that his salary was $100,000 a year, the press knew that Cousy had been given a sweetheart deal by Max Jacobs; the *New York Times* estimated that it was $150,000 a year and that in addition to high salary and stock options, he had been promised player-control and trade authority.

A lot of people were shaking their heads when informed of Cousy's hiring. It just didn't seem like a good fit. Bob Cousy, a lifelong easterner and pro basketball legend who probably could have had any job in the game back in the east that he wanted, suddenly packing up his family and coming to the edge of the Midwest to coach basketball. As it turned out, it was all about money and going forward, even Cousy would jest that he was overpaid. For those meager 4,000 but fiercely loyal Cincinnati Royals fans that still went through the turnstiles of Cincinnati Gardens, Cousy's arrival would be bad news in the making.

Both Oscar Robertson and Jerry Lucas were present at the news conference and expressed opinions on Cousy's hiring. Oscar Robertson reinforced that reasoning. "I had no idea whatsoever Bob would get this job," said Robertson. "With a person of his caliber, we ought to play to sell-out crowds next season."[2]

Jerry Lucas felt that as Bob Cousy was a former player, he would have an advantage as a coach over one without that experience.

The bottom line on Max Jacobs' reasoning for hiring Cousy was that with his name, he had the potential to attract fans for his sagging franchise.

The fallacy in Jacobs' reasoning was that he already had two of the biggest names in professional basketball playing on his team, Oscar Robertson and Jerry Lucas, and fans weren't knocking the doors down at Cincinnati Gardens to see the Royals play.

When Jacobs hired Cousy, there was immediate speculation as to how he would interact with his old NBA rival Oscar Robertson. Previously, the relationship between the two had been competitive, player vs. player. Now, with Cousy the coach and Robertson the player, that relationship would be asymmetric with Cousy in control, and some wondered if it would lead to conflict.

When asked how he thought he would interact with The Big O, Cousy gave a vague reply, "I haven't had that much exposure to him. I don't know how our personalities will blend. I do know every player who gives 100% can take advantage of me. Oscar has always shown me he's always done this."[3]

Oscar Robertson was of the opinion that all of his past rivalry on the court with Cousy was yesterday's news. It had been a professional relationship and he couldn't conceive of any grudges or issues carrying over from their playing days. What was there left for Cousy to prove? If anything, The Big O felt he and Cooz would be able to merge their skills and experience and the team would benefit greatly from the strategy they formed.

At that point in time, Robertson was concerned with the more recent decisions that the previous Royals management had made. He felt that Ed Jucker had lost control of the Royals and that the team lacked bench strength. Robertson also was critical of outgoing general manager Pepper Wilson's first round draft pick that had just occurred in April when he passed up former University of Cincinnati standout forward Rick Roberson in favor of guard Herm Gilliam of Purdue.

Robertson was also quick to point out that since he had joined the Royals in 1960–61 only two of their first-round draft picks had made the team—himself and Jerry Lucas.

But in retrospect, the shocking reality for Oscar Robertson was that he was about to experience with Bob Cousy the worst interaction he'd ever had with any coach in his career at any level; high school, college, or professional.

Cousy came to Cincinnati with a mindset that he had to recreate the Cincinnati Royals in the Boston Celtics image. In order to be a winner, the Royals needed to be a fast-break, running team with a hard-nosed defense like what he knew from his playing days in Boston. He wanted to keep all five men moving purposefully. In Oscar Robertson, he had the best middle-man in the game to accomplish it. Cousy also felt that the Royals needed to use their bench more.

Even today Jerry Lucas is quick to point out, "The Royals already had a fast break offense when Cousy took over as coach."[4] That was a fact, but they didn't use it much.

Under Ed Jucker, the Royals had used an offense that was slow and deliberate with a lot of picks and screens and a defense that had a tendency to slough off and concede outside shots to opponents in order to prevent layups. It was very similar to the game plan used by the Cincinnati Bearcats' George Smith when Jucker was an assistant coach.

But Oscar Robertson felt the Royals needed to run more. "I think that pro ball is all running," he said. "You're not going to be able to shoot jump shots all night and win. I think our style had been all wrong."[5]

It begged the question, where was Cousy going to go with the style of play he expected from the Royals? Critics of Cousy's intentions to remake the Royals' offense pointed out that he had two of the game's best men at handing off the ball to someone who can score—but who would that player be that could score at will?

The other part of Cousy's strategy was a continual focus on winning. "I told my college players unless they were ready to be sore losers, they should drop off the team," said Cousy. "But you've got to be able to reach your leaders. Oscar and Luke are the key guys. They're the best players. The guys respect them. It's as simple as that."[6]

Cousy had heard a rumor that Oscar Robertson and Jerry Lucas didn't get along. Both Robertson and Lucas were present for the news conference at the Cincinnati Club to announce Cousy as the new Royals coach. Cousy intended to immediately investigate the matter. He told Robertson and Lucas to meet him in a private room. There Cousy put it on the line, asking both Robertson and Lucas if there was any truth to the rumor of there being friction between the two of them. Each said they got along fine.

About six months after that meeting took place, Jerry Lucas remarked about it during an interview with Milton Richman of UPI. "Cousy had a meeting with Oscar and myself and said to us we'd be the key to anything that would happen in Cincinnati," said Lucas. "That's the way things began, but they deteriorated from that point."[7] Lucas went on to say that as soon as they got into training camp, Cousy decided he wanted a different type of play; he told management that it might take three years to get where he wanted to be and that he needed certain power to get there.

Bob Cousy brought with him an assistant coach by the name of Draff Young, a black man who had played college ball and with the Harlem Globetrotters. Cousy felt since the Royals would be the first team he had coached that had a majority of black players, that Young could function as a liaison between the black players and him, possibly advocating for issues that they might be reticent to discuss with a white coach. While it is more speculation than established fact, Young's primary role may have been to be an intermediary between Cousy and Robertson, who Cooz just didn't seem really comfortable being in a coach-player relationship with.

With a new general manager, coach, and assistant coach on board, Max Jacobs decided to spend some cash on a few upgrades at Cincinnati Gardens. The original scoreboard from 1949 was still being used. So, Max splurged on a new scoreboard that provided fans with player's totals for points scored and rebounds.

The previous season, there had been no radio coverage of Royals games. So, prior to the 1969–70 season, Max Jacobs sold the radio rights, and then one of Cousy's acquaintances from Boston, Dom Valentino, was hired to do play-by-play for the Royals over 50,000-watt WLW radio. Jacobs then began a campaign to increase the Royals' TV coverage, and Cousy agreed to make several pre-season appearances on TV and radio shows to promote the Royals.

On the first day of practice, Cousy demonstrated that he would be more of a drill sergeant than a coach. He accused veteran players of being out of shape and threatened those he felt were not working hard in practice. He seemed to be especially critical of Jerry Lucas. Cousy felt that Lucas was not giving all he had and quickly reached the conclusion that he was out of shape and too slow for his offense.

While Jerry Lucas is regarded as one of the game's all-time rebounders, he was a run-and-gun type player, who did not play like the power forwards in today's game who play above the rim. Although he made three first-team All-NBA teams and two second-teams in his first five years in the league (1964–1968), Cousy was critical of him.

Bob Cousy was of the opinion that Jerry Lucas lacked the fire in his belly necessary to become a great basketball player in the NBA—a superstar. He felt Lucas used only 80% of his massive individual ability and lacked the competitive spirit necessary to excel in an emotional game such as basketball. According to Cousy, "people with less talent could shut-off Lucas, nullify him and Lucas seemed unwilling or unable to get that other 20% out of himself to get by those people. Luke came to play basketball the way a lot of people go to the office: they punch in at nine, sip coffee and eye the clock, then leave promptly at five."[8]

It appeared to Cousy that Lucas was more interested in talking about his fast-food business than the Royals' fast breaks. Often, before a game, Lucas would be in the Royals locker room talking about business rather than basketball. That left a very poor taste in the coach's mouth. It was clear that Lucas' days as a Cincinnati Royal were numbered.

Jerry Lucas was a very good basketball player and an excellent, unselfish team player. But he was also a very intelligent person, and as much as he loved the game, he didn't see a need to live, breath, and die for it. Lucas had a broader agenda in life.

It's clear that Cousy's displeasure with Lucas was personal. Cousy's maligning of Lucas as a basketball player borders on the compulsive-obsessive when it is taken into account that in his book, *The Killer Instinct,* published a few years after he had quit coaching in the NBA, nine pages into the very first chapter, he cites Jerry Lucas as the poster boy for the epitome of a player that never used his full potential.

Jerry Lucas would not be the only Royals player that would be in Cousy's doghouse. During training camp in 1969, Walt Wesley was traded to Chicago for Norm Van Lier who had just been drafted by the Bulls out of St. Francis College (PA).

In an exhibition game against Chicago at Illinois State University, Norm Van Lier got into a fight with the Bulls' Jerry Sloan that became so fierce the two combatants rolled off the court into the halls of the arena and knocked over a popcorn maker. Meanwhile, while play continued at the other end of the court, the other players were looking for Van Lier and Sloan. Cousy was thrilled with the rookie Norm Van Lier's competitive nature and admired him more than any other player he had ever coached. Still, Van Lier would eventually fall into Cousy's disfavor and be traded back to the Chicago Bulls during the 1972 season.

It wouldn't be long before Cousy would start having problems with Oscar Robertson, who he would conclude had gained weight, slowed down, and was incapable of leading his fast-break offense for 48 minutes and without him, the team had a tendency to stall. He and Joe Axelson had decided that Norm Van Lier, just 22 years old, could take over the older Robertson's job of running the offense, and almost immediately The Big O was controlling the ball less. Cousy wanted Robertson to shoot less and pass more as he wanted to shift the emphasis of the Royals' offense from the guards to the front line.

Bob Cousy did inherit some serious competitive problems with the Royals, but he immediately created a problem by trading 6'11" Walt Wesley for Norm Van Lier. It left Jerry Lucas with his bad knees as the big man in the Royals forward wall, and after him, there wasn't much strength around or under the basket. So, it begged the question, who did Bob Cousy think was going to lead his fast-break offense or take all those passes from Robertson and Van Lier after he traded Walt Wesley?

The Royals' backup center was Cincinnati Gardens crowd sentimental favorite 33-year-old Connie Dierking. A former University of Cincinnati Bearcat, Dierking was a 12-year professional veteran, having played three years in the defunct ABL and nine in the NBA. While Dierking was 6'9", gutsy, capable of scoring, and gave everything he had, he was flatfooted, slow, and incapable of playing above the rim.

The NBA game was increasingly going above the rim and Connie Dierking, playing his early 1950s-style basketball, was going to be pitted against players in the middle, such as Lew Alcindor, Willis Reed, Zelmo Beaty, Elvin Hayes, Nate Thurmond, Luke Jackson, Wes Unseld, and Wilt Chamberlain; all younger men, bigger, stronger, and more agile.

Bob Cousy and Joe Axelson determined that the solution to the dilemma faced by the Royals upfront was to sign 6'5" veteran forward Johnny Green, who had just been cut by the Philadelphia 76ers. While Green could jump like he was four inches taller, he was 36 years old and incapable of playing 48 minutes any longer.

The NBA was looking towards its 24th season in 1969–70 with great anticipation of a banner year. A rookie superstar, Lew Alcindor, (soon to become Kareem Abdul-Jabbar), was about to start his career playing for the Milwaukee Bucks, and Connie Hawkins, an ABA All-Star who had been barred from playing in the NBA since 1962, had jumped leagues to join the Phoenix Suns.

In addition, the NBA continued to expand adding three new teams: the Cleveland Cavaliers, Buffalo Braves, and Portland Trailblazers, to make it a 14-team league.

Also, there were five new coaches, including Tom Heinsohn, who would be taking over for Bill Russell, who, after leading the Boston Celtics to their 11th NBA championship in 13 years, retired. Lenny Wilkins became player-coach at Seattle. In Los Angeles, after failing to win with Jerry West, Elgin Baylor, and Wilt Chamberlain, Butch van Breda Kolff hung it up and moved on to take the coaching job in Detroit. His was being replaced in LA by former Providence College coach Joe Mullaney. And, of course, Max Jacobs had thrown so much money at Bob Cousy that it forced him out of retirement to become coach of the Cincinnati Royals.

On September 13, with the season about a month away from starting, Bob Cousy surprised everyone when he announced his intention to seek permission to return as an active player for the Royals. Everyone was asking the same question—what the hell is going on with Cooz? Former Celtics teammate Frank Ramsey asked him if he was crazy. He was a middle-aged man with two teenage daughters, and if he would be successful in receiving permission from the Boston Celtics, who had him listed on their voluntary retired list, he would be the oldest player to ever play in the NBA at 41 years old.

Cousy explained that he would not be attempting to play half of a game or make a major contribution, but there were two reasons he wanted to be reactivated as a player. First, said Cousy, "There are certain changes I have to effect here—both defensive and along the lines of fast-breaking. I feel if I can somehow move up and down the court quickly enough, I can affect the changes more quickly—especially with the younger players."[9]

The second reason was that he was of the opinion that he could add to the box office appeal of the Royals both at home and on the road.

So Cousy had the romantic notion in his head that he could be "hands-on" while running up and down the court on his 41-year-old legs to teach Oscar Robertson, Jerry Lucas, Adrian Smith (all NBA All-Stars), and his other Royals how to play fast-break basketball, while at the same time, attracting scads of fans willing to pay to witness such a spectacle.

It was not only the stuff of pulp fiction but the epitome of egocentricity for Cousy to attempt to activate himself at 41 years old. If Boston simply agreed, which was unlikely, the Royals needed only to notify NBA commissioner Walter Kennedy of the move. But the reality was that seeking active status for Cousy came with consequences. Red Auerbach hadn't become some kind-hearted old fool! Cousy's former coach in Boston was now the Celtics' general manager and wanted compensation to release his name from the retired list.

The fact that Red Auerbach would want to be compensated by the Royals in such a matter had precedence, and Cousy should have been aware of it. Auerbach had attempted to pull the same trick in 1960 when Lakers owner Bob Short, who had just moved his team from Minneapolis to Los Angeles, inquired about the Celtics releasing Bill Sharman from his contract so that he could become coach of the Lakers. The deal fell apart when Auerbach demanded Jerry West, who had just been the Lakers number-one draft choice, be sent to Boston in the deal.

The deal would eventually be done when Royals general manager Joe Axelson sent some of Max Jacobs' cash to Boston and threw in a player for good measure, 26-year-old Bill Dinwiddie, a 6'7" forward who was recuperating from a knee operation.

However, the process had caused some hard feelings between Bob Cousy and his long-time friend Red Auerbach. It had taken eight weeks of posturing and back-and-forth bickering between the two to reach an agreement. While Cousy was attempting to convince Auerbach that his expected playing time of two minutes a game would really be promotional and that he didn't expect to make any significant contribution, Auerbach wasn't buying it. Auerbach was of the opinion that in those two minutes, Cousy could get the ball to Oscar Robertson for one shot that might win a game.

While waiting for resolution on his active status, on October 15, 1969, Bob Cousy made his NBA coaching debut at Madison Square Garden, losing to the New York Knicks, 89–94, before a small crowd of just under 6,000 fans.

The Royals then traveled to Boston to play Cousy's old Celtics team. A huge crowd of 13,755 turned out in Boston Garden to welcome Cooz home. Later, Cousy would say he was more nervous about this game than any in his career. The Royals were triumphant, 110–108, giving their coach his first win in the NBA.

At halftime, the Royals headed to the locker room with a 50–42 lead, only to see the Celtics, led by John Havlicek, score 39 points in the third quarter to take the lead, 81 to 75. But with two minutes remaining, jump shots by Oscar Robertson, who finished with 25 points, and Luther Rackley, who scored 17, put the Royals ahead for good. Also, for the Royals, Tom Van Arsdale scored 22 points and Johnny Green, 19 points, but Jerry Lucas scored just 5.

For the Boston Celtics, Larry Siegfried and John Havlicek both scored 20 points, and Henry Finkel, a big lumbering 7'0", 240-pound center, who was Bill Russell's replacement, scored 21 points before fouling out.

Four games into the season, the Royals, with a record of 1–3, were in sixth place in the Eastern Division. Jerry Lucas was averaging 10.3 points per game, 2.3 assists, and 11.3 rebounds.

For six years playing with the Cincinnati Royals, Jerry Lucas was averaging 19.9 points per game and held almost every club rebound record. He had also been an All-Star every year and was named the 1964 All-Star game MVP. At that time, Lucas was the eighth leading rebounder in NBA history.

Bob Cousy has maintained that at that point in the season, Jerry Lucas came to him and said that he had reached the conclusion that with his bad knees he couldn't play defense the way he wanted him to. Then, Lucas asked to be traded—preferably to San Francisco. Cousy states that he told Lucas he would talk to Joe Axelson and see what could be done.

According to Cousy, it was a mobility problem with Lucas, if one man can't keep up with the pace, the whole system breaks down.

"He was doing the job off the boards," says Cousy. "And he was doing it well—although he did not have the height or awesome strength of some of the truly 'big men' in pro basketball. But we needed a lot more speed out of him."[10]

In an interview for this work, Jerry Lucas denies that scenario. "I didn't ask to be traded," said Lucas. "I was shocked when I found out that I had been traded. I don't think Joe Axelson had anything to do with my trade. I didn't really know him, and I never met Max Jacobs. Cousy wanted to change everything. It was agreed that when he took over, he could make all the decisions and that included getting rid of players of All-Star caliber."

In regard to Bob Cousy's opinion that he only gave 80% on the court, Lucas responded, "I was motivated to play in every game I ever played in at all levels, high school, college, the Olympics and the pros."[11]

Cousy rubbed salt in any wounds Jerry Lucas may have had over being traded when he stated, "I had concluded that Jerry wasn't physically or psychologically capable of playing the fast-breaking offense and aggressive defense I wanted. I didn't want to bring in young players who might absorb his attitude."[12] It really annoyed Cousy that Lucas talked about outside interests in the locker room; he wanted his players to come into the arena talking basketball.

But Cousy really throws the knockout punch in insults toward Lucas when he states in his book, *The Killer Instinct,* that he and Joe Axelson began looking around the league for a team to trade Lucas to, but only the San Francisco Warriors showed any interest in him—the team where he wanted to go in the first place.

When Bob Cousy was asked in early 2015 to recall the circumstances involved with trading Jerry Lucas, he sort of took the 5th Amendment approach, stating he's now 86 years old and his long-term memory is no longer sharp. "I could attempt to answer some questions, but my testimony would not be accepted in court—I'd be faking," said Cousy.[13]

That being the case with Cousy, it sets up a huge dichotomy in seeking the truth of the matter when taking into consideration the assertion of Lucas that he never asked to be traded.

If there was ever an athlete who personified the trait of having a photographic memory, it was Jerry Lucas. Teammates were constantly amazed at how he was capable of keeping game statistics in his head. It's a fact that later in his playing career, Lucas memorized the first 200 pages of the New York City telephone directory. Lucas could even take any word and then instantly reorganize the letters in it into alphabetical order. Following his basketball career, Jerry Lucas would write a series of books to help readers memorize things. Lucas' first book, *The Memory Book,* was published in 1974.

On October 24, 1969, Bob Cousy traded Jerry Lucas to the San Francisco Warriors. The Cincinnati fans were shocked and so was the most of the NBA. The trade seemed bizarre because, in return, the Royals didn't receive a player anywhere near the All-Star caliber of Lucas.

Bob Cousy maintained that he and Joe Axelson attempted to get Jeff Mullins, a guard who was averaging 22.8 points per game, from the Warriors. But what they got was Jim King, a 6'2" guard, who was a veteran of seven years in the NBA, and Bill Turner, a 25-year-old, 6'7" forward, who had been a reserve on the Warriors for the past three seasons. Unfortunately, Jim King would make no contribution to the Royals because shortly after reporting, he broke his leg.

The assertion of Cousy, that no team other than the San Francisco Warriors wanted Lucas, was not accurate. Gene Shue, coach of the Baltimore Bullets, was very interested in acquiring Jerry Lucas. Shue said that he had been listening to radio broadcasts of Royals games and realized that Lucas was not fitting into Bob Cousy's plans for running a strong defensive team. He said that he had talked to Cousy two days prior to the trade and offered him Ray Scott for Lucas.

Ray Scott was a 6'9" center-forward drafted by the Detroit Pistons out of the University of Portland in the 4th round of the 1961 NBA draft and later traded to the Baltimore Bullets. He had played in the NBA for ten years and was never selected as an All-Star.

When Gene Shue learned what the Royals got in return for Lucas from San Francisco, he said, "What kind of a deal is that? I was on top of this all the way. I can't tell you what we were offering, but it was a lot more than you got."[14]

When Bob Cousy was informed of Gene Shue's comments, he remarked, "He offered us John Barnhill and Barry Orms earlier this year. It's none of his business. Whatever he has to say, he has an ulterior motive. It's nice to be an expert. Someday I may be as smart as him."[15]

The Lucas trade was further complicated by the fact that during the past summer, Jerry Lucas had indicated that he was considering retirement. In a concession to Lucas, Bob Cousy and Joe Axelson signed an addendum to his contract stating that the Royals would not trade him unless he agreed to it. So it begged the question of whether or not Jerry Lucas would have reported to Baltimore.

Jerry Lucas and his wife, Treva, had come to enjoy living in Cincinnati immensely. They owned a home in the upper-middle-class suburb of Indian Hill and were close to family still living in Middletown, Ohio. Furthermore, while playing for the Royals, Jerry was close to the restaurant chain that bore his name that he operated which had bothered Bob Cousy so intensely.

But all of this domestic bliss surrounding Lucas was a little too distracting for Bob Cousy and Joe Axelson, and it's clear that neither wanted him on the Royals.

Apparently, Lucas had been expecting a trade for some time. Treva Lucas told the press that they had enjoyed living in Cincinnati the past six years and made many friends in the community. Treva wouldn't scold Bob Cousy for trading her husband. "It could prove to be very beneficial for the Royals and us, too," she said. "I'm sure he's doing the right thing. I have confidence in him. I think he's a fine coach."[16]

So, Jerry Lucas resolved that his future was in the words of the old song, "California, Here I Come," and headed west.

Back east, the future of the Cincinnati Royals remained to be seen.

Oscar Robertson became concerned when Cousy announced that he wanted Norm Van Lier to handle the ball more—thereby moving him off screens and finishing plays. During his entire ten years with the Royals, Oscar Robertson had been running the offense.

Oscar stated in his biography, *The Big O—My Life, My Times, My Game,* the problem with making Van Lier the playmaker was that he wasn't tall enough to see over the player who guarded him. It not only delayed Van Leer's passes but also made him susceptible to the presence of double-teaming. The result was that the Royals had trouble getting into their offense.

When he arrived in Cincinnati, Bob Cousy had announced that he was going to implement a youth movement on the Royals. That certainly seemed like a good idea. A few of the Royals starters were over 30 years old: Adrian Smith was 33; Johnny Green, 36; Connie Dierking, 33; and Oscar Robertson, 31. But then, Cousy contradicted his plans when he decided to insert himself on the active roster—he was 41!

On November 18, after a couple of months of haggling, the Royals and Celtics reached an agreement on removing Cousy from the Boston inactive list. Cooz was free to suit up, but he suddenly came up injured with a pulled muscle in the groin during a practice session.

A few nights later, on November 21, at Cincinnati Gardens, the "Wizard of the Hardwood" made his return on the court, and his performance left a lot to be questioned. The Royals won the game defeating the Chicago Bulls 133–119 with The Big O scoring 41 points and Tom Van Arsdale, 19.

The game was hardly the grand promotion that Cousy had promised with him playing—only 3,450 fans showed up. It was reported later that one fan out driving his car and listening to the game on radio rushed to the Gardens to buy a ticket when he heard that Cousy was going to play.

In the third period, when Cooz stood up and took off his warm-up jacket, the small crowd rose to their feet with a standing ovation for him. Cousy entered the game and helped Oscar Robertson and Norm Van Lier break the Bulls' zone press.

At the beginning of the 4th period, Cousy remained on the bench, but with the Royals leading by 20 points, he replaced The Big O for the final 5 minutes and 28 seconds of the game and fans began to see just how rusty his skills had become while not playing in the NBA for the past 6½ years. His passes bounded off other player's hands or went awry. On six or seven occasions, Cousy threw the ball away.

However, Cousy's wife Missy, who was on hand, quickly came to the defense of her husband. "It would seem to me," said Missy, "that when they're open in the corner, that they would know that they're going to get the ball."[17]

Cousy finished with 3 points and 2 rebounds. His self-assessment of his return as a player was critical but not convincing. "I thought I was terrible really. I'm going to have to get myself back in shape. I felt confident and the legs didn't feel too bad. I think I'm capable of playing a little better than that."[18]

On November 28, Bob Cousy made another appearance on the court in Cleveland where the Royals were playing the high-flying New York Knicks. With about one minute and thirty seconds left in the game, Oscar Robertson fouled out after scoring 33 points with the Royals leading 101–98. Then, Cousy put himself in and promptly threw the ball away. That was followed by a foul, the Knicks sank two free throws, and then Cousy turned the ball over again.

With 16 seconds remaining and the Royals leading 105–102, Cousy called a timeout so the Royals could bring the ball in near midcourt. He passed the ball to Tom Van Arsdale, but Dave Debusschere stepped in front of him, stole the ball, then scored to cut the Royals' lead to 105–104. Then, as Van Arsdale started to bring the ball up court, Willis Reed tapped it away in the direction of Walt Frazier. So, Van Arsdale fouled Frazier who then made both free throws to give the Knicks a 106–105 victory. It was New York's eighteenth straight win. Later, Cousy was to say that he felt sad that he had put himself in the game, but as he looked down the bench, he didn't see anyone he felt could keep their cool in that situation.

What Oscar Robertson didn't know at the time, was that Bob Cousy and Joe Axelson had already started shopping him around to other NBA teams. They had offered Robertson to the New York Knicks in exchange for Cazzie Russell and Dave Stallworth. But when the Knicks, coached by Red Holzman, suddenly went on an 18-game winning streak between October 24 and November 28, they cut off the trade talks with the Royals.

While going forward in the season Cousy would play less, he suddenly came under fire from some members of the press and other players for using his reactivation as a player as subterfuge to make himself eligible for the player's pension fund.

According to Cousy, Max Jacobs had informed him that, as he had returned as a player, if he would contribute about $20,000 for the years he had been out of the NBA, he would be eligible to collect about $10,000 a year when he reached the age of 65.

Regardless of the criticism, Cousy felt that he had been the first president of the NBA players' association, worked hard for the establishment of the pension fund, and deserved to be included. But in the end, he quit without qualifying.

Towards the end of December, Bob Cousy came to the conclusion that 33-year-old, nine-year NBA veteran guard Adrian Smith, like Jerry Lucas, didn't fit into his plans for the running Royals either. On Christmas Day 1969, Smith was traded to the San Francisco Warriors for a future second-round draft choice.

Cousy decided to trade Smith because he was satisfied with the way Norm Van Lier was playing in the backcourt with Oscar Robertson. Once again, Cousy stated that the only team interested in Smith, who was making $35,000 a year, was the San Francisco Warriors—they wanted him to take the pressure off of Jeff Mullins.

The Warriors were coming to Cincinnati to play the Royals on Christmas Day. As Bob Cousy didn't want to be the "Grinch that Stole Christmas," he told San Francisco general manager Bob Feerick that he wanted to wait until after the game to tell Smith that he had just been traded. To that end, he promised to keep him out of the game. But the game went into overtime and Cousy had to use Smith. The Warriors won 124–120. Adrian "Odie" Smith took the trade hard, broke down, and cried. However, Smith's wife was furious with Cousy and never spoke to him again.

Royals fans were absolutely dumbfounded; Bob Cousy had traded two All-Stars in Lucas and Smith and gotten little in return for either. In fact, the Royals got players for both who were incapable of making the Royals' starting lineup.

As the Royals struggled to play .500 ball, two days after Christmas, on Saturday, December 27, 1969, a huge holiday crowd of 11,665 fans packed Cincinnati Gardens. It was the largest crowd to ever see a Royals game in the Queen City. But those fans were not there to see Bob Cousy or The Big O. The Milwaukee Bucks were in town with the NBA's prized rookie center Lew Alcindor.

In late November, the Royals had defeated the Bucks 129–104 in Milwaukee. At the time, Lew Alcindor was apparently still adjusting to the NBA game. Connie Dierking had dominated Alcindor underneath the basket and, at one point, was scoring a basket a minute while out-positioning him for rebounds.

Surprisingly, the Royals defeated the Bucks again 112 to 110 in overtime giving them a season record of 17–21. It was Milwaukee's only loss in an eleven-game stretch.

Oscar Robertson led the Royals with 31 points supported by Connie Dierking and John Green who both who scored 14 points.

Oscar Robertson in action.

For the Bucks, Flynn Robinson, soon to be a member of the Cincinnati Royals, was the leading scorer with 41 points followed by Lew Alcindor with 29.*

At the All-Star Game break on January 7, 1970, the Royals had a record of 22–23.

As the second half of the 1969–70 season began, the Royals kept losing, and fans kept hearing rumors, often fueled by the media, that Oscar Robertson was not fitting into Bob Cousy's

* After winning his first NBA Championship in 1971 with the Milwaukee Bucks, at the age of 24, Ferdinand Lewis Alcindor, Jr. adopted the Muslim name Kareem Abdul-Jabbar.

running game. Oscar was hearing the rumors, too, and when the Royals were on the road, opposing players would ask him what he knew about the possibility of being traded. All the rumors appeared to have an isolating effect on Robertson.

Oscar considered Cincinnati home and really didn't want to be traded. But he knew his departure was inevitable, and so in order to ease the emotional pain, he reverted into his customary defense mechanism that Cincinnati was a racist city and the local media was biased against him, therefore he didn't care where he went.

Robertson wasn't alone in his feelings about Cincinnati not being a bastion of racial tolerance. Bob Cousy had expressed serious doubts, too, and it made him wonder if Cincinnati had a future in the NBA. Shortly after it was announced that Cousy would be the new coach for the Royals he started receiving unsigned hate mail letters. Cousy cites one example of such a letter that read, "Who the hell wants to go to your games and watch those niggers run up and down the court?"[19]

Considering Robertson's feelings and Cousy opinions in regard to the spirit of racial tolerance in Cincinnati, it was just a bit surprising that almost 12,000 of those alleged "Queen City bigots" came out to Cincinnati Gardens during the Christmas-New Year's holiday week to see Lew Alcindor play. From a historical perspective, one can only say "go figure!"

Still, at times, one has to admit that there was some credibility to Oscar Robertson's racial sensitivity toward Cincinnati, but you would hardly think that it would be a member of the press that would take the lead in reinforcing his negative feelings. But that is exactly what happened following a Royals 129–122 victory over the Baltimore Bullets in late January 1970.

Barry McDermott, a sports reporter for the *Cincinnati Enquirer,* wrote a column that appeared in the paper the following morning that included an asinine analogy, comparing the play of Oscar Robertson, who scored 41 points and had 15 assists, and Johnny Green, who scored 19 points with 12 rebounds in 32 minutes, to sanitation workers. At the same time, McDermott stated that they were the "Frick and Frack" of the Cincinnati Royals.*

It is a fact that in most American municipalities for over a hundred years the overwhelming number of employees holding

---

* According to *urbandictonary.com*, Frick and Frack are defined as "two people, usually employees of a company, who are deemed to be incompetent, lazy, or wasting time continuously by doing things other than working."

the position of sanitation worker, AKA garbage man, have been black. In fact, Oscar Robertson's father for a time had made a living as a sanitation worker in Indianapolis. But for a reason only known to him, Barry McDermott wrote in his column, "With all the sanitation workers out on strike in Cincinnati, ageless Johnny Green looks like the best garbageman in town. And if Johnny is cleaning up in the back of the truck, Oscar Robertson has to be up front at the wheel."[20]

In defense of Barry McDermott, one could make the inference that he was only writing the lead-in for his column based on post-game comments made by the Bullets' Kevin Loughery, who said, in regard to the brilliant play of Johnny Green in favor of his lay-ups, throw-ups, and fancy play around the basket, "It's not garbage what he's doing. Everybody else in the league would do it but it takes talent. Everybody would like to get two footers all night."[21]

Nonetheless, the column bothered an already supersensitive Oscar Robertson, and it should have. The Big O was playing his heart out with trade rumors swirling around him, and out of the blue, a sportswriter unwittingly insults both him and his father.

In an attempt to bring clarity to the social consciousness of Oscar Robertson, Bill Furlong of *Sport* magazine wrote in early 1970 that he saw race from the inside where no white man could venture. "[Robertson] knows that there are times when the worst thing that can happen to a black in America is fame. It gives him a sense of claustrophobia—he doesn't know he's been confined to a ghetto until he gets a chance to leave it."[22]

As Bob Cousy continued to remake the running Royals, by February, only seven of the fourteen players that had been at training camp were still on the roster, and soon the biggest name on the team would be packing his bags, too.

Cousy was less than candid with his critique of how The Big O fit into his plans for the Royals. "Oscar can go out there and score 40 points every night—he's that kind of player," said Cousy. "And we might win a few more games if he did. But if we want to be the kind of team we can be, we've got to establish the habits that will give us continuity in our offense and our defense. And to do that, Oscar has to keep the ball moving when somebody else can do the scoring."[23]

The rumors of an Oscar Robertson trade really heated up in late January 1970, and then the rumors became a reality. On

January 28, a sports reporter intercepted Oscar on his way to the locker room at Cincinnati Gardens and asked him how he felt about the trade. Shocked, Robertson called his attorney, Jake Brown, who confirmed that he had been traded to Baltimore for Gus Johnson.

That night, the Royals, playing the Milwaukee Bucks, entered the fourth quarter only 2 points down, but Oscar Robertson sat out the first five minutes of the period and they lost the game by 12 points, 114–126. Robertson finished with 23 points while Jim McGlocklin and Lew Alcindor both scored 33 points, and Flynn Robinson added 23 for Milwaukee.

Two days later, general manager Joe Axelson confirmed the trade stating that he and Cousy felt that they could better themselves. That meant that while they were rebuilding the Royals, they came to the conclusion that Oscar Robertson was more useful as barter than a building block.

While Baltimore was willing to increase Robertson's $125,000-a-year salary by $30,000 to $50,000 and give him a two-year contract extension, Cousy and Axelson had failed to read the fine print in Robertson's contract that stated he had a no-trade clause. So Robertson nixed the deal. He was willing to consider going to Baltimore for a $700,000-a-year, no-cut contract, but that was unlikely to happen.

When informed of the clause in Robertson's contract by Jake Brown, Bob Cousy, Joe Axelson, and Ambrose Lindhorst, the Royals attorney, were smitten; The Big O had them all by their—whatever. The Royals could trade Robertson, but he would have to approve the deal. Nonetheless, Jake Brown assured the three that he and Oscar would cooperate with them. Brown even offered to let them know what teams Oscar would be willing to be traded to.

Oscar Robertson had come to Cincinnati 14 years ago, and over that span of time, the community had become home to him. He had a wife and three children, owned property, and had business interests in the city. But Robertson quickly came to the conclusion that if Bob Cousy wanted him gone, then it was time to go, but he would be the one to decide where he was going to.

The Cincinnati print media, led mainly by the *Cincinnati Enquirer,* driven mostly by the fact that Oscar Robertson had never been friendly with them, began to take the side of Bob Cousy and the Royals management in the trade dilemma. Instead of criticizing Robertson's game, they began to launch personal attacks on him, suggesting, for instance, that despite Bob Cousy doing everything in his power to appease The Big O, he was never anything but bitter. The newspaper went on to state that for years Robertson had scorned the Royals management and ridiculed Cincinnati and its fans and would grow old a bitter man convinced that it was all a plot.

As the switchboard in the Royals front office began to light up with protest calls, Bob Cousy started to put an economic spin on the reason he wanted to trade Robertson, stating that the Royals were going to show a considerable loss for the season and that they could not continue to pay out a Wilt Chamberlain size contract when they were only drawing 3,500 fans a game and losing $300,000 a year.

"I feel that $125,000 is good compensation," said Cousy. "He's been an All-Star and he's done a job as a player. He's contributed something to Cincinnati and Cincinnati has compensated him. The fact is that a superstar in this price range has to draw people. Oscar draws people. Unfortunately, he draws people for everyone else during the year. He draws people on the road."[24]

With the trade rumors out in the open and Robertson's veto of the deal with Baltimore, skeptics were now wondering if The Big O would begin to "dog it" on the court—just going through the motions. Bob Cousy was not concerned about that possibility as he felt that Robertson's stature as a player would not allow him to do that.

Then, on February 1, suddenly another problem occurred, Oscar Robertson revealed that he had suffered a groin injury. The Royals' team physician examined him, confirmed the injury, and recommended that he be out two weeks.

Following the botched Baltimore trade attempted by Bob Cousy, Joe Axelson, and Ambrose Lindhorst, according to Robertson, everyone, including the *Cincinnati Enquirer,* turned up the heat to run him out town; Robertson cites in his biography a story in the *Enquirer* that stated, in part, that the reason the Royals attempted to trade Robertson was because Bob Cousy didn't think basketball was a one-on-one game. That was the philosophy he carried with him from winning multiple championships in Boston. In the article, it stated, "The Royals would never lose if Oscar and one player from the other team could play one-on-one for 48 minutes. But basketball is not this way and the Royals with Robertson have never been a champion."[25]

Bob Cousy, the Royals management, and Oscar Robertson were at loggerheads in their dispute, and it all seemed to be a complex matter driven by the personality conflicts existing among the parties as much as money. Oscar told the press, "under no circumstances will I play for this organization after this season."[26]

With Oscar Robertson out of the line-up on February 6, the Royals were defeated by the New York Knicks, 135–92. The 43-point margin was the largest of the season for New York. It was the Royals' fourth loss in a row.

While Robertson was out, Tom Van Arsdale attempted to kick his game into high gear, and on a couple of occasions, scored more than 30 points, but the Royals only won 3 games while losing 8 during The Big O's period of recuperation.

Robertson finally returned to the line-up on February 21. According to Bob Cousy, he was happy to have Robertson back, and Robertson was happy to be back, playing at his customary high level. The Big O scored 28 points and the Royals defeated the Chicago Bulls 127–119. The win left the Royals with a record of 30–39 with 13 games remaining and the season was over for them.

Oscar Robertson played his last home game for the Cincinnati Royals on March 20, 1970, against his old teammate Jerry Lucas and the San Francisco Warriors. The Warriors won the game 118–111 as Lucas, on those supposedly bad knees, scored 31 points and hauled in 25 rebounds. Oscar scored 24 points and later stated that he didn't shoot in the final nine minutes of the game out of defiance.

Following the game, when reporters asked Bob Cousy about Oscar's noticeable shutdown in the game, he was indifferent: "Leave me alone, will you babe? I pass. There's one game left. Leave it go, I pass."[27]

The final game for the 1969–70 Royals took place the following day at Madison Square Garden where the Royals beat the New York Knicks 136–120. In his final game with the Cincinnati Royals, Oscar Robertson scored 29 points.

The transplanted Boston Celtics style of basketball that Bob Cousy attempted to use with the Cincinnati Royals hadn't worked—while he didn't have the right players for the offense he wanted, he continued to pretend that he did. As a result, the Royals finished in fifth place in the NBA Eastern Division with a record of 36–46, five games worse than they had finished the previous season under Ed Jucker. It was the third consecutive season that the Royals had failed to make the playoffs.

Attendance at Cincinnati Gardens had improved slightly by 800 per game with the Royals averaging 4,869 per game while the team continued to play a barnstorming schedule with thirteen games played on neutral courts including four in Cleveland, three in Omaha, two in Memphis, two in Oakland, and one each in Kansas City and Columbia, South Carolina. All of that occurred while Bob Cousy and Joe Axelson traded or attempted to trade three of the most talented players on the team in Oscar Robertson, Jerry Lucas, and Adrian Smith and received no player of equal talent in return in any of the deals.

During the 1969–70 season, Bob Cousy had played a total of 34 embarrassing minutes for the Royals spread over seven games and compiled a season statistical record of 0.7 points per game, 1.4 assists, and 0.7 rebounds.

The soon-to-be-departing Oscar Robertson, on the other hand, finished the season scoring 25.3 points per game with 8.1 assists and 6.1 rebounds.

At least there was a consolation prize for the Cincinnati Royals in 1969–70; after a decade of trying, the Royals finally finished ahead of the Boston Celtics. With Bill Russell's retirement, the Celtics collapsed, finishing in sixth place in the NBA Eastern Division with a record of 34–48.

The irony in the fact that Royals finished ahead of the Celtics was that it permitted Boston to have a higher draft pick in 1970 and allow them to select a player that would eventually lead them back to the top of the NBA.

For nearly the entire decade of the 1960s, the New York Knicks had been the doormat of the NBA, finishing fourth (last) in the Eastern Division every season from 1959–60 to 1966–67. Then, as a result of each year's draft and some key trades, the Knicks began to improve. As they steadily added players, such as Willis Reed, Dick Barnett, Walt Frazier, Dave Debusschere, Bill Bradley, and Cazzie Russell, by 1969–70, the Knicks had become NBA champions.

The key to the Knicks' success leading up to the 1969–70 championship was having balance in scoring, three regulars with consistent scoring averages every year in Willis Reed, Dick Barnett, and Dave DeBusschere.

In route to the 1969–70 NBA crown, the New York Knicks defeated the Milwaukee Bucks 4 games to 1 in the Eastern Division Finals, then won the championship finals, beating the Los Angeles Lakers 4 games to 3.

The Milwaukee Bucks, with NBA Rookie of the Year Lew Alcindor, had collapsed in the playoffs against the New York Knicks. Alcindor had finished the regular season with averages of 28.8 points per game, 14.3 rebounds, and 4.1 assists. He had been asked to do it all as the Bucks outside shooters couldn't score and the inside men had trouble breaking through.

In the final game of the Division Finals, Alcindor was dominated by Willis Reed, being pushed around until he fouled out. It fueled speculation that Oscar Robertson might be the player the Bucks needed to put them over the top.

The Phoenix Suns called Joe Axelson and offered Gail Goodrich, Jim Fox, and Gregg Howard a 6'9" player from New Mexico who had played in Italy during the past season, but Robertson and his attorney quickly turned down the trade.

Robertson, with a no-trade clause in his Royals contract, had indicated that he might be agreeable to a trade with Milwaukee. Playing with a big man such as Lew Alcindor might give him a chance to win a championship before his playing days ended.

On April 21, Oscar got his wish when the Royals traded him to Milwaukee for Flynn Robinson and Charlie Paulk. While Royals fans were familiar with Robinson, they didn't know much about Paulk. Bob Cousy had never seen Paulk play, but Joe Axelson had and felt that since he could play both forward and center, he might be just the man that the Royals needed. At the time, Charley Paulk, a former NAIA All-American from Northeastern State College in Tahlequah, Oklahoma was serving with the U.S. Army in Viet Nam.

Oscar Robertson had pretty much self-engineered his trade to the Milwaukee Bucks. The financial aspects of getting him to sign his contract with the Bucks were a piece of cake. All that Robertson asked for was a three-year contract at $175,000 a year, about $50,000 more than he had made with the Royals and the inclusion of the no-trade clause.

Bob Cousy felt pretty good about the trade if for no other reason than the Royals would now be his team and not Oscar Robertson's. Furthermore, Robertson had found it difficult to fit into Cousy's patterns of play and now he could find a player who didn't.

In his official statement announcing the trade of Robertson to the Milwaukee Bucks, Bob Cousy said in part, "We are pleased that this situation has been resolved to the mutual satisfaction of both Oscar and the Royals. I would like to repeat what I have stated on many occasions this year, that Oscar has done an outstanding job for the Royals and deserves the complete support and loyalty of the fans."[28]

While the press had been highly critical of Robertson in his year of silent discontent with the Royals, Bob Cousy had allowed it to continue. Cousy and Axelson were telling the public and the press that the whole affair was about a new contract that Robertson wanted, one they couldn't afford. But there was a lot more to it. The fact was that Oscar Robertson had been pushed out the door of Cincinnati Gardens by Cousy and Axelson.

Bob Cousy said that in games Oscar carried a chip on his shoulder toward referees. "No one could look more startled than Oscar when a foul was called on him," said Cousy. "It was often said that he went through his career absolutely certain that he had never committed a foul."[29]

As Oscar prepared to leave Cincinnati for Milwaukee, the press in the Queen City didn't cut him any slack. Jim Schottelkotte of the *Cincinnati Enquirer* wrote, "The problem with Oscar is that we babied him here too much. He was our first bonafide super sports hero, the best ever to play the game, but nobody dare criticize him. When someone finally did, Oscar didn't know how to handle it. In the future, those of us in the public media ought to remember it."[30]

There was a subtle ambiguity expressed by Oscar Robertson about leaving Cincinnati. He stated that when his basketball-playing days were over, he would return and make the city his home. In a response to the circumstances surrounding his trade to the Milwaukee Bucks, Robertson stated, "The attitude here was one in which I could not go on with. They traded me in mid-season. I just wasn't wanted. I knew then it was time to get away."[31] Then, in response to having criticized the city and the Royals, Oscar said, "I've never knocked the town. The fans were driven away. The Royals never made a draft choice that helped the team. Only two of their No.1 draft choices remained around for a while, me and Lucas."[32]

Whatever the case may have been, if he criticized the city or not, one thing was certain, Oscar Robertson was absolutely blind to one aspect of his exodus from Cincinnati—the sentiment of the fans. Oscar Robertson never fully comprehended his status as a Cincinnati sports hero. He was always concerned with what the sportswriters were saying about him rather than what the fans thought about him. Even though the University of Cincinnati won two consecutive NCAA National Championships and narrowly missed a third, losing in a double overtime after he had graduated, The Big O was considered Cincinnati Bearcats basketball and still is to this very day. It would be nearly impossible to find one person today in Cincinnati that would argue that Oscar Robertson doesn't deserve the statue of his likeness that sits on the University of Cincinnati campus. He's the man!

The only other athlete that could possibly challenge Robertson's huge historical popularity in Queen City sports history is Pete Rose.

Had Oscar Robertson left the NBA in the spring of 1970 and ran for Cincinnati City Council in the fall, he would have won in a landslide...and immediately would have become the most popular politician in the city—hands down. The people of Cincinnati loved him. But the only way Oscar could see the world was through a victim's lens.

It made no difference if Bob Cousy and Joe Axelson felt Robertson could not be part of their system, most of the Royals' fans would have preferred to lose with Oscar rather than win without him. Still very few of those fans believed that Oscar should have stayed—they knew under the circumstances it was in his best interest to go. They sympathized with his plight and openly criticized Bob Cousy as being arrogant and self-serving. Oscar was the franchise. The overwhelming majority of Cincinnati Royals fans felt cheated with Oscar Robertson going to Milwaukee for Flynn Robinson and some unknown guy who was serving his country fighting in the jungles of Viet Nam. The Robertson trade became a trivia question in Cincinnati taverns for years to come: "Who Was Oscar Robertson Traded For?"

But The Big O turned his back on his fans. To bring closure to his fourteen years on the hardwood in Cincinnati, Oscar Robertson needed to say goodbye to them, and he never did.

12

The Royals Move to Kansas City

& Bob Cousy Resigns

With Oscar Robertson traded to Milwaukee and Jerry Lucas traded to San Francisco, Bob Cousy could now begin to build the Royals into the team he wanted. The first step in the process was for Cousy and Joe Axelson to get players in the 1970 NBA draft they hoped to build around.

Bob Cousy wanted a center that could mirror the extraordinary abilities of his former Celtics teammate Bill Russell. He wanted a player like Russell who had the ability to grab rebounds, protect the rim, and start the fast breaks for the racehorse guards that he preferred.

The player that Cousy coveted was Dave Cowens, a 6'9" center out of Florida State University. Cowens had grown up across the Ohio River from Cincinnati in Newport, Kentucky and played high school basketball at Newport Central Catholic High. The upside on Cowens was that he was strong, could jump, and was extremely fast for a big man—just the kind of center Bob Cousy wanted to lead his fast break. The downside on Cowens was that he had a tendency to foul out of games.

But there was a problem, according to Bob Cousy, Dave Cowens had sent him a letter informing him that he did not want to play for the Royals, and therefore, not to draft him.

The Cincinnati Royals had the fifth draft pick right behind the Boston Celtics, who, by virtue of finishing behind the Royals, had the fourth pick. Regardless of how Cowens felt about being drafted by the Royals, Cousy was determined to draft him if he was available when the Royals' first pick was up.

The 1970 NBA draft was held at 11:00 A.M. on March 23 in New York via a telephone hook up with all the teams. As they waited for the draft to begin, Bob Cousy, Draff Young, Joe Axelson, and assistant general manager Larry Staverman huddled together in the Cincinnati Gardens Lancer Room listening to elevator music coming over the phone line. Finally, at 12:30 P.M. commissioner Walter Kennedy announced that the time to begin was at hand.

Detroit picked first and chose Bob Lanier.

San Diego was second and selected Rudy Tomjanovich.

Atlanta was next and a muffled response came over the phone line. Walter Kennedy told Hawks general manager Marty Blake to talk louder. He stated again that the Hawks take Pete Maravich.

Playing at LSU, Pete Maravich had become the all-time college scorer, averaging more than 40 points a game for three years in a row.

Nonetheless, Bob Cousy was relieved when Atlanta took Pete Maravich. There were still two big centers available, Dave Cowens and Sam Lacey. "This is how ludicrous this thing has become," said Cousy later. "You sit there and hope you don't have to take Maravich."[1]

Boston was next, and Cousy could feel his heart sink in his chest as he heard Red Auerbach bark over the phone line that the Celtics chose Dave Cowens of Florida State.

Dave Cowens would revitalize the Boston Celtics. Along the way to the Naismith Basketball Hall of Fame, between 1970–71 and 1979–80, Cowens would be an eight-time NBA All-Star and lead the Celtics to two NBA Championships in 1974 and 1979.

The Royals drafted next and took Sam Lacey, a 6'10" center out of New Mexico State.

In the second round, using the 19th pick obtained from San Francisco in the Adrian Smith trade, the Royals selected Nate "Tiny" Archibald, a 6'0" guard out of the University of Texas in El Paso.

Other than Dave Cowens, the only other players that Cousy and Axelson really wanted and did not get were former Cincinnati Bearcat center-forward Jim Ard, who was selected by Seattle, and Gregg Howard from New Mexico, who was selected by Phoenix. But the Royals were relieved when the Suns drafted Howard. There had been reports that while he was playing in Italy the previous season, he was arrested on drug charges and also a rape charge. As it turned out, Howard was a bust in the NBA, playing only two seasons.

The rival ABA had held its draft in January, and some of the biggest college stars available had already signed contracts such as Dan Issel of Kentucky, Charles Scott of North Carolina, and Rick Mount of Purdue.

The ABA, hoping to force a merger with the NBA, was driving player's salaries up considerably. The New York Nets had offered Bob Lanier $1.3 million and that forced the Detroit Pistons to sign him for $1.2 million over five years.

Because the Carolina Cougars had offered "Pistol" Pete Maravich a substantial contract, it forced the Atlanta Hawks to sign him for $2 million over five years.

Oscar Robertson had been an All-Star every one of his ten years in Cincinnati. One of the reasons that Bob Cousy traded Oscar was that he was concerned that he was going to ask for a contract calling for $200,000 a year for three years. Due to pressure coming from the ABA, to sign Nate Archibald the Royals had to pay him $465,000 for three years. Nonetheless, for just $135,000 more the Royals could have kept Oscar Robertson. Sam Lacey signed for less than Archibald.

In 1970–71, to keep pace with the ABA and not cede any potential market to the rival league, once again the NBA expanded. It awarded three new franchises to Cleveland (Cavaliers), Buffalo (Braves), and Portland (Trailblazers). As the NBA was now a 17-team circuit, it divided the teams into two conferences with four divisions. In the East Conference were the Atlantic and Central Divisions, and in the West Conference were the Midwest and Pacific Divisions. The Cincinnati Royals joined the new Central Division with Baltimore, Atlanta, and Cleveland.

The 1970–71 Cincinnati Royals roster included nine players (57%) that had not been on the roster the previous year. Of all the players drafted by Bob Cousy and Joe Axelson, only three rookies made the team, Sam Lacey, Nate Archibald, and Greg Hyder, a 6'6" forward from East New Mexico.

Bob Cousy felt that with Norm Van Lier playing alongside Nate Archibald at guard, Tom Van Arsdale and Charlie Paulk as the forwards with Sam Lacey in the pivot, and Johnny Green coming off the bench, he had the players necessary to play his intense defense/fast-break offense game.

But after the Royals started the 1970–71 season with five straight losses, the reality sunk in that Cousy still had some work to do with remodeling the team. By Thanksgiving, the Royals were 7–13.

In January 1971, Bob Cousy would be elected to the Naismith Memorial Basketball Hall of Fame along with Bob Pettit and the late Abe Saperstein, founder of the Harlem Globetrotters, who had died in 1966.

However, Cousy's pending enshrinement in Springfield did little to elevate the Royals in the standings. On January 9, 1971, the Royals at 19–23 were still fighting to get their record above .500. It didn't help matters much that they were still losing home-court advantage by continuing to play so many games on neutral courts. With the season about half over, the Royals had already played three of their home games in Omaha and one in Madison, Wisconsin. Later, they played games in Toronto, Ontario, and Eugene, Oregon.

The 1970–71 Cincinnati Royals failed to make the playoffs for the fourth year in a row finishing third in the Central Division of the NBA East Conference with a record of 33–49 while home attendance at Cincinnati Gardens dropped by 15.5% from the previous season.

While Bob Cousy was content with the hard work of Tom Van Arsdale and praising the play of Norm Van Lier and Nate Archibald, he was blaming the Royals' inability to win games on Sam Lacey. He felt that he was not aggressive enough; he'd let his man get position on him and didn't understand that when you let the opposing center get the ball in low, you're going to get burned. Furthermore, Cousy felt Lacey lacked confidence and that he couldn't get the job done without giving him a pep-talk before taking the court.

According to Cousy, Sam Lacey didn't even know where the weak side of the court was. Cousy stated that once in practice, he shouted at Lacey to go to the weak side (where the ball isn't)! But Lacey immediately ran to the strong side (where the ball is). So Cousy called him over to where he was standing. "'Sam,' I asked, 'what does weak side mean?' Lacey looked at the floor and said, 'I don't know.'"[2]

Sam Lacey had been an All-American at New Mexico State and was the number five pick in the 1970 NBA draft. In the opinion of the *New York Times,* Sam Lacey had a fine rookie season.

Although Lacey would go on to play thirteen years in the NBA and average 10.3 points and 9.7 rebounds per game, he could never make the grade with Cousy.

One night during Lacey's rookie year in 1970–71, after the Royals had played that night in Boston, Cousy got together for a post-game dinner with one of his former Celtics teammates, Tom Heinsohn, who was, at that time, coach of the Celtics. Almost immediately, Cousy began complaining to Heinsohn about Sam Lacey; he couldn't do this, he couldn't do that, he didn't take to being coached very well.

Finally, Heinsohn interrupted Cousy stating that he needed to take a realistic look at the circumstances surrounding Lacey. Heinsohn reminded Cousy that the Royals had signed him for a lot of money, so Lacey must feel that the team's management thought pretty highly of him. Then, Heinsohn said, "His wife thinks he's great. His mother thinks he's great. His agent thinks he's great. You're the only guy telling him he's not great. So, Cooz, who do you think he's going to listen to?"[3] Sam Lacey finished the 1970–71 season scoring 13.5 points and grabbing 11.3 rebounds per game.

Tom Van Arsdale led the Royals in scoring with 22.4 points per game, 6.1 rebounds, and 2.2 assists per game.

As for Cousy's fast-break guards, Nate Archibald scored 16.0 points per game with 5.5 assists and 3 rebounds. Norm Van Lier scored 10.1 points per game, had 10.1 assists, and 7.1 rebounds.

The Royals third guard, Flynn Robinson, one of the key players in the Oscar Robertson trade, spent most of the season on the bench. While Robinson scored 13.3 points per game, his average playing time was just 19.3 minutes per game. At the end of the season, Robinson was traded to the Los Angeles Lakers. According to Joe Axelson, Robinson did not fit in with the Royals. However, Robinson fit in beautifully with the Lakers. Backing up Jerry West and Gail Goodrich, Robinson was one of the key players that led the Los Angeles Lakers to the 1972 NBA Championship. Lakers' radio broadcasters referred to Robinson as "Mr. Instant Point."

It was a fact that Joe Axelson had not even read Oscar Robertson's contract when he attempted to trade him to the Baltimore Bullets. Whether or not Axelson or Bob Cousy, had attempted to belittle the contributions of Oscar Robertson to the Cincinnati Royals was conjecture. Robertson's exit from Cincinnati had been filled with innuendos and bitterness.

It was amidst such ballyhoo that The Big O arrived at the Milwaukee Bucks training camp in the summer of 1970. For fourteen years, playing at the University of Cincinnati and with the Cincinnati Royals, Oscar Robertson had worn the familiar number 14 on his jersey.

Jon McGlocklin had been wearing number 14 for the Milwaukee Bucks and out of deference to The Big O, he offered his jersey number to him. But Robertson refused McGlocklin's offer. Instead, he took number 1. Robertson proclaimed that coming to Milwaukee was a new basketball life for him. Cincinnati was in the past and the only thing that mattered was winning with the Bucks.

The Milwaukee Bucks, with coach Larry Costello, had built a team very wisely—one that some analysts felt had the potential to be an instant dynasty. Of course, the Bucks had been fortunate to have the first pick in the 1969 draft and be able to select Lew Alcindor who had been on championship basketball teams almost his entire life. First, at Power Memorial High School in the Bronx where he led the team to a series of New York City championships; then, at UCLA where he played on three consecutive NCAA championship teams coached by John Wooden.

But aside from drafting Alcindor, the Bucks had also made two very wise trades. In acquiring Oscar Robertson from Cincinnati and Bob Boozer and Lucius Allen from Seattle, they had given up the same number of players and got $100,000 in cash.

While the record showed that Oscar Robertson was the third highest scorer in NBA history, it was apparent to all observers that The Big O they were witnessing in a Milwaukee Bucks uniform was not the player of the past. He was visibly older, somewhat heavier and was less of a dribbler and more defensive minded.

But being on the Bucks gave Oscar Robertson a chance to finally play with an extremely good center and it gave Lew Alcindor the opportunity to play with an extremely good play-maker. To that end, The Big O scored less as Jim McGlocklin was a spectacular outside shooter and instead ran a deliberate offense and set-up play for Alcindor and Bob Dandridge. With Robertson on the court, it made it much easier for Lew Alcindor, Bob Dandridge, and Gregg Smith to get open.

To get full utility out of all this talent, Larry Costello and his assistant coach, Tom Nissalke, watched hours of game films and set up hard, well-organized practices filled with grueling repetition drills. Everything became business-like for Costello, Alcindor, Robertson, and the rest of the team. As a result, the 1970–71 season was a cakewalk for the Milwaukee Bucks.

With their starting five shooting better than 50%, early in the season, the Bucks won 16 consecutive games and later won a record 20 consecutive games on their way to setting a league-best record of 66–16.

Led by Lew Alcindor, who had averaged 31.7 points per game with 16 rebounds and 3.3 assists, and Oscar Robertson, who had averaged 19.4 points per game with 5.7 rebounds and 8.2 assists while being named an All-Star for the 11th time.

In the playoffs, the Bucks made quick work of the San Francisco Warriors in the West Conference Semi-Finals, winning the series 4 games to 1. Then, the Bucks dispatched the Los Angeles Lakers with Jerry West and Elgin Baylor out with injuries, 4 games to 1 in the Conference Finals.

In the finals, the Bucks defeated the East Conference champion, the Baltimore Bullets, 4 games 0 to win the 1971 NBA Championship with Oscar Robertson scoring 30 points in the final game. It was only the second finals sweep in NBA history, the first being Boston over Minneapolis in 1959. Lew Alcindor was named the Finals MVP having averaged 27.0 points per game, 18.5 rebounds, and 2.8 assists.

The Bullets had been riddled with injuries to key players such as Wes Unseld, Gus Johnson, and Earl Monroe. While Monroe did score 26 points in game one, had he been healthy, the matchup of him against Robertson might have been a classic.

The 1971–72 season would be the NBA's twenty-fifth anniversary as a league. Prior to the season, Lew Alcindor changed his name to Kareem Abdul-Jabbar. The Milwaukee Bucks finished first again in the Midwest Division with a record of 60–23.

A lot of fans and people in the media believed that the Milwaukee Bucks were going to be the next dynasty in the NBA. But a funny thing happened on the way to the coronation; the Bucks lost the West Conference Finals to the eventual NBA champion, the Los Angeles Lakers, 4 games to 2.

There has remained speculation that the Bucks didn't win back-to-back NBA championships because following the 1970–71 title run, management broke up the team.

Oscar Robertson addressed the issue stating, "After the championship, they did something which was really foolish. They

Oscar Robertson – Milwaukee Bucks. (Courtesy of Vernon S. Braver, Public Doman via WikiMedia Commons.)

traded Gregg Smith, Bob Boozer, and Dick Cunningham. You had people who really did not understand what a team concept means. You win a championship and make a trade of any key ballplayer, and it's the kiss of death."[4]

In 1972–73, the Bucks again won the Midwest Division and lost the West Conference Finals to the Golden State Warriors (the former San Francisco Warriors who had moved to Oakland prior to the season), 4 games to 2.

For the fourth consecutive year in 1973–74, the Milwaukee Bucks won the Midwest Division, this time with a record of 59–23. The Bucks advanced to the NBA Finals but were defeated by the Boston Celtics led by Dave Cowens, John Havlicek, and JoJo White in a seven-game series.

The seventh game of the series, played in Milwaukee and won by Boston 102–87, was Oscar Robertson's last game in his brilliant 14-year NBA career. The Big O, who was now 35 years old, scored only 6 points and was just 2 for 13 shooting field goals and 2 for 2 at the foul line.

The Milwaukee Bucks decided that they didn't need Oscar Robertson anymore and failed to offer him a new contract. So, Robertson was a free agent, but rather than pursue his NBA career any further, he chose retirement.

Although The Big O had won an NBA championship ring with the Bucks, he left Milwaukee just as unhappy as he had left Cincinnati, holding the belief that the Bucks had lowballed him.

The year after Oscar Robertson retired, although the Milwaukee Bucks still had Kareem Abdul-Jabbar in the frontcourt, they did not qualify for the playoffs, finishing in 1974–75 with a record of 38–44.

It had been a wonderful experience for Kareem Abdul-Jabbar to play with Oscar Robertson and is a memory that he has always cherished. In 2014, freelance journalist Jon Saraceno asked Kareem Abdul-Jabbar, "Who was the best basketball player not named Kareem Abdul-Jabbar?" Kareem's reply without hesitation was, "LeBron James is an incredible talent, but Oscar Robertson in his prime would blow people's minds today."[5]

Through the 2017–18 season, Oscar Robertson is the twelfth-leading scorer in NBA history with 26,710 career points, is sixth all-time in assists with 9,887, and eighteenth in field goals made with 9,508. He was a twelve-time All-Star, and he remains the only player in NBA history to average a triple-double for a season. In 1961–62, The Big O finished the year averaging 30.8 points per game, 12.5 rebounds, and 11.4 assists.

By contrast, more modern era players, such as LeBron James, have had 28 triple doubles in a season, Michael Jordan had 27, but in 1961–62, Oscar Robertson had 41.

Oscar Robertson's legacy, however, is larger than his career statistics. During the early part of the 1969–70 season, as president of the NBA Players Association, Robertson, along with player representatives that included Paul Silas, Dave DeBusschere, John Havlicek, and Larry Fleisher, the players association attorney, had been working on a plan to end the NBA's reserve clause.

Four days before leaving the Cincinnati Royals in April 1970, Oscar Robertson became part of one of the most important court cases in NBA history. The landmark case known commonly as the Oscar Robertson suit, filed by the NBA's Players Association, of which Robertson was president, against the league, stalled a proposed merger between the NBA and the ABA. The anti-trust suit, filed in New York District Court, challenged the merger as a violation of the Sherman Antitrust Act, as well as the legality of the college draft and the NBA's reserve clause that prohibited free agency. In 1975, six years after the suit was filed, the NBA, in an out-of-court settlement, agreed to merge with the ABA in 1976–77.

The draft remained intact. But drafted players now had the right to refuse to join the teams that had drafted them, sit out for a year and then re-enter the draft. In addition, teams were no longer required to provide compensation when signing a free-agent player which in the future, would lead to such high-profile free agency signings as LeBron James leaving the Cleveland Cavaliers in July 2010 ("This fall, I'm taking my talents to South Beach and joining the Miami Heat."). The settlement led to the signing of more free agents and eventually led to even higher salaries for all players.

In the spring of 1971, Max Jacobs moved the Royals' business operations, along with the team's financial records, to Buffalo. In December, Joe Axelson went to Buffalo and met with Max Jacobs. Axelson told Jacobs that the Royals were not going to make it in Cincinnati. So they had two choices, sell the team or move it. Jacobs accepted Axelson's recommendation, and they began looking for a city to relocate the franchise. It was now only a matter of time before the Cincinnati Royals no longer existed.

In the regular 1971 NBA draft, Joe Axelson and Bob Cousy drafted ten players and then one in the league's first hardship draft. None of those players would improve the Royals. Of those ten players taken in the regular draft, five would never play one game in the NBA. Two others would play just one season, while Ken Durrett, a 6'7" forward from La Salle University, would play four years in the NBA and John Mengelt, a 6'2" guard from Auburn, would play for ten years.

It cost the Royals $1.4 million over three years to sign Ken Durrett. He had injured his knee in his senior year at La Salle. While doctors told Cousy and Axelson that Durrett was able to play, his knee became problematic during the 1971–72 season, and he would have to be operated on.

The blue-chip player obtained by the Royals was Nate Williams, a 6'5" guard/forward from Utah taken as the number one pick in the hardship draft. Williams would go on to play 12 years in the NBA.

The hardship draft had come about as a result of a court case challenging the NBA's eligibility requirements. Spencer Haywood had played junior college basketball at Trinidad State Junior College in Colorado in 1967–68. Then, he played on the 1968 U. S. Olympic Team that won a Gold Medal in Mexico City. Haywood transferred to the University of Detroit, wherein the 1968–69 season, he averaged 32.1 points per game and led the nation in rebounding with 21.5 per game.

Feeling he had nothing more to accomplish at the collegiate level, Spencer Haywood signed a contract with the Denver Rockets of the ABA that did not have a restriction on signing college undergraduates. One again, Haywood excelled becoming the ABA Rookie of the Year in 1969–70 while averaging 30.0 points per game.

Then, the next year, Haywood, just 21 years old, attempted to jump leagues and signed a contract with the NBA's Seattle Supersonics.

At that time, the NBA prohibited signing college players before their class had graduated. The NBA and all of its teams immediately objected to the Sonics signing Haywood because he had not gone through the regular draft. Therefore, the Sonics had no right to sign him.

The NBA filed suit against Spencer Haywood and the Seattle Sonics. Haywood's stance was that he was the sole wage earner in his under-privileged family and subsequently was a "hardship case," and the NBA with its eligibility rule was blocking his right to earn a living.

The case quickly wound its way through the justice system and was heard by the U.S. Supreme Court that ruled 7–2 in Haywood's favor.

On September 10, 1971, the NBA held its first "hardship draft" or supplemental draft for college underclassmen. In 1976, the need to prove a hardship would be removed from the requirement for underclassmen who wished to enter the NBA draft and replaced by the early entry procedure whereby any player with remaining college eligibility could enter the NBA draft on the condition that he notified the league office at least 45 days before the draft.

The 1971–72 Cincinnati Royals season would be a complete disaster. The squad would be the last Royals team to play in the Queen City and would finish with the worst win-loss record in eleven years and third poorest of any team since the franchise was relocated from Rochester.

The roster that Bob Cousy and Joe Axelson chose for the 1971–72 Royals included five veterans: Johnny Green, now 38 years old; Darrall Imhoff, 33; Tom Van Arsdale, 28; Matt Guokas, 27; and Norm Van Lier, 24; along with three second-year players: Nate Archibald, Jake Jones, and Sam Lacey; and six rookies: Nate Williams, Ken Durrett, John Mengelt, Sid Catlett, Jake Jones, and Gil McGregor.

Matt Guokas had come to the Royals in a trade with the Chicago Bulls for Charlie Paulk. Cousy had come to the conclusion that Paulk, like so many other of his players, wasn't aggressive enough. It begged the question of if the only person who could have lived up to Cousy's expectation under the boards was someone like Hulk Hogan.

Nonetheless, in all fairness to Cousy, he may have been right about Charlie Paulk. His NBA career lasted only five years and 120 games. But now both players, Charlie Paulk and Flynn Robinson, obtained in the botched Oscar Robertson trade by Cousy and Axelson were with other NBA teams leaving the Royals with nothing in return for a future Hall of Fame player.

After defeating Phoenix 110–95 on November 7 at Cincinnati Gardens with the usual crowd of 3,076 diehard fans, surprisingly, the Royals found themselves in first place in the Central Division of the East Conference with a record of 3–6.

It was ridiculous and apparent that the Royals needed to improve to stay ahead of Atlanta and Baltimore. Joe Axelson was stating that he was looking into some trades.

Meanwhile, it was a surprise to no one that Bob Cousy was once again blaming the Royals' poor play on Sam Lacey, even though he had scored 18 points and had 17 rebounds in the win over Phoenix. In the past two games, Lacey had scored 35 points and grabbed 33 rebounds.

Everything was on Sam Lacey's shoulders, Cousy and Joe Axelson expected him to carry the team. Next up for the Royals was the Boston Celtics in a game at Omaha, and Joe Axelson was telling the press that whether or not he makes a trade might depend on how the Royals do against the Celtics. What Axelson was really saying was it all depended on how Sam Lacey did against the Celtics.

"A big part of Sam's problem," said Cousy, "is that he's not in the best of shape. I'm convinced that's why he has been tiring. I'm going to run him, run him and run him."[6]

It turned out that things didn't go well for the Royals in the game at the Omaha Civic Auditorium witnessed by 6,035 fans. The Royals were behind the entire game and defeated by the Celtics 120–109 as Dave Cowens scored 30 points and had 19 rebounds. For the Royals, Sam Lacey had one field goal for 2 points and was simply unable to contain Cowens. Bob Cousy actually gave up on Lacey and replaced him with rookie Gil McGregor.

Following the game, Cousy was livid. Nate Archibald and Norm Van Lier had been sulking because Cousy had been starting Matt Guokas at guard. "The rookies, as well as the veterans, are letting it go in one ear and out the other," said Cousy. "I'm beginning to wonder if we've got a bunch of prima donnas. Somebody gets their feelings hurt; we take a guy out of the game at a certain time and guys are sulking. It looks like we're dealing with a bunch of 12-year-olds."[7]

In regard to Dave Cowens pushing Sam Lacey around and then Gil McGregor, Cousy stated that it had been a rough game out there and it wasn't all Lacey's fault because Cowens is quicker than he is. But Cousy added, "They came to play and banged us around. And if [Lacey] and McGregor allow Cowens to intimidate them again next week, I'm going to fine them both $500."[8]

Bob Cousy had a very young team; nine of his players had a total of three years' NBA experience and for the third time in three years as coach of the Royals, at the preference of himself and Joe Axelson, he was starting the rebuilding process all over again. Cousy had hoped that his young players would adapt to the pro game quicker than they were. It was apparent that his patience in getting the job done was waning.

Sam Lacey was a good basketball player, so respected that eventually his number 44 would be retired by the Sacramento

Kings and hang high above the rafters at Sacramento's arena. But Bob Cousy was never going to turn Lacey into the new Bill Russell.

In a frantic attempt to keep the Royals' 1971–72 season from going down the drain, two days after the loss to Boston at Omaha, Cousy and Axelson traded Norm Van Lier to the Chicago Bulls for Jim Fox, a 6'10" center. Fox had been an eighth-round draft choice by the Royals in 1965 and later traded along with Happy Hairston to the Detroit Pistons for Tom Van Arsdale and John Tresvant.

Bob Cousy said that it was the most difficult trade he had ever had to make as Van Lier had given him 200%. That, of course, was an astronomical rating considering that Cousy felt Jerry Lucas had only given him 80%.

But with Nate Archibald starting to demonstrate the ability to control the ball and score a lot of points, Cousy was of the opinion that the team could not have two guards on the court who wanted to control the ball, so he traded Van Lier.

At the time, Norm Van Lier, a black man, was dating Cousy's oldest daughter Marie, who met him when she came to Cincinnati from the east on vacations. So, there were some individuals who were convinced that Van Lier was traded to break up the couple's interracial relationship. But Cousy denied that and told various people that Norm would have made a great son-in-law.

In regard to Jim Fox, Cousy stated, "Who knows, acquiring Fox might result in improvement in the play of Lacey and Darrall Imhoff. Neither has been playing up to his potential. If I have to, I'll use three different players at center."[9]

Cousy would have the opportunity to try his triple-platoon center strategy almost immediately on November 10 against the New York Knicks. Superstar center Willis Reed had been hobbling around with a sore knee, was sidelined most of the game, and only able to play the entire third quarter. As a result, the Royals, led by Nate Archibald with 22 points and Sam Lacey with 16 rebounds, defeated the Knicks 99–85.

Although the Royals had won, Bob Cousy was disappointed with Sam Lacey's shooting performance. The big center had made only 4 field goals out of 14 attempts while being guarded by Jerry Lucas who had 21 rebounds and 17 points. Bob Cousy, not wanting to give much credit to the play of Jerry Lucas simply said that Lacey had been given a lot of chances and should have had a field day.

Sam Lacey was very aware of all the criticism of his play in the Cincinnati newspapers. "They can write anything they want," said Sam. "I just don't give a damn. I just play the best I can. I'm doing the best I can."[10] Lacey attributed his poor shooting performance against the Knicks to attempting to make hook shots while working inside. However, he had a tendency to palm the ball when he shot.

Jerry Lucas had been doing a great job filling in at center for the aching Willis Reed and did indeed put pressure on Lacey. Playing about 30 minutes a game since Reed became injured, Lucas was the Knicks' leading rebounder with 236 grabs in 384 minutes played so far in the season.

Jerry Lucas' business holdings had been considered by Bob Cousy to be an enormous distraction to his game. But by 1971, things weren't going well in the world of hamburgers and milkshakes for Jerry Lucas. He was experiencing financial problems and been forced to declare bankruptcy in his business holdings when his fast-food franchise, Jerry Lucas Beef and Shakes, went belly-up. Then, following the 1970–71 season, the San Francisco Warriors traded Lucas to the New York Knicks for Cazzie Russell.

But in the Bob Cousy-Joe Axelson Cincinnati Royals saga it would be Jerry Lucas who had the last laugh. Critics of Lucas had pointed out that although he played on the Cincinnati Royals with Oscar Robertson, he never won a championship in his prime years and was traded twice. First, to the Golden State Warriors in 1969 for Jim King and Billy Turner because Bob Cousy wanted to put more speed and hustle into the Royals' game. Then a little over a year later in May 1971, Lucas was traded by Warriors to the New York Knicks.

In 1972, Jerry Lucas would finally make it to the NBA Finals with the New York Knicks, but they lost to the Los Angeles Lakers 4 games to 1.

The next season in 1972–73, Jerry Lucas got his championship ring as the New York Knicks turned the tables on the Los Angeles Lakes, defeating them in the finals 4 games to 1. Lucas played a formidable role in the Knicks championship coming off the bench playing 28.2 minutes per game, averaging 9.9 points per game, 7.2 rebounds, and 4.5 assists.

The night of the Royals vs. Knicks game, Cincinnati Gardens was only about 25% full with 3,483 fans in attendance. A curious situation occurred when, for some reason, there was considerable enthusiastic and loud support from those fans for the visiting New York Knicks. Sportswriters and others there for the game were amazed at this circumstance as various groups of fans in the arena were overpowering the sparse Royals fans in their vocal support of the Knicks. Many observers thought that perhaps all the cheering for the Knicks was actually Royals fans cheering for Jerry Lucas.

But when a few of the media members investigated, they discovered that the Knicks were being supported by several hundred college students who were from New York and New Jersey that attended the University of Cincinnati and Xavier University. With the indifferent and passive attitude of the sparse Royals fans that night, the students' boisterous support of the Knicks had literary turned a road game in Cincinnati Gardens into a home game for the New Yorkers.

Cousy was very happy with the win and at the moment, the Royals clung to the Central Division lead by two games over Baltimore.

On November 27, another young NBA team that included a grizzled old veteran came to Cincinnati Gardens—they were reigning NBA champion, the Milwaukee Bucks. The largest crowd of the year, 8,858, showed up to witness the play of Kareem Abdul-Jabbar and Oscar Robertson, and no one was surprised with the result. The Bucks defeated the Royals 114–81. It was the lowest point total scored by a Royals team since the Boston Celtics held the Royals to 87 points in a 1966 game.

Early in the fourth period, the Bucks led by 39 points when Kareem Abdul-Jabbar was taken out of the game. Jabbar had scored 20 points with 16 rebounds for the night.

Oscar Robertson led the Bucks with 25 points and 14 assists. The Big O, who held almost every pro basketball record in Cincinnati Gardens, set another with 9 assists in the third quarter. Asked if it made any difference that he was playing against his old team, Robertson just shrugged his shoulders.

Circumstances for the Royals were about to get a lot worse. Between December 12, 1971, and January 9, 1972, the Royals would lose fourteen straight games leaving them with a season record of 10–31. Finally, on January 11, the Royals would defeat the Buffalo Braves 109–107 in overtime on a basket by Sam Lacey to end their agony. At that point, the season was half over, there were 40 games remaining, and to make the playoffs the Royals would need to win about two-thirds of them.

On February 16, Wilt Chamberlain scored 19 points for the Los Angeles Lakers in a losing effort vs. the Phoenix Suns. In the third period, Chamberlain became the first player in NBA history to score 30,000 points in his career. In a recent game, Chamberlain had surpassed Bill Russell's career record for rebounds.

Two days later, on February 18, the Cincinnati Royals would begin another losing streak. This time the Royals lost eight games in a row leaving them with a season record of 18–44.

Then, suddenly the Royals went on a hot streak, winning four games in a row to make their record 22–44. Despite their poor record, they were only 6½ games behind Atlanta for second place.

After beating Buffalo 100–97 on February 24 at the University of Dayton arena in front of 2,422 fans, everyone seemed pumped up. Nate Archibald had scored 32 points and Tom Van Arsdale, 19. Sam Lacey, who had scored 20 points and grabbed 15 rebounds, was all smiles as he told the press, "We needed this one tonight. So we worked the last eight minutes. Everyone was after loose balls and rebounds."[11]

The Royals then departed on a west coast road trip, February 25 to March 1, and lost four straight games in Los Angeles, Seattle, Oakland (Golden State), and Houston to limp home with a record of 22–48.

For three months, as the Royals continued to flounder, Joe Axelson had been looking for a new home to relocate the team. On March 15, the players, their fans, and the community at large in Cincinnati got the disappointing news that the Royals were being moved to Kansas City next season.

Joe Axelson had received an offer to buy the Royals from Peter Graham, a San Diego financier. But it was turned down on the recommendation of Royals attorney Ambrose Lindhorst as unsatisfactory. Eventually, a group of ten Kansas City businessmen would buy the Royals for $5 million, but at the present, Max and Jeremy Jacobs still owned the Royals and would continue to control it throughout the transfer.

The only concern expressed by the Jacobs brothers in authorizing the franchise shift to Kansas City was in regard to Cincinnati Gardens, which they still owned. It was a no-brainer that they couldn't sell hot dogs in an empty auditorium. The brothers were quickly relieved when informed by Axelson that for the coming year, the Gardens had about 200 days and nights of events booked including an ice show, circus, wrestling, the Harlem Globetrotters, and a few college basketball games, including the annual sell-out—a shootout between crosstown rivals, Cincinnati vs. Xavier.

While Ambrose Lindhorst held a somber and stuffy press conference in Cincinnati to announce the move of the Royals, Joe Axelson and his assistant, Larry Staverman, held a warm and fuzzy welcome wagon news conference in Kansas City. Staverman was familiar with the city as he had been a player with the Kansas City Steers in the defunct ABL.

Chastising Cincinnati and the Royals fans, Axelson remarked to the Kansas City press, "We have tried every promotion under the sun. But you can't build a crowd on gimmicks. An average of 3,500 customers this year represents the NBA's lowest attendance figure. This number also represents a drop of about 500 a game from last season. Kansas City is a good basketball town, Cincinnati is not. Xavier [University] and [The University of] Cincinnati have good basketball teams and don't even fill small buildings with students getting in free."[12]

The move of the franchise was a strange situation. In actuality, the Royals were not moving to Kansas City but were going to become a regional team playing in both Kansas City and Omaha. Since Kansas City already had a Major League Baseball team called the Royals, the name of the basketball team would be changed to the Kansas City-Omaha Kings.

The plan was for the Kings to play 21 home games in Kansas City, ten in Omaha, and ten in St. Louis.

The act of becoming a regional team infuriated some of the Royals players. Tom Van Arsdale, the Royals players' union representative, informed NBA commissioner Walter Kennedy and players' association attorney Larry Fleisher that the move was bush and the players were threatening to fight it.

Van Arsdale told the press, "None of us are happy. How can you be happy playing 61 games on the road? It's ridiculous."[13]

Sam Lacey was taking the move more personal. "Hey you're never home man," said Lacey. "I don't like the idea of moving anyway. I like the city. I'm used to it."[14]

The San Francisco Warriors players had been confronted with a similar situation a year ago when the Warriors management wanted to play half their home games in San Diego and half in Oakland while changing the team name to the Golden State Warriors. To that end, players' association attorney Larry Fleischer informed Walter Kennedy that the players were not going to be in a situation where they were a floating franchise. The team name was changed and a compromise was reached as the Warriors played all but six of their home games in Oakland.

Everybody had their opinion of what happened to cause the Royals to fail in Cincinnati. Some were saying that fans, angered by Bob Cousy and Joe Axelson trading Oscar Robertson and Jerry Lucas, stopped going to Royals games. Some blamed very difficult accessibility of getting to Cincinnati Gardens—it was a fact that there was very little public transportation to the Gardens. Others blamed the success of the Cincinnati Bengals, the rise of the Big Red Machine (Pete Rose, Johnny Bench, Tony Perez, Joe Morgan, etc.), or the popularity of college basketball in the city with Cincinnati and Xavier.

Some explanations were downright silly, such as the notion advanced by *Cincinnati Enquirer* sportswriter Jim Schottelkotte that the domination of the sport by blacks had added to its demise in Cincinnati.[15]

The racial theory for the demise of the Royals in Cincinnati just doesn't cut the mustard. When the Royals first made Cincinnati their home in 1957–58, they were a predominately white team and averaged 3,643 fans per game. Their last season in Cincinnati, in 1971–72, the Royals were a predominately black team and average home attendance was 3,688.

The reason for professional basketball failing in Cincinnati is more complex. There were some who felt the absentee ownership of Max and Jeremy Jacobs was a large part of the problem. It's true that the Jacobs brothers were very busy running their concessions empire and relied heavily on Bob Cousy, Joe Axelson, and Ambrose Lindhorst to make autonomous business decisions relative to the Cincinnati Royals.

According to Oscar Robertson, Bob Cousy was trusting Joe Axelson to make decisions on players, and he didn't know a basketball from a pumpkin.

When Bob Cousy was asked what went wrong in Cincinnati, he replied, "Let's blame it all on Joe Axelson, he's dead so he can't defend himself."[16]

While Cousy appears to be avoiding the issue, his suggestion could be taken as tongue-in-cheek. But forty-five years after the fact, the actions and non-actions of Joe Axelson appear to be pretty much the bottom line on the demise of the Cincinnati Royals. Joe Axelson did not know how to build a successful professional basketball team. Axelson was constantly jumping into empty pools with trades and draft choices that didn't make any sense, and he didn't have a clue on how to promote the team or the league. It was as if he was marketing challenged. Beyond that, Axelson kept appealing to absentee ownership in Buffalo to help him find the solution to the Royals' difficulties rather than working with local entrepreneurs and local government officials.

There could have been a different outcome to the Royals' dilemma if Joe Axelson had any business foresight rather than tunnel vision. In just a few years after the Royals left Cincinnati for Kansas City, a new 14,000-seat basketball/hockey arena was built downtown next door to Riverfront Stadium that was very accessible to fans throughout the city, suburbs, and Northern Kentucky by both public transportation and interstate highways. Parking was also part of the plan, and in the winter, 4,500 parking spaces would be available next door in Riverfront Stadium and an additional 18,000 parking spaces in downtown Cincinnati within ten minutes walking distance of the arena.

Furthermore, in the early 1970s, about the time Joe Axelson and Bob Cousy were packing their bags for Kansas City, Cincinnati was about to experience an urban renaissance as the city fathers continued to implement its 1948 Master Plan for development.

The construction on Riverfront Stadium that seated 60,000 for football and 52,000 for baseball, was completed at the same time that the construction of a new convention center opened which spawned lots of investment in new restaurants, bars, and three new hotels downtown; even the city's historic public meeting place, Fountain Square, had been torn down and rebuilt. The core area of the city had become very popular with the 20-something crowd and "Yuppies." There were rock concerts, a taste of Cincinnati festival, Oktoberfest, and a Labor Day extravaganza on the Ohio Riverfront that as a stand-alone event attracted nearly 250,000 persons annually and culminated with one of the largest pyrotechnical displays in the nation.

The move of the Royals from Cincinnati Gardens, located fifteen miles from the core area of the city sandwiched in between a heavily industrialized area, a dowdy drive-in-movie theatre, and a poor black ghetto neighborhood, served by almost no public transportation, would have been replaced by a brand-new arena in new booming downtown Cincinnati.

If Bob Cousy could have hung in there just a couple more years and Joe Axelson would have had one iota of vision, they would have had a brand-new home for the Royals and a generation of thousands of new young and very enthusiastic fans that would have supported the Royals along with their corps of 2,500 loyal rooters from Cincinnati Gardens.

If Joe Axelson would have worked with city officials, they could have solved the Royals' attendance dilemma—but he didn't have the communication skills and never tried. The Cincinnati Reds had faced a similar situation in the late 1960s and both the City, led by Mayor Eugene Ruehlmann and various private entities such as the *Cincinnati Enquirer,* and private individuals went into action to protect everyone's interest.

At that time, there was a unique aspect of Cincinnati's economic demographics in that the city had a relatively small number of powerful and wealthy families. These families all knew each other and sometimes worked harmoniously together. Had Joe Axelson attempted to interface with some of these privileged Cincinnatians he would have been welcomed and found them to be strong advocates for finding a viable solution to his organization's needs.

But never did Bob Cousy, Joe Axelson, or Ambrose Lindhorst ever ask for any civic or private assistance and the phone never rang in city hall nor in the Hyde Park Country Club.

Bob Cousy was ambivalent towards Cincinnati and Joe Axelson was only interested in attempting to impress Max Jacobs and become a big shot. It's doubtful if Axelson had ever heard of the Cincinnati Chamber of Commerce.

It made no difference to Ambrose Lindhorst if he was serving the Jacobs' interest in Cincinnati, Kansas City, or Timbuktu. Lindhorst was simply a loyal legal servant, or pawn, depending on your point of view, of the Jacobs brothers. He saw the world in terms of contracts, with one glaring omission: Oscar Robertson's.

Max and Jeremy Jacobs didn't deal with municipalities; they felt more comfortable dealing with intermediaries of a different stripe. Like their late father, Louie, they didn't see much need to leave Buffalo for any reason; they also held his belief that same sun that shined in Cincinnati shined in Buffalo and Kansas City, too. So, the Jacobs brothers trusted Joe Axelson to be their noble centurion in the Midwest region of their vast sports concessions business empire.

But it turned out that the modus operandi of Joe Axelson that "the grass is always greener on the other side of the fence," didn't necessarily prove to be a truism. Consequently, the transfer of the Royals to Kansas City would eventually fail, too, and the westward trek of the franchise to find the promised land would continue on to Sacramento.

The Royals played their last home game at Cincinnati Gardens on Friday evening March 24, 1972, with 4,052 fans on hand to say farewell. While it seemed a little out of place, at halftime, Connie Dierking was inducted into the Royals Hall of Fame. The Royals defeated the Baltimore Bullets handily, 132–114, with Nate Archibald scoring 38 points. For good measure, Sam Lacey had 24 points and John Mengelt tossed in 22.

While one banner hanging in the stands proclaimed "Welcome ABA." It had been a quiet and dignified end to Royals' era in Cincinnati.

Bob Cousy was silent and seemed to be relieved that it was all over. He had been homesick for his family and friends back east and found living and competing in Cincinnati depressing. He disliked Cincinnati Gardens and playing games before the small crowds.

As the press spoke with various players, Tom Van Arsdale said that he was putting his house in Cincinnati up for sale and going to buy one in Phoenix where his brother Dick played for the Suns.

When Baltimore forward Gus Johnson was asked what he would remember about Cincinnati Gardens he replied—"Lucas." Both Gus Johnson and Jerry Lucas had been rookies in 1963 and went head-to-head in some memorable battles under the basket. That year, Johnson finished second to Lucas in the NBA Rookie of the Year balloting.

The Royals still had two more road games to play before bringing the curtain down on the 1971–72 season. They went to Milwaukee where, on Saturday evening, they were defeated by the Bucks 119–95.

The final game of the season took place the next day on Sunday, March 26 in Cleveland before 10,289 spectators as the Royals defeated the Cavaliers 135–122 with Nate Archibald scoring 45 points and John Mengelt, 28.

The Royals finished their swan song season in the Queen City with a record of 30–52, missing the playoffs for the fifth-straight year while having a sparse season attendance average of 3,368 fans per game. Realizing that the curtain had come down on their Royals, perhaps 2,500 people in Cincinnati were angered or hurt, but it was all over and the transfer of the franchise to Kansas City could begin in earnest.

When Walter O'Malley took the Brooklyn Dodgers to Los Angeles in 1958, the LA city fathers nearly paid the Dodgers to play in their community.

While the Royals, soon to become the Kings, were provided with incentives to relocate to Kansas City/Omaha they didn't realize any multi-million-dollar sweetheart deal for relocating. Still, there were modest incentives.

Kansas City Mayor Charles Weaver agreed to charge the Kings $500 per playing date in Municipal Auditorium and provide the team with free office space at a cost of $25,000 to $30,000 a year. Also, the city agreed to build a new arena in the next few years. Lastly, Kansas City agreed to underwrite the Kings' attendance.

It was agreed that the Kansas City-Omaha Kings would not play any home games in St. Louis which disarmed the players who opposed it. Instead, in 1972–73, the Kings' schedule would include 26 home games to be played in the Municipal Auditorium in Kansas City and 15 games in Omaha Civic Auditorium.

The KC facility had been built in 1935 and had a seating capacity of 7,300. So, Bob Cousy, who had been depressed by playing in old Cincinnati Gardens, built in 1949 with a seating capacity of 14,000, was now going to play the majority of his home games in a building that was fourteen years older than the Gardens and had half the seating capacity.

The Kings' secondary home, the Omaha Civic Auditorium, was constructed in 1954 and had a seating capacity of 10,960.

At the end of the 1971–72 season, Bob Cousy had come to the end of his three-year contract that he had signed with Max Jacobs to coach the Royals. Jacobs asked Cousy to stay on during the team's transition to Kansas City because he felt it would be bad public relations if a name coach departed in the process. Once again, Jacobs threw a six-figure contract at Cousy and he agreed to stay. Cousy's public explanation for his continuing on was that he wanted to finish the building of the team he had started.

The Kings were switched to the Midwest Division with Milwaukee, Chicago, and Detroit. In the end, neither having Cousy stay on as coach nor the switch to a new division did anything to improve the play of the Kings. In 1972–73, the Kansas City-Omaha Kings finished fourth in the Midwest Division with a record of 36–46. The Royals-Kings team had now missed the playoffs for the sixth straight year.

If there was one glaring consolation for the Kings in their first year in Kansas City/Omaha, it was that 6'0" Nate "Tiny" Archibald had suddenly become one of the NBA's biggest stars. In 1972–73, Archibald led the NBA in scoring with an average of 34.0 points per game and assists with 11.4 per game. His 34.0 points per game was the highest ever in the history of the franchise, beating Oscar Robertson's 31 points per game in 1963–64, and he nearly beat Robertson's assists per game record of 11.5 per game set in 1964–65.

Archibald gave the credit for his quick rise to stardom to Bob Cousy. "He's helped me as a basketball player," said Archibald. "He's taught me how to utilize my talents most effectively, how to take charge and run a team. He's made me a much better player."[17]

According to Cousy, Archibald absorbed coaching well and despite his size, he was getting his points and knew what to do with the ball. "The kid is the first to practice and the last to leave," said Cousy. "He's worked hard to adapt himself to the needs of the team."[18]

While it was mutual admiration between Archibald and Cousy, to some observers, having a high scoring guard with the ability to find the open man seemed like Cousy was going back to square one. Hadn't he swapped out another high scoring, high assists man in Oscar Robertson in order to implement a running team with a balanced scoring attack? Perhaps after four years of coaching in the NBA, Bob Cousy had just given up and decided to let events on the court take their own direction.

On November 21, 1973, the Kings lost to Philadelphia 103–90 in a game played at Omaha. It was the Kings' fourteenth loss in twenty games in the 1973–74 season. Following the game, Bob Cousy resigned as coach.

Max Jacobs accepted Cousy's resignation and assistant coach Draff Young was appointed interim coach, and then lost the next four games in a row. Phil Johnson was named as the Kings' new coach and guided the team through the balance of the schedule winning 27 games and losing 31. The Kings finished the season in fourth place in the Midwest Division with a record of 33–49, missing the playoffs for the seventh straight year.

In 1974–75, the Kansas City-Omaha Kings began play in the newly constructed 18,344-seat Kemper Arena and would finally make it to the NBA playoffs again but lose in the first round in the West Conference Semi-Finals.

In the 1975–76 season, although the Kings still played a few games in Omaha, they would drop the name of that city and become the Kansas City Kings.

Hard times in the standings and low attendance would continue for the KC Kings throughout the rest of the late 1970s. On June 4, 1979, a storm with 70 mph winds swept through downtown Kansas City, ripping the roof off Kemper Arena, and the Kings would be relocated to Municipal Auditorium.

In 1983–84, the Kings would be sold to a group of investors from Sacramento, California for $19.5 million, and the following season, on April 14, 1985, the NBA Board of Governors would officially approve the transfer of the franchise to Sacramento where they remain today.

In Kansas City, the Kings had no more success in the standings and box office as they had in Cincinnati. In January 1985, Joe Axelson announced that the Kings were moving from Kansas City to Sacramento. At the news conference announcing the move, Axelson stated that the only hope for Kansas City getting another NBA team would be through expansion. Kings fans called Axelson "Fat Joe," and at the team's final home game at the Kemper Center in Kansas City, they wore masks of his face. On May 31, 2008, Joe Axelson died at the age of 80 in Coronado, California.

Following the death of their father, Louis, in 1968, Max and Jeremy Jacobs worked diligently to remove the taint of underworld connections to the Emprise Corporation's brand and to expand the concessions enterprise giant into new markets.

After divesting the company in the Kansas City Kings, the decade of the 1970s would be a turbulent time for Emprise. The company was constantly confronted with scandals and suggestions of corruption. In 1972, a House Select Committee on Organized Crime held hearings that led to questions about Emprise Corporation's connections with organized crime figures.

It was about the same time that Emprise was convicted of racketeering in concealing its ownership along with known organized crime figures Anthony J. Zerilli and Michael S. Polizzi in the Frontier Hotel-Casino in Las Vegas. In 1970, a Federal Grand Jury in Los Angeles had found that Emprise had made substantial loans to front men for the allegedly mob-related owners. While the mobsters received five-year prison sentences, Emprise was fined $10,000 and the late Louie Jacobs and his son, Max, were named as unindicted co-conspirators.

Also, in 1972, the U.S. Justice Department began an investigation into possible antitrust violations by Emprise. Papers filed in Buffalo alleged that Emprise, with its enormous lending power, had an unfair advantage over other companies in the sports concessions business.

Emprise was facing similar antitrust suits in Atlanta stemming from investigations of the company's racetrack operations in the southeastern part of the United States.

At that time, the Jacobs still owned the Cincinnati Royals and the U.S. Senate was holding hearings on a bill that would permit the NBA to merge with the ABA. In order for the merger to be approved, the NBA had to get a specific exemption from antitrust laws.

Sam Steiger, a Republican Congressman from Arizona, offered testimony to the committee stating that several NBA teams were reluctant to submit their tax returns in order to prove the financial necessity of the merger. Steiger cited the Cincinnati Royals as a prime example.

Steiger stated to the committee that the concession business was the most consistent profit maker in sports. He pointed out to the committee that Emprise, as the concessionaire to the Washington Senators, had made $1.7 million in the last three years while Bob Short the Senators owner had lost so much money that he had to move to the team to Texas.

Then, in summation, Steiger took it a step further in trying to connect the dots between organized crime and Emprise. "Their history is replete with business associations with underworld and organized crime," said Steiger. "Basketball very properly demands the most exemplary behavior of its players, and yet there is no apparent harm in the sole owner of a basketball club having criminal associations with criminals."[19]

While no action was taken by the committee against the Jacobs brothers or Emprise, the stigma of the hearings remained.

Through it all, Jeremy and Max Jacobs continued to expand their business and Emprise thrived. In 1975, the brothers individually bought the Boston Bruins of the NHL. They also bought Boston Garden, where the Bruins played their home games, from the Storer Broadcasting Company.

Nonetheless, by the end of 1976, the company's fitness to administer its contracts had faced challenges in eight of twenty-eight states in which it held liquor licenses, as well as six of the nine states in which it had pari-mutuel operations.

While several states restored Emprise's operating licenses on appeals, a plea for a presidential pardon was denied in 1977. This action led a number of states to deny Emprise licenses due to having laws prohibiting convicted felons (the Las Vegas case) from holding liquor licenses.

In 1977, Jeremy and Max Jacobs decided that their enterprise needed a facelift, so they dissolved Emprise and began a new parent holding company, Sportsystems Corporation, to oversee the company with annual revenues of $225 million. By now, the company had become diversified and was not only in the concessions and racetrack business but also had subsidiaries in steel, smelting, and appliance distribution.

In 1980, the name of the parent company was changed again, this time from Sportsystems to Delaware North Companies, Inc. (DNC). By the end of the 1980s, the company seemed to have recovered from the rocky period of controversy in the 1970s and was now positioning itself to enter new markets such as conventions centers, international airports, and even National Parks.

Today, Delaware North Corporation is run by a third generation of the Jacobs family, Jeremy Jacobs' sons, Jerry Jr. and Lou, who serve as co-CEOs. It is a vast conglomerate with annual revenues exceeding $3 billion from a portfolio that includes management of hotels, resorts, and gaming facilities, the Kennedy Space Center, and Wembley Stadium in London. DNC ranks number 169 on *Forbes'* list of largest privately held companies in the U.S.

Circumstances for the Kings didn't improve much in the Golden State. In the forty-five years since the team was relocated from Cincinnati to Kansas City and finally to Sacramento, the Kings have only made the playoffs fifteen times and reached the conference finals twice before losing. The Sacramento Kings last made the NBA playoffs in 2006.

Entering the 2018–2019 season, the Sacramento Kings franchise has not won an NBA championship since 1950–51. It is the longest team championship drought in NBA history and one of the longest non-title stretches in American professional sports.

The Sacramento Kings have retired ten jersey numbers dating back to the franchise's origins in Rochester, five of them were worn by former Cincinnati Royals players: (1) Nate Archibald, (12) Maurice Stokes, (14) Oscar Robertson, (27) Jack Twyman, and (44) Sam Lacey.

In the history of the NBA, only Wilt Chamberlain, Bill Russell, and Bob Pettit—all taller than Jerry Lucas—averaged more rebounds. The fact that Sacramento Kings have neglected to retire Lucas' number (16) is a glaring oversight.

Jerry Lucas was the first player to win a championship at four levels: high school, college, NBA, and Gold in the Olympics. Lucas left the NBA after a 12-year career in 1974. He was elected to the Naismith Memorial Basketball Hall of Fame in 1980. In 1996, Lucas was selected as one of the NBA's fifty greatest players. Now 78 years old, Lucas lives in California.

After retiring from professional basketball in 1975 as the NBA's All-Time assists leader, Oscar Robertson returned to live in Cincinnati. In 1980, he was elected to the Naismith Memorial Basketball Hall of Fame and in 1996, was selected as one of the NBA's fifty greatest players.

In 2003, Oscar Robertson's biography, *The Big O—My Life, My Times, My Game,* was published. In the book, Robertson states that his motivation for fighting to get rid of the NBA's reserve clause began in 1970 when he was president of the National Basketball Players Association and Joe Axelson attempted to trade him from the Cincinnati Royals without ever reading his contract.

In 1971, Bob Cousy was elected to the Naismith Memorial Basketball Hall of Fame, and in 1996 was selected as one of the NBA's fifty greatest players.

Eventually, Oscar Robertson (University of Cincinnati) and Bob Cousy (Holy Cross) would be immortalized with statues of their likenesses on their alma mater's campuses.

Although nearly a half-century has passed, it is apparent that unresolved conflict still exists between Bob Cousy, now 90 years old, and Oscar Robertson, now 80 years old, over their Cincinnati experience. In 2018, both Cousy and Robertson appeared in the

Oscar Robertson statue at the University of Cincinnati. (Courtesy of John Ruschulte.)

ESPN documentary *Basketball—A Love Story,* and when questioned about their player-coach relationship with the Royals, both were standoffish with their responses.

While Bob Cousy and Oscar Robertson respected each other's ability as players they never respected each other's concept of what a team player represented. Cousy wanted to change Robertson's game, have him shoot less and pass more. There was never a remote chance that their personalities and philosophies would blend in a player and coach relationship in Cincinnati. But what is more surprising is that Bob Cousy and Joe Axelson showed such blatant disrespect for The Big O, the finest all-around player in the history of the game, by trading him and receiving so little in return. Cousy's actions with the Royals destroyed his professional coaching career. There was no second chance for Cincinnati either; with the departure of the Royals, professional basketball has never returned to the Queen City. After resigning from the Kansas City Kings, Bob Cousy would never coach another professional basketball team. Jerry Lucas was not surprised by Cousy's failure as an NBA coach; in his opinion, "Great players never make great coaches."[20]

Bibliography

Books

Associated Press Sports Staff, Supervising Editor: Will Grimsley, Photo Editor: Thomas V. diLustro, (basketball by Mike Recht). *A Century of Sports.* N.p.: Plimpton Press, 1971.

Benson, Michael. *Everything You Wanted to Know about the New York Knicks: A Who's Who of Everyone Who Ever Played on or Coached the NBA's Most Celebrated Team.* N.p.: Taylor Trade Publishing, 2007.

Cousy, Bob, with John Devaney. *The Killer Instinct.* New York: Random House, 1975.

Halberstam, David. *The Fifties.* New York: Fawcett Columbine, 1993.

Madden, Bill. *Steinbrenner—The Last Lion of Baseball.* New York: itbooks, 2010.

Pluto, Terry. *Tall Tales—The Glory Years of the NBA, in the Words of the Men Who Played, Coached, and Built Pro Basketball.* New York: Simon & Shuster, 1992.

Robertson, Oscar. *The Big O—My Life, My Times, My Game.* N.p.: Rodale, 2003.

Rosen, Charley. *The Wizard of Odds—How Jack Molinas Almost Destroyed the Game of Basketball.* New York/London/Sydney/Toronto: Seven Stories Press, 2001.

Russell, Bill with Alan Steinberg. *Red and Me—My Coach, My Lifelong Friend.* New York: Harper Collins, 2009.

Simmons, Bill. *The Book of Basketball—The NBA According to the Sports Guy.* New York: Ballantine Books, 2009.

Stewart, Mark. *Basketball—A History of Hoops.* New York/London/Hong Kong/Sydney: Franklin Watts, 1998.

Taylor, John. *The Rivalry—Bill Russell, Wilt Chamberlain and the Golden Age of Basketball.* New York: Ballantine Books, 2005.

West, Jerry and Jonathan Coleman. *West by West—My Charmed, Tormented Life.* New York: Little Brown and Company, 2011.

Journals

Cook, Kevin. "The Rochester Royals—The Story of Professional Basketball, Rochester History." Edited by Ruth Rosenberg Naparsteck. *City Historian* LVIII, no.1 (Winter 1996).

Research Papers

Compiled by Robert Bradley, with special thanks to Steve Dimitry, Roger Davis, Roger Meyer, and Dick Pfander. "History of the American Basketball League." APBR.org, http://www.apbr.org/ablhist.html.

Robert Bradley. "The History of NBA Labor—Association for Professional Basketball Research" APBR.org, www.apbr.org/labor.html.

Libraries

Boston Public Library
Monmouth County Library (NJ)
The New York Public Library
The Public Library of Cincinnati and Hamilton County

Magazines

Horizons, University of Cincinnati Magazine 25, no. 6 (Spring 1996).
Sport 29, no. 1 (January 1960).
Sport 49, no. 2 (February 1970).
Sports Illustrated 36, no. 22 (May 29, 1972).

Newspapers

Asbury Park Press
Boston Globe
Boston Herald
Cincinnati Enquirer
Cincinnati Post & Times-Star
New York Post
New York Times

Websites

www.allstatesugarbowl.com
www.basketball-reference.com
biography.yourdictionary.com/bob-cousy
www.buffalonews.com/business
www.fresnobee.com/sports/outdoors/article24790630.html
www.floridabulldog.org/2013/12/broward-commision-skips-bids-award-15-year-ai
www.goholycross.com/sports-baskbl/archive-files/careers.pdf
www.libraryweb.org/-rochhist'v58—1996/v58i1
www.nba.com/history
www.sandiegoreader.com
www.si.com/vault
www.spectatorarchive.library.columbia.edu
www.sportsecyclopedia.com/nba/rochester/rochroyals
sports.espn.go.com/espn/blachhistory2009/news/story?id=3932017

Notes

Chapter 1

1. "Mother Recalls Cousy Prophecy," *Boston Globe*, March 18, 1963, 24.
2. *New York Times*, March 17, 1946, 53.
3. Arthur Siegel, "Young Referee Found Cousy For Julian, HC," *Boston Globe*, March 18, 1963, 31.
4. "Top 25 Sports Moments," *Holy Cross Magazine*, http://magazine.holycross.edu/issue.
5. Bob Cousy with John Devaney, *The Killer Instinct*, (New York: Random House, 1975), 18.

Chapter 2

1. Chris Broussard, "Pioneer with Early Black Pro Team Looks Back," *The New York Times*, February 15, 2004, sec. 8, 2.
2. Broussard, "Pioneer with," sec. 8, 2.
3. www.goduquesne.com/sports/m-baskbl
4. Ed Linn, "The Wonderful Wizard of Boston," *Sport* 29, no. 1 (January 1960): 59.
5. Linn, "The Wonderful," 59.
6. Arthur Siegel, "Young Referee Found Cousy For Julian, HC," *Boston Globe*, March 18, 1963, 31.
7. Linn, "The Wonderful," 60.
8. *Boston Globe*, March 18, 1963, 31.
9. Bill Russell with Alan Steinberg, *Red and Me—My Coach, My Lifelong Friend* (New York: Harper Collins, 2009), 44.

Chapter 3

1. Dave Anderson, "The Opportunity to Walk," *The New York Times*, Sports of the Times, http://partners.nytimes.com/library/sports/backtalk/021701.
2. Anderson, "The Opportunity," Sports of the Times.
3. "Nat Holman—The Man, His Legacy and CCNY," The City College Library, http://digital-archives.ccny.cuny.edu/exhibits/holman/basketball_scandal.html.
4. Alfred E. Clark, "Judge in Fix Case Condemns Kentucky Teams and Coach," *The New York Times*, April 30, 1952, 1.
5. Clark, "Judge in Fix Case," 1.
6. "George Mikan vs. The Knicks," In *NBA.com: Encyclopedia*, www.nba.com/encyclopedia/finals/MikanvKnicks.html.
7. John Taylor, *The Rivalry—Bill Russell, Wilt Chamberlain and the Golden Age of Basketball* (New York: Ballantine Books, 2005), 37.

8. Terry Pluto, *Tall Tales—The Glory Years of the NBA, in the Words of the Men Who Played, Coached, and Built Pro Basketball* (New York: Simon & Shuster, 1992), 21.

Chapter 4

1. David Halberstam, *The Fifties* (New York: Fawcett Columbine, 1993), 697.

2. John Taylor, *The Rivalry—Bill Russell, Wilt Chamberlain and the Golden Age of Basketball* (New York: Ballantine Books, 2005), 77.

3. Bill Russell with Alan Steinberg, *Red and Me—My Coach, My Lifelong Friend* (New York: Harper Collins, 2009), 39.

4. Russell with Steinberg, *Red and Me—My Coach,* 130.

5. Clifton Brown, "The Foundation of a Dynasty," in *NBA.com: Encyclopedia,* http://www.nba.com/encyclopedia/celtics_1957.html.

Chapter 5

1. Kevin Cook, "The Rochester Royals—The Story of Professional Basketball," *Rochester History*, Edited by Ruth Rosenberg Naparsteck, vol. LVIII, no. 1 (Winter 1996): 13.

2. Cook, "The Rochester," 15.

3. Associated Press, "Royals Seek New Home," *The New York Times*, March 14, 1957, 37.

4. "Stokes Still in Coma, May Be Encephalitis," *Cincinnati Post*, March 17, 1958, 1.

5. Aram Goudsouzian, "Can Basketball Survive Chamberlain?" http://www.kshs.org/publicat/history/s005/wtumn, 167.

Chapter 6

1. Indiana University Department of History, "A Closer Look at Indiana's Klan," *Indiana Magazine of History*, http://www.iub.edu-imaghist/for_teachers/mdrnprd/stmp/Klan.html.

2. Zak Keefer, "Bob Collins Championed Attucks amid Threats, Bigotry," *The Indianapolis Star,* http://www.indystar.com/longformsports.

3. Bill Simmons, *The Book of Basketball—The NBA According to the Sports Guy*, ESPN books (New York: Ballantine Books, 2009).

4. Haldane Dosher Higgins, "Inspired by Oscar, Letters," *University of Cincinnati Magazine* 45, no. 1 (March 2015): 3.

5. "Who Named Oscar the 'Big O'?," *The University of Cincinnati News Record*, April 24, 1970, 8.

6. Oscar Robertson, *The Big O—My Life, My Times, My Game* (n.p.: Rodale, 2003).

7. Wally Forste, "Oscar Scores Big 56; Corny Musketeer Ace," *Cincinnati Post*, January 10, 1958, 20.

8. Louis Effrat, "Robertson Sets Garden Scoring Mark as Cincinnati Routs Seton Hall Five," *The New York Times*, January 10, 1958, 27.

9. Effrat, "Robertson Sets," 27.

10. Wally Forste, "Ozz's Lead Slim Over Wilt," *Cincinnati Post*, January 13, 1958. 13.

11. Dick Forbes, "Mendenhall 'Clobbered,' Referee Missed It—Smith," *Cincinnati Enquirer*, March 15, 1958, 11.

12. Dick Forbes, "Bearcats Wallop Wichita, 88 to 74," *Cincinnati Enquirer*, February 22, 1959.

13. Stan Olson, "California Dreamin' a Reality," *Knight-Ridder/Tribune News*, http://www.chicagotribune.com.

14. Olson, "California Dreamin'."

15. Jerry West and Jonathan Coleman, *West by West—My Charmed, Tormented Life* (New York: Little Brown and Company, 2011), 58.

16. Steve Kornacki, "Michigan Great Russell Reflects on 'The House That Cazzie Built,'" October 29, 2014, http://www.mgoblue.com/sports/m-baskbl/spec-rel/102914aac.html.

17. West and Coleman, *West by West,* 103.

Chapter 7

1. Terry Pluto, *Tall Tales—The Glory Years of the NBA, in the Words of the Men Who Played, Coached, and Built Pro Basketball* (New York: Simon & Shuster, 1992).

2. Oscar Robertson, *The Big O—My Life, My Times, My Game,* (n.p.: Rodale, 2003).

3. Robertson, *The Big O.*

4. Jerry West and Jonathan Coleman, *West by West—My Charmed, Tormented Life* (New York: Little Brown and Company, 2011), 104.

5. William Leggett, "The New Kid on The Block Takes on The Champ," *Sports Illustrated*, November 14, 1960, www.si.com/vault/1960/11/14/585198.

6. Leggett, "The New Kid on the Block."

7. Bill Madden, *Steinbrenner—The Last Lion of Baseball* (New York: it-books, 2010), 42.

8. Madden, *Steinbrenner—The Last,* 43

9. Kevin Grace and Gregg Hand, *The University of Cincinnati,* (Montgomery, AL: Community Communications, 1995), 152.

10. Arthur Daley, "Paying the Piper," *The New York Times*, July 13, 1962, 15.

Chapter 8

1. Bob Cousy with John Devaney, *The Killer Instinct*, (New York: Random House, 1975), 9.

2. Jerry Lucas, telephone interview by the author, March 30, 2015.

3. Harry Reckner, "Auerbach, Fan Exchange Blows," *Cincinnati Post*, December 2, 1962, 23.

4. Pat Harmon, "Oscar Again Helps Win All-Star," *Cincinnati Post*, January 17, 1963, 25.

5. Bill Russell with Alan Steinberg, *Red and Me—My Coach, My Lifelong Friend*, (New York: Harper Collins, 2009), 167.

6. Jerry Nason, "Cousy Day," *Boston Globe*, March 19, 1963, 23.

7. Nason, "Cousy Day," 23.

8. Nason, "Cousy Day," 23.

9. Joe Looney, "Cousy's Celts Topple Nats," *Boston Herald*, March 18, 1963, 24.

10. Will McDonough, "Cousy's Smile Talks," *Boston Globe*, March 18, 1963, 24.
11. AP, "Celts Clip Nats in Cousy Final," *Cincinnati Enquirer*, March 18, 1963.
12. Jim Schottelkotte, "Can Royals Do It Again in Celts' Lair?," *Cincinnati Enquirer*, March 31, 1963, 1D.
13. Jim Schottelkotte, "Auerbach Credits Royals' Reserves," *Cincinnati Enquirer*, April 1, 1963, 40.
14. Oscar Robertson, *The Big O—My Life, My Times, My Game*, (n.p.: Rodale, 2003), 167.
15. Harry Reckner, "Xavier Floor is 'Neutral'," *Cincinnati Post*, April 1, 1963, 17.
16. Jim Schottelkotte, "Cincinnati Royals Sold to Local Businessman," *Cincinnati Enquirer*, April 1, 1963, 1.
17. Al Heim, "'I'd Listen'—Juck; Grace Surprised," *Cincinnati Enquirer*, April 2, 1963, 27.
18. Jim Schottelkotte, "Sale to Hensel Needs Sanction," *Cincinnati Enquirer*, April 3, 1963, 21.
19. Jim Schottelkotte, Royals Set for Celts Tonight, *Cincinnati Enquirer*, April 3, 1963, P21.
20. http://enquirer.com/editions/2002/05/18/spt.
21. Jim Carfield, "Big O's 36 Ruin Celts; Garden Final Wednesday," *Boston Herald*, April 8, 1963, 23.
22. Cliff Keane, "C's Tee Off on Referees," *Boston Globe*, April 8, 1963, 18.
23. Harry Reckner, "Embry Rebounds as Royals Win," *Cincinnati Post & Times-Star*, April 8, 1963, 25.
24. Harry Reckner, "Royals Shoot for Money," *Cincinnati Post & Times-Star*, April 10, 1963, 27.
25. Keane, "C's Tee Off on Referees," 17.
26. Carfield, "Big O's 36 Ruin," 24.
27. Bill Anzer, "Lucas Would Prefer to Play for Royals," *Cincinnati Enquirer*, April 8, 1963, 35.
28. Jim Schottelkotte, "Royals in Underdog Role Against Celts," *Cincinnati Enquirer*, April 10, 1963, 19.
29. Harry Reckner, "'Won't Be Back'—Charley Wolf," *Cincinnati Post & Times-Star*, April 11, 1963, 23.
30. Cliff Keane, "Cool Movie Heats Sam," *Boston Globe*, April 11, 1963. 47.
31. Jim Carfield, "Celtics Romp into Finals," *Boston Herald*, April 11, 1963, 38.
32. Reckner, "'Won't Be Back,'" 23.
33. Reckner's Notes, *Cincinnati Post & Times Star*, April 11, 1963, 23.
34. Jim Schottelkotte, "Hensel O.K. With Brown, Celts' Owner," *Cincinnati Enquirer*, April 11, 1963, 36.
35. Cousy and Devaney, *The Killer*, 3.
36. Robertson, *The Big O*, 169.
37. Jerry West and Jonathan Coleman, *West by West—My Charmed, Tormented Life* (New York: Little Brown and Company, 2011), 84.

Chapter 9

1. *The Heights*, February 25, 1966—Boston College, http://newspapers.bc.edu/egi-bin/bostonsh?a=d&d=bcheights19660225.2.70.
2. Jim Schottelkotte, "Royals Are Not for Sale; Hensel Loses Out," *Cincinnati Enquirer*, October 3, 1963, 1.
3. John Underwood and Morton Sharnik, "Look What Louie Wrought," *Sports Illustrated*, May 29, 1972, 42.
4. Underwood and Sharnik, "Look What Louie," 46.
5. Howard M. Tuckner, "Tall Sure-Shot," *The New York Times*, April 13, 1958, SM42.
6. Oscar Robertson, *The Big O—My Life, My Times, My Game*, (n.p.: Rodale, 2003), 173.
7. "NBA All-Star Ultimatum Paid Off for Players," *Los Angeles Times*, http://articles.latimes.com/2011/feb/16/sports/la-sp-all-star-strike-20110217.
8. "NBA All-Star."
9. Bob Cousy, "A Former Coach Tells of the Evils of College Recruiting," *The New York Times*, January 25, 1976, 226.

Chapter 10

1. Jerry Lucas, telephone interview by the author, March 30, 2015.
2. Terry Pluto, *Tall Tales—The Glory Years of the NBA, in the Words of the Men Who Played, Coached, and Built Pro Basketball* (New York: Simon & Shuster, 1992).
3. Jerry West and Jonathan Coleman, *West by West—My Charmed, Tormented Life*, (New York: Little Brown and Company, 2011), 63.
4. Jim Schottelkotte, "Challenge Lures McMahon," *Cincinnati Enquirer*, April 6, 1967, 35.
5. "The Mob—Part 2, $7 Billion from Illegal Bets and a Blight on Sports," *LIFE*, September 8, 1967, 92, https://books.google.com/books.
6. Bob Cousy with John Devaney, *The Killer Instinct*, (New York: Random House, 1975), 65.
7. "The Mob—Part," 92.
8. *Organized Crime in Sports: Before the Select Committee on Crime*, 738–739, http://njlaw.rutgers.edu/collections/gdoc/hearings/7/73601062b/73601062b.html.
9. Dave Anderson, "Personal Reminiscence—Defining 'The Cooz': A Personal Essay," *Holy Cross Magazine* 43, no. 1 (Winter 2009): 23, http://www.holycross.edu/magazine.
10. Dave O'Hara, "Bob Cousy Denies Any Wrong Doing," *The Day* (New Haven, CT), September 8, 1967, 17.
11. O'Hara, "Bob Cousy," 17.
12. John Bach, *University of Cincinnati Horizons*, May 2000.
13. Jerry Lucas, telephone interview by the author, March 30, 2015.
14. Oscar Robertson, *The Big O—My Life, My Times, My Game*, (n.p.: Rodale, 2003), 220.
15. Sam Goldaper, "N.I.T. Rings Down Curtain for Cousy," *The New York Times*, March 9, 1969, S3.

16. "Cousy to Retire as College Coach," *The New York Times*, January 21, 1969, 54.
17. Sam Goldaper, "To His Fans, Cousy Goes Out Like Champion," *The New York Times*, March 23, 1969, S5.
18. Goldaper, "To His Fans," S5.

Chapter 11

1. Barry McDermott, "'O' Lucas Applaud Cousy's Running Game," *Cincinnati Enquirer*, May 18, 1969, 13.
2. Sam Goldaper, "Cousy is Signed to Three-Year Pact at $150,000 to Coach Royals in NBA," *The New York Times*, May 10, 1969, 20.
3. Jim Schottelkotte, "Cousy's First Act," *Cincinnati Enquirer*, May 10, 1969, 13.
4. Jerry Lucas, telephone interview by the author, March 30, 2015.
5. McDermott, "'O' Lucas Applaud," 13.
6. Schottelkotte, "Cousy's First," 13.
7. Milton Richman, "Bob Cousy versus Robertson: No Room For Both in Cincy?," *Washington Afro-American*, February 10, 1970, http://news.google.com/newspapers?nid=2238&dat=19700210&id=dc01AAAAIBAJ&sjid.
8. Bob Cousy with John Devaney, *The Killer Instinct* (New York: Random House, 1975), 9.
9. UPI, "Cousy at 41, Seeks to Return as Player," *The New York Times*, September 14, 1969, 29.
10. Bill Furlong, "Bob Cousy vs. Oscar Robertson: The Struggle to Remake the Royals," *Sport*, February 1970, 82.
11. Jerry Lucas, telephone interview by the author, March 30, 2015.
12. Bob Cousy with John Devaney, *The Killer Instinct* (New York: Random House, 1975), 116.
13. Bob Cousy, letter to the author, February 26, 2015.
14. Barry McDermott, "Royals Deal Lucas For Two; Bullet Coach Blisters Trade," *Cincinnati Enquirer*, October 25, 1969, 9.
15. McDermott, "Royals Deal," 9.
16. "Jerry Had 'Inkling,' Says Wife," *Cincinnati Enquirer*, October 25, 1969, 9.
17. Barry McDermott, "'I Was Terrible,' Says Cooz," *Cincinnati Enquirer*, November 22, 1969, 14.
18. McDermott, "'I Was Terrible,'" 14.
19. Cousy with Devaney, *The Killer Instinct*, 141.
20. Barry McDermott, "Robertson, Green Just Too Tough for Bullets," *Cincinnati Enquirer*, January 26, 1970, 39.
21. McDermott, "Robertson, Green," 39.
22. Furlong, "Bob Cousy," 81.
23. Furlong, "Bob Cousy," 81.
24. Barry McDermott, "It Was Oscar For Gus, But O Wanted $700,000," *Cincinnati Enquirer*, February 1, 1970, 1.
25. Robertson, *The Big O*, 237.
26. Thomas Rogers, "Robertson is Out of Royal Line-Up," *The New York Times*, February 7, 1970, 47.
27. Robertson, *The Big O*, 241.

28. "Paulk Key Man in Oscar Trade," *Cincinnati Enquirer*, April 22, 1970, 23.
29. Cousy with Devaney, *The Killer Instinct*, 128.
30. Jim Schottelkotte, "There Was No Other Way," *Cincinnati Enquirer*, April 22, 1970, 23.
31. Bill Anzer, "'Hasn't Hit Me Yet' Says Oscar of Deal," *Cincinnati Enquirer*, April 22, 1970, 23.
32. Anzer, "'Hasn't Hit," 23.

Chapter 12

1. Barry McDermott, "Working in The Market," *Cincinnati Enquirer*, March 24, 1970, 2.
2. Bob Cousy with John Devaney, *The Killer Instinct* (New York: Random House, 1975), 146.
3. Bill Simmons, *The Book of Basketball—The NBA According to The Sports Guy* (New York: Ballantine Books, 2009), 111.
4. "'Big O' Completed Bucks Championship Run," http://www.nba.com/history/finals/19701971.html.
5. Jon Saraceno, "A Conversation with...Kareem Abdul-Jabbar," *AARP Bulletin/Real Possibilities*, January/February 2015, 4.
6. Earl Lawson, "Royals Turn to Lacey," *Cincinnati Post & Times-Star*, November 8, 1971, 17.
7. Barry McDermott, "Cousy Flays Royals After Loss to Celtics," *Cincinnati Enquirer*, November 9, 1971, 21.
8. McDermott, "Cousy Flays," 21.
9. Earl Lawson, "Cousy Pained to Deal Norm," *Cincinnati Post & Times-Star*, November 10, 1971, 23.
10. Barry McDermott, "Nate-Sam Show Puts Knicks to Sleep," *Cincinnati Enquirer*, November 11, 1971, 51.
11. Tom Callahan, "Royals' Streak at 4," *Cincinnati Enquirer*, February 5, 1972, 25.
12. Tom Callahan, "Royals Leaving Cincinnati for Kansas City," *Cincinnati Enquirer*, March 15, 1972, 21.
13. Tom Callahan, "Royals' Players Vow to Fight 'Bush' Move," Cincinnati Enquirer, March 15, 1972, 1.
14. Callahan, "Royals' Players," 1.
15. Jim Schottelkotte, "The Demise of the Royals," *Cincinnati Enquirer*, March 15, 1972, 21.
16. Bob Cousy, letter to the author, February 26, 2015.
17. "To Many, Tiny Archibald Is Big Man," *The New York Times*, March 18, 1973, 219.
18. "To Many," 219.
19. Leonard Koppett, "Royals Owners Linked to Crime in Senate Hearing," *The New York Times*, January 26, 1972,
20. Jerry Lucas, telephone interview by the author, March 30, 2015.

About the Author

William A. Cook is the author of numerous books including twelve on baseball history and two on true crime, and has appeared in productions on ESPN2 and the MLB Network. A former healthcare administrator and township councilman in North Brunswick, New Jersey, he lives in Manalapan, New Jersey.

Printed in Great Britain
by Amazon